Miriam's Miracle

A Medical Memoir
Wrapped in a Love Story

Mark and Miriam Johnson

Published by SuburbanBuzz.com LLC

ISBN: 978-1-959446-29-3

DEDICATION

This book is dedicated to our son, Matthew. You were only nine when Mom had her accident, and today, you are in your thirties with a wife and son of your own. The story on these pages consumes a large portion of your life. To the extent possible, we tried to shield you from as many burdens as possible and provide you with as normal of a childhood as we could. Your contribution helped us to cope daily; your presence helped us to look beyond the trees and take in the forest. You provided your mother with a reason to persevere and not give up. Her greatest regret is the years she/we lost from your childhood.

Many details from those years have been mercifully forgotten as fresh memories replace the old, partially out of self-preservation. Some of this will all be new information for you because, as I said, we tried to shield things from you that we could. You were a child, and our adult burdens were not yours to shoulder. We are grateful for your presence in our lives.

CONTENTS

ACKNOWLEDGMENTS

Overwhelming gratitude continues to dominate my thoughts. Father Time has affected the other cast members in our drama: Attorney Fred has retired and is enjoying his grandchildren. Dr. Robel, last we knew, was about half retired. Our dear friend Celia (a.k.a. St. Tulia) passed away more than 10 years ago. We also miss Kay Shepherd, who helped us in many different ways. There are many others with whom we've just lost contact.

Also, to the dear friends and relatives who have read, corrected, and suggested changes to the early manuscript, including encouraging me to not throw it away and quit. To "the pros" Melanie Saxton and Holly Chervnsik for helping turn the raw pages of manuscript into a real book.

A special thanks needs to go to a dear friend who came once a month for several years to our home and gave us all haircuts. They usually brought a meal with them when they came!

Another family transported Matthew to and from school for several years, thank you!

We are also grateful for the army of caregivers who helped to facilitate Miriam's life and our family's sanity; some remain close friends years after their employment ended.

Our church family has been mentioned elsewhere in the book, but they deserve an additional expression of our gratitude. For nearly two decades Miriam's name was a fixture at the top of the prayer list on the weekly newsletter. We were never forgotten, and their literal and figurative embrace really helped buoy our spirits through the difficult years. Now we give collective praise for answered prayer!

My parents, Miriam's sisters, my brother and his family were all an important part of our safety net. They rose to the need, no matter how great, to help keep us going.

INTRODUCTION
The Locusts

Sometime before I became part of her life, a young, broken woman who had been run over by life was counseled by a young pastor named Charles. During their time together, he gave her a verse from the Old Testament Book of Joel that she often thought about in the ensuing years.

"I will restore to you the years the locusts have eaten..." Joel 2:25

In October 1983, this same pastor married the young woman and me. Miriam and brother Charles may have thought that this union would enjoy a happily ever after as we danced through endless fields of daisies. That was the fulfillment of this very personal prophecy. While it is true the locusts were held at bay for the first five years of our marriage, when they returned, they were legion, and they were relentless. They devoured nine years of our son's childhood, and then, as that crisis was beginning to mercifully diminish, they returned with reinforcements.

This time, the attack lasted more than two decades, turning my dear wife into a pain-infused shell of her former self.

In 1678, John Bunyan penned his timeless classic *Pilgrim's Progress*. In this masterfully crafted and arguably divinely inspired allegory, he writes about Pilgrim and his progress toward the Celestial City. In the story, Pilgrim faces many challenges that mirror what we still face today. I admit to drawing inspiration from Bunyan with some of the metaphors used in this book.

Unfortunately, this is not an allegory but a real-life story about a

1

journey through a life-altering crisis. During the early morning hours of October 10, 1997, with the simple ring of a telephone, our family's footing upon the "trail of life" was lost, and we began a slow slide/skid/tumble downhill. Time and momentum gathered until it seemed, at times, as though we were in free fall. "Safety lines," formed by a braid of faith, family, and friends, were sheathed by a very frayed Workman's Compensation system. Somehow, this combination managed to keep us from going splat at the base of the cliff. I agree with Bunyan that life can be portrayed as a challenging journey full of surprises and uncertainties. Life portrayed as scaling a mountain seems an appropriate metaphor for our pilgrimage to the awaited hereafter.

Some people intentionally choose a more difficult path than is necessary by making poor choices; for others, fate chooses it for them. A few people appear to saunter through life, basking in sunshine and frolicking in green pastures. But for most, life is more of a stony, steep path littered with adversity, seasoned by glimpses from magnificent vistas. A few of us lose our footing altogether and end up dangling from a rope beside a vertical face of life's mountain.

Join us on our journey. Laugh with us, cry with us, and get angry, but do not pity us. We have much to be thankful for and do not have to look far to find people experiencing even more difficult times. The couple whose child has cerebral palsy or the person caring for a quadriplegic family member have life sentences that will not end until death intervenes. Though worse off than ours, perhaps these families simply have not had the time or opportunity to document their crisis, or they remain silent due to the wishes of their loved ones.

The story that follows is 22 years in the making. I began putting it into book form in 2005 but lost interest when I realized there was no ending. Who wants to read a book with no ending? Good or bad, there must be an ending. And then something miraculous happened. If you don't believe in miracles, perhaps this book will change your mind. During the fall of 2019, an ending arrived in a rather dramatic fashion, and my interest in the book project was renewed.

What follows is a story about an amazing woman who refused to give up on life or her faith following a tragic accident. It is also a story about God's faithfulness. There is a story here for a variety of palates. What is your pleasure? If you want a love story, our story checks that box. If you're interested in a story about triumph over tragedy, you're in luck.

Prefer a medical drama shrouded in mystery? I can offer one of those, too. If you prefer legal drama, you, again, have come to the right place. What you will not find is fiction.

Unfortunately, this is a real story that is stranger than any fiction I could compose. I have had a front-row seat for the duration and can hardly believe many parts of it myself. If you tend to cry, get a fresh box of tissues. But be patient, and you will probably also enjoy some good belly laughs. Keep the tissues close; if you make it all the way to the end, you may shed tears of joy. We occasionally refer to the prophetic verse and the locusts, but now more in jest. Better memories are replacing the devoured years. Four years after she took her first halting steps, as this book is finally being finished, I find that I'm still overwhelmed that she/we have had our lives restored to us. This is something for which I give thanks daily. It is time to share a remarkable story.

~ **Mark Johnson**

CHAPTER 1
A Snapshot of Our Life

Sunday, December 16, 2001

It's nearly 9 a.m., and Miriam and Matthew are in the spa. She's working on her first cup of coffee while he's nursing a finger that he may have broken playing basketball a couple of days ago. He also has a sore throat, so I'll take him to urgent care for an x-ray and an exam later this morning. We won't be attending church once again, but we hope to make the Christmas program tonight.

I have emptied the bedside potty, prepared Miriam's ice water, and spent some time with her in the spa. I am now trying to steal a few minutes to write.

"Mark."

"What?"

"I'm ready to get out."

I push the pause button on my life and tend to an imminent need. Yes, I'm tired of this four-year-long ordeal that has consumed our lives, careers, and financial security and is taking a good whack at our future. But my love for her causes me to persevere, trying to imagine how difficult this is for her.

She has now been in and out of the shower and is situated in her recliner, enjoying breakfast and her second cup of coffee. The Sunday paper is rustling in her hands as I return to the laptop.

We were planning our life together 18 and half years ago and trying to set some goals, and I don't recall including debilitating afflictions or a perpetual state of crisis in our plans. I remember talking about children and buying a home of our own someday.

"Ooooohhh." The voice beside me wails as she lifts her left leg and holds it in my direction. This is when I'm supposed to locate the exact spasm on her left foot.

"Where is it?" I ask while grabbing the foot and applying pressure in a likely spot.

"In the middle near the arch," she explains through moans and tears.

I look into her face, searching for approval while applying all of the finger pressure my bulk is capable of placing on one spot. I hold this until the spasm abates, and she tells me to let go. After less than 15 seconds, this one has mercifully moved on. The next one may be in her big toe, the heel, on the ball, or between any two toes and could occur within the next few seconds or might wait several minutes or even hours. The only thing we know for sure is that it is coming — sometime.

As best as I can tell, the pain is like someone taking a hot poker from the fire and jabbing it into her foot at random. The pain comes from the nerves in her foot misfiring or shorting out. These spasms arrive without warning and at the speed of light. They can range from an intense searing agony that can last several minutes (that's several hours in agony time), to a quick jolt that stays just long enough to make her nearly jump from her chair before leaving just as fast. Sometimes it is a simple cramp she can work out herself that lasts only a few seconds; the worst ones bring tears, wailing, a leg that shakes uncontrollably, a loss of bladder control, and can require outside assistance to get the cramp to let go.

Occasionally, nausea joins in the fun to help season the moment with memorable highlights. I go to great lengths to see that she is not left alone. These days, workman's comp pays an attendant to stay with her nine hours per day, five days a week, but that was not always the case. Matthew, myself, my family and friends take care of the rest. With this comprehensive effort, she is not alone more than a few hours per week, usually only a few minutes at a time.

CHAPTER 2
The Beginning

The stream gurgled as it flowed over and around Miriam and me, as we lay in a stream that runs through Victoria Bryant State Park, located near Franklin Springs, Georgia. It was a June day in 1983. We absorbed the summer sun while basking in the glow of our mutual affection. I took this opportunity to ask the cute little brunette laying in the stream at my side if she would marry me. She promptly offered an affirmative answer, whereupon we climbed back on my motorcycle and rode the 30 miles back to our respective homes. As the motor purred between our legs, I thought about what I had just done. I was overwhelmed by emotions ranging from joy and excitement to apprehension and anxiety. She sure acted more confident than I felt. She, too, may have been wondering about the commitment she had just made.

Four months later, on the prettiest October morning God ever made, we stood before a church full of people and pledged to cling to one another for better or for worse. How could we have known what lie ahead? We were a pair of 20-something kids embarking on an adventure together. She was a beautiful bride, walking toward me, her father on her arm. The white dress accented well her dark hair and radiant smile. Looking at her took my breath away. *Wow*, I thought, *I get to be married to her?*

We honeymooned in Williamsburg, Virginia. Perhaps the first omen concerning our future life together arrived during our trip home when the car began making noises unbecoming to a smooth-running piece of machinery. Although the car was only a few years old, was comfortable to ride in, and delivered fantastic gas mileage, mechanically, it resembled a loose formation of parts careening down the highway. A few weeks later, I traded her good-looking, comfortable, air-conditioned Chevy Citation for an older, uglier, un-air-conditioned, but far more dependable Toyota Corolla. The dealer traded us even up. Miriam probably should have recognized a developing trend and left me on the spot, but she probably decided that she surely had already seen the worst and would hang around to see if something better came our way...

Our son arrived shortly after our fifth anniversary, following two miscarriages, a difficult pregnancy, and a touch and go delivery that ended with a successful C-section. Before his first birthday, health problems came to light involving his immune system. By the summer of 1997, he was finally doing much better, had not been hospitalized for almost a year, and was coming off many of his medications. He was nine by then and had managed to keep our lives pretty exciting with countless trips to see specialists and weeks and weeks spent in hospitals, trying to get well enough to return home until the next inopportune incident involving high fevers and infections "of unknown origin."

During the Summer of 1997, we embarked on a business adventure (in retrospect, more of a brain cramp) of enormous magnitude. I decided the time had come to "grow" my little furniture business and begin making hardwood flooring. I rented a building, leased machinery, hired some good help, and set up production. Three months later and five days before our 13th anniversary, I was awakened by a phone call in the early morning. The voice on the other end explained that my wife had fallen while working and was in the emergency room. "She cannot drive home and will need to be picked up," the voice explained. In another lifetime, should this happen again, I will tell the voice that they have the wrong number, roll over and go back to sleep, hoping it to be just a bad dream.

If a phone call bearing bad news is not answered, will the bad news go away? Frivolous philosophy aside, this phone call marked the beginning of an ordeal that would strain us, test us, realign our priorities, and generally change our lives. It reminds me of a song sung on the children's television show, *Lamb Chop*, called *The Song That Doesn't End*. I should write a play. I could title it: Leg that Won't Heal. So far, my play would have eleven acts featuring six surgeons spread over four hospitals and three states. The supporting cast would include a legion of physical therapists, nurses, attendants, several lawyers, a judge, and a brown-colored hairball with four legs, a curly tail, and M&M eyes we call Missy.

This is our story, composed from journal entries, correspondence, and entries from an e-rag I named the *The Knee Gazette*. I first started writing simply to document events for future reference, but it quickly became an outlet for my own frustrations. Letters were written to the medical team, the legal team, or to the case manager, all in an attempt to keep Miriam's case moving along. Eventually writing became a way to keep friends and relatives up to date with developments; a few have suggested I write a book

Emergency Room Visit 1

When I arrived at the E.R. and asked for Miriam, I was led through a pair of large double doors and into a large room surrounded by smaller ones. My wife waited in one of the smaller rooms. One wall was made of glass, which allowed the medical personnel to observe the patients in each room from the central desk, which was in the center of the large room.

My bride was lying on a gurney. As I entered the room, she turned her head and forced a brave smile. She was embarrassed, she was angry, and she was hurting. Her eyes were red and her make-up, or what was left of it, was smeared.

"The E.R. doctor says my knee is sprained," she told me as we were driving home. "He also thought it might be a good idea to have it looked at by an orthopedic specialist." Then she began to explain what had happened.

"The housekeeping staff had been working on waxing different parts of the lab. An alarm went off on one of my machines, so I headed toward it. There were none of the signs or the tape that normally marks off an area where they are working on the floor, so I had no warning. The wax had just been laid and was wet and fresh. When I came around a corner my last footfall had no grip, and my foot just started spinning. I reached for the machine, but it was too far away. I remember seeing my foot and leg spin completely around and heard a sound like glass being ground into concrete by the sole of a hard shoe. I remember seeing people spinning; their eyes were big as saucers. I was screaming. My leg hurt so bad. I told them to bring me a wheelchair. I locked the

9

wheels and crawled up into it, and they pushed me to the E.R."

I took her home, tried to make her comfortable, and spent my first day away from the plant since opening it only a few short months before. I called my partner and told him what had happened. An appointment was made to see Dr. Max Robel, a well-respected orthopedic surgeon in Athens.

A few days later, we were in his office. Miriam was sitting on the exam table with her legs dangling off the edge. Dr. Robel is tall and thin with a pleasant demeanor and a personality that puts patients quickly at ease. It was a quick examination, followed by a diagnosis delivered with a tone of certainty that left little room for doubt.

"You have severed, or nearly severed, your Anterior Cruciate Ligament (ACL). Enough time must pass to let the swelling subside. We'll operate in a month. Until then you will need to get some physical therapy. Do you need something for pain?"

"What is the ACL?" I asked, not realizing that within a couple of years we would become lay experts on the subject.

"The Anterior Cruciate Ligament essentially holds the lower leg in proper relation to the upper leg," Dr. Robel patiently explained.

"Why do we need to wait a month before surgery? How long will the recovery take?" The questions began to come in a flood, but most of them came to mind after we had left the office. As I recall, the answers left out a bunch of information. It is my opinion that if patients understood how painful the recovery would be, there would be a lot fewer ACLs reconstructed. This began a doctor/patient relationship that lasted more than two decades. Dr. Robel was an anchor, a common denominator providing continuity through difficult storms.

Friday, November 9, 1997

The month of waiting in a state of suspended animation finally ended in an operating room. A month after her fall and two days after surgery, Miriam is finally showing some improvement.

Saturday, November 10

The three days and two nights since surgery have been the toughest. She is in pain and is heavily medicated; her mind is fogged in, and she is nauseated. The agonized groans of pain have ceased, and she can get up with assistance and use the bathroom instead of the bedpan.

Friday night we slept little, with her needing constant attention for either nausea, positional adjustments or pain medication.

I brought her home today. The nausea is relentless. She is constantly heaving, even though the lack of solid food causes most of the heaves to be dry. Her stomach is sore and her head aches from the heaving, and then, of course, there is the understandable and expected pain from the freshly carved upon knee.

Making her comfortable here at the house is going to be challenging. She requires constant attention. I missed work Friday and again today. Tomorrow friends will stay with her so I can go to the plant for a noon meeting.

Today, we are putting up the Christmas tree. Matthew has grown enough that he is really a big help. Miriam and Matthew usually do the inside decorating while I'm at work; this year, Mom sits in her director's chair on wheels and directs the activities. I am thankful the wheelchair is only temporary.

Saturday, January 3, 1998

Miriam's knee is not doing well. She is still in almost constant pain. On her best days, she looks good and appears to have good mobility until evening when she begins to stiffen up. Her worst days are when the weather is changing. Her schedule is centered around physical therapy, light housework, computer work, and an occasional trip to the grocery store. Her evenings are spent sitting in her recliner, occasionally whimpering in pain. She sleeps with a heating pad on her knee and is usually in bed by 9:30.

A few weeks ago, she was fitted with a brace that allowed her to 'walk' again. It brought tears to our eyes as she displayed elation at being able to walk without crutches or get around without benefit of the wheelchair. This brace, which allows her to walk while protecting the knee from additional injury is her constant companion, unless she is in bed or bathing. She is supposed to wear it for the next year.

Monday, January 5, 1998

We've been to Dr. Robel's office twice today, plus two hours of physical therapy. Then we took the out-of-work paperwork to the Altma Hospital laboratory. I took her to the pharmacy for prescriptions and to the mall for recommended shoes, and the day is shot. Miriam's knee has stolen another day from our lives and my business.

According to the x-rays, her bone plugs are secure and have not popped loose. Dr. Robel says she is on schedule, with slower progress than some and faster progress than others. He also excused her from work for eight more weeks. If she can return then, she will have been out of work for five months! The bad news is she is progressing normally, and nothing can be done she is not already doing to speed up the recovery process. She is going to hurt. Walking from the parking deck to the lab and back required nearly 10 minutes and sapped her energy.

Sunday, April 5, 1998

The anger grows with each passing day and every step backward.

Miriam turned in a two-week notice in February after one week on light duty. The work was not the problem; the pain caused by walking (on crutches) from the parking deck to the laboratory was too much for her. After picking up the pieces of her shattered emotions for those days, I told her to quit. The job just was not worth the agony it was causing her. Without the accident, she would still be working her weekend night shift.

April 27, 1998

On April 10, she went back into the operating room. This operation was more of a reconnaissance and clean-up procedure than the last one, so the trauma was much less. Her nausea was better this time, perhaps due to having an epidural instead of general anesthesia. We were able to come home that same afternoon, which was helpful! Her range of motion, in some respects, is better than before the surgery, so maybe there is some reason for hope.

Dr. Robel initially said it would be two to three months before he decides whether to repeat the November ACL procedure or whether this one will rehab satisfactorily. Seventeen days later, the surgery has failed to yield the desired results. Her knee still slips whether she is wearing the brace or not. Since the surgery, she has had perhaps four good nights of sleep.

The thought of going through another ACL reconstruction and the resulting recovery is terrifying. She doesn't deserve this fate and frankly, neither do Matthew or me.

Sunday, May 10, 1998

It is Mother's Day. This morning, we went to church and later had the same crowd we ate with last night over to our house for Mother's Day dinner. Smoked turkey and last night's leftovers made a simple but nice meal. This morning, during a hymn, Miriam's knee shifted while standing completely still — a painful first. She enjoyed the remainder of the service from the comfort of the pew.

Tomorrow, we return for another scheduled visit with Dr. Robel. I am sure he will be distressed to learn that twice this week, Miriam's knee has given way and caused her to fall; once at home, where she had to call a neighbor to help her get back up, and once in my office when coming out of the bathroom. These are terribly painful and usually require several hours to recover her normal level of mobility.

During the May 11 visit with Dr. Robel, the decision was made to proceed with the ACL reconstruction using her hamstring. The graft had loosened and would have to be redone. Dr. Robel would assist Dr. Hayes and this time they would do a hamstring graft. The first ACL reconstruction was performed using the middle third of the patella tendon, which is the tendon that connects the bottom of the kneecap with the top of the tibia. For the second ACL reconstruction, with the middle third of the patella on her left leg already missing, they plan to "harvest" part of the hamstring from the back of the left leg. He also decided to have her fitted for a new, more elaborate brace.

Letter to Dr. Robel

May 13, 1998

Please help come up with a plan to eliminate the kind of night dawn mercifully ended. It went like this:

5:30 p.m.

Miriam took a Motrin.

9:00 p.m.

Miriam took a Tylox, then a sleeping pill, as she prepared for bed.

10:20 p.m.

I find her still awake as I prepare for bed. We sleep in separate rooms so I can get most of a night's sleep.

Midnight

I am awakened by her moans of pain. I get the TENS unit for her and help her to the bathroom. Her knee is having spasms. Could this in any way be connected to the knee having to adjust to the Protonics brace? The brace has increased her mobility and decreased her pain while walking, at least for half of the one day she has had it, but I wonder if there will be an adjustment period as the leg muscles adjust to a new form of support and resistance.

4:30 a.m.

More spasms create cries of agony I can no longer ignore. By this point she has slept sporadically, but the sleeping pill has not worked as the pharmacist promised it would, or she needs a stronger pain medication that will last longer than four hours, or we need a better schedule for the medications we already have.

She has been very diligent with every aspect of the rehab process we have control over, but the absence of progress is taking a toll on her as well as the rest of us. Seven months have gone by since her accident and six since her surgery, but despite the long journey, we have traveled nowhere.

I look forward to hearing from you soon,

Mark Johnson
Husband, and round-the-clock caretaker.

Journal

May 27, 1998

In preparation for Friday's rebuild on Miriam's knee, we have reassembled command central. This is an attempt to put her "life" within arm's reach for her post-op recovery period. Her large recliner/bed/dining table is accompanied in that corner of the room by an old desk, an old nightstand, a floor lamp and a coffee table. On the desk sits the telephone, a pitcher of ice water, some reading material and a boom box tuned to her favorite radio station. In the desk drawers are her medications, some CDs, and a few snacks to take with her medications. Under the desk, the pillows and blankets are stored. Her crutches lean against the wall between the desk and the coffee table; an assortment of immobilizers and braces, complete with leggings and extra padding lie near the crutches. In the right arm of the large chair is stored the fold-away table; in the left, an assortment of remote controls for the boom box, the TV, and the chair control (heat & vibration). From the chair, she has a variety of entertainment to choose from: she can watch the fish in the aquarium, birds feeding at one of our four feeders, or watch the TV.

The big difference between this ACL surgery and the last is that now we know what to expect and, hopefully, we are better prepared, physically and mentally. Miriam is remarkably brave in the face of the hell we know is coming. Recently, we have encountered two former ACL patients who had strong comments about the pain associated with the procedure.

The first was the youth pastor at our church. His comment about Miriam's upcoming rerun: "They could offer to pay me a million dollars and I wouldn't go through that again."

The other was a woman we met at the grocery store. She was still wearing a tell-tale brace, so we engaged her in conversation. Her injury occurred on Christmas Eve in a skiing accident. Her surgery was in January. She had already quit therapy and was going up and down stairs (Miriam was talking from a wheelchair at the time)! Her assessment of the pain during recovery: "I've gone through natural childbirth twice, and tendon replacement in my arm, but that pain didn't come close to what was experienced after ACL surgery!"

15

CHAPTER 3
Operation Day

On May 29, 1998, we faced another major surgery. I captured this adventure in my journal, a habit by now.

4:50 a.m.

I am up before the alarm to get showered and everyone else ready for the day. By six, I have her at the hospital, and Matthew farmed out to a neighbor.

6:30 a.m.

Pastor Ray arrives in our pre-op room.

6:45 a.m.

Dr. Robel arrives. A discussion occurs about the best choice of anesthesia for the surgery; an epidural wins out. Hopefully, this will make her recovery less traumatic.

7:10 a.m.

Pastor Ray prays with us. I kiss her and watch her get wheeled away. My eyes mist over as I marvel at her bravery.

7:40 a.m.

They call from the operating room and tell me the procedure has begun.

9:45 a.m.

Dr. Robel comes out to report the procedure has gone well and that Dr. Hayes has done "a magnificent job."

10:00 a.m.

Pastor Johnson prays with me and leaves. Family friend Linda Hamby was here for about an hour, leaving about 9:15.

11:15 a.m.

My contemplations are interrupted by a recovery room worker coming to report that Miriam is doing well but is shivering with cold. He says that it will be 30-40 minutes before I can see her.

12:15 p.m.

I was allowed to see Miriam for a few minutes. She looks good and is not in pain. The epidural is working! She is buried under a pile of blankets and is attached to a patient warming machine, which blows warm air into an air mattress like device to assist with warming.

12:30 p.m.

I go to the room and await her arrival. Her mother soon arrives with some flowers and her pastor.

12:50 p.m.

Miriam is wheeled in. I am distressed to learn the epidural has been removed.

1:05 p.m.

It doesn't take long for pain to begin. I have flashbacks to November's surgery, but so far nausea has not been a problem.

1:44 p.m.

Miriam received her first shot of morphine. Her right leg is still completely numb. Unfortunately, it was the left knee that was operated on, and those nerves are wide awake!

1:55 p.m.

She is sleeping now but occasionally utters a deep agonizing moan that wakes her momentarily.

6:10 p.m.

I needed to run an errand. As I was leaving, they were putting her on a bed pan. Somehow, she got the bed wet and remained that way until the nurse was sternly encouraged to change the sheets. When the meal came, she could not eat. The nausea arrived while I was out.

6:30 p.m.

Miriam is writhing in pain now. The morphine pump is so far not producing measurable relief. Her agony is intense. Dr. Robel and Dr. Hayes have been in. They were both dismayed that the epidural had been removed in post-op. Were the orders written and not followed, or never written? We will never know the answer, but Miriam is paying the price for someone's inability to read and follow orders. They want to put her on a motion machine when, and if, the pain is at a tolerable level.

May 30, 1998

I spent the night on a cot at her side. The morphine, Toradal, and Percoset did not provide enough relief to allow her to get comfortable, and the Phenergan and Tigan failed to suppress the nausea. It was a rough night; however, not quite as bad as I remember the first night after surgery in November. This morning her gut ached from all the heaving, which followed every spasm in her knee. It is a vicious cycle. The morphine dries her mouth, drinking and the IV drip fills the bladder, which requires her to be lifted onto and off the bedpan, which has led to some of the worst spasms. Dr. Hayes and Dr. Robel are both expected this AM. Hopefully, a strategy for dealing with this pain will be developed.

I've missed so much work between the surgeries, doctor visits, and her really bad days. Today I am still the president and majority stockholder in a fledgling wood products company headquartered in Greensboro, GA. How much longer we will even exist is in question. The time and attention I've been unable to give my company has not helped solve any of the problems and challenges associated with a young operation having 20 employees.

Our nine-year-old son has done a good job of rising to new challenges and responsibilities. He often has the supper table set and something on the stove or in the oven when I get home in the evening. He also helps with laundry and has been very understanding when Mom's medical needs interfere with his schedule. Our one-morning-every-other-week cleaning lady has been increased to once a week to help keep the health inspector at bay. Naturally, I pick up the rest of the slack that I can get to; what I cannot, often does not get done. Miriam is not satisfied with any of the above. Before her accident, she worked

32 hours a week on weekend nights at the hospital and helped me at the flooring plant during the week, in addition to being a wife and mother.

As I write this, I have been interrupted 15-20 times to adjust her in the hospital bed, get her something, or to hold her up while she tries to vomit. I feel helpless. When she is having a spasm or cramp or a bout of nausea, there is nothing I can do to ease her agony.

9:20 a.m.

The physical therapist just left. While here, the therapist re-interpreted the doctor's instructions for the constant motion machine (CPM) and reset it. She interpreted "30-70 degrees as is able to tolerate the pain" as 70 degrees high and 30 degrees low. The nurse that set up the machine understood it meant 30-70 degrees was the high and the low was 0 degrees or full extension. When this caused pain, the low was increased to 7 degrees—"Far too much extension for a fresh ACL," the nurse commented. I am fuming! Is it possible another incompetent medical "professional" has compromised another of Miriam's surgeries? I could not compose fiction this horrifying! Expecting someone to read the instructions and pay attention to what they are doing is just too much to ask, I guess.

11:00 a.m.

Dr. Robel poked his head in the door and announced that another epidural has been ordered. Within five minutes they came and unplugged the bed and wheeled her away. It appears we won't be going home anytime soon.

1:00 p.m.

Miriam has returned to the room and already is more relaxed. While downstairs, they checked her blood pressure every few minutes because evidently the epidural lowers the blood pressure. She was also told that the protocol required the nurses on the floor to check her blood pressure every 15 minutes. I go home for the afternoon, leaving her in the capable hands of her older sister.

6:45 p.m.

I return after a nap and a shower and feel like a new man!

According to the vital signs stat sheet laying on the counter, her blood pressure hasn't been checked for hours. Shocking, I know. They do appear to be monitoring respiration and pulse.

Dr. Robel was in earlier this evening. He wants to keep her until Tuesday! He plans to remove the epidural on Monday and is planning a strategy for us to deal with the pain after we get home. The anesthesiologist that put in this epidural came to check on Miriam. She remembered Miriam's case from the November visit because of the difficult time Miriam had. Neither doctor recalls having a case where a patient's body reacted to severe pain with this kind of nausea without the anesthesia or narcotics playing a role. I think these people enjoy a challenge; it is probably boring to deal with normal patients all the time.

Matthew is spending another night with the Adams family, who live across the street.

Maybe Matthew and I can go to church together in the morning. I got to see him this afternoon while I was at home. I do not like us not being all together. If Miriam is still doing well tomorrow night, I will spend the night at home with Matthew. "No honey, I promise it has nothing to do with wanting to sleep in my own bed without any interruptions, honest! It really is for Matthew's benefit!" Her expression is very clear; it's obvious she's not buying what I'm trying to sell.

June 2, 1998

Last night was spent at home with Matthew. My own bed sure felt good! By 7:30, I am back in her hospital room in anticipation of being able to take her home this morning. This knee will be treated as if it is made of glass for three months!

10:30 p.m.

We arrived home around noon after getting several prescriptions filled. I got her to sit up in the recliner, gave her some drugs, and left for the plant. I arrived for work at 1:45 in the afternoon.

3:45

I received a call from Matthew: "Dad, mom's throwing up." I left immediately. I figure it's a bit much to ask a nine-year-old to be the sole caretaker of such a sick patient. When I got back to the house, she looked bad, but the nausea had settled down. I gave her some food

21

and began building the drugs in her system back to a level where the pain and nausea were again under control. I was at work all of two hours, after spending an hour on the road driving to and from.

June 3, 1998

It was quite a night. I slept in a chair beside Miriam. Morning came way too soon. By the time I got her bathed, fed, drugged, and dressed, it was after eight before I was able to leave for the plant. When I talked to Miriam this afternoon, she complained of a fever and said her mouth had broken out in ulcers. She reminded me that the same thing happened in November.

June 6, 1998

10:15 a.m.

It's Saturday morning and we slept in. This week has been one of mental and physical fatigue, so some extra rest is appreciated. Since Miriam came home Tuesday, she has left her chair only to take "bird baths" and use the potty chair, except for going to physical therapy yesterday morning! Monday morning, we go to see Dr. Robel (more missed work for me). Then she goes to PT. Other than the necessary outings she is confined to her chair. I put the continuous passive motion machine (CPM) on the chair at night, but during days her leg is propped up on a stack of pillows. Often it is iced down with the Cryo Cuff apparatus, that circulates cold water to the joint. By tenish, Matthew and I had made a dent in the housework, and once again, home is at least one rung above a pig's wallow!

June 10, 1998

Miriam has been in severe pain. Dr. Robel boosted the oxycontin dose from 10 mg to 40mg, but it didn't help much. Her screams of pain severely affected my night's sleep. I was awake from 3:30 on, and I am not in very good shape this morning.

I managed to escape to the plant, arriving about 2:45 in the afternoon. Where do I start on a pile of work that has been building during my absence?

At 4:45 p.m., Matthew calls and says, "Mom is throwing up, I'm going to call Julie."

Neighbor Julie took Miriam to therapy this morning, but she threw up before they left, once again in Julie's van. When they arrived at the Sports Medical Center, Henry was alarmed at her condition and called Dr. Robel. Dr. Robel wanted her taken to the emergency room for a shot of Phenergan and a bag of fluids to ward off further dehydration. Miriam called me from the ER at about 1 p.m. Although distracted, I worked until 4:30 p.m. and came home. Note to self: Remember to block all calls coming from an ER; they are never good news.

Miriam was in her chair in a drug-induced fog, but thankfully not hollering in pain or heaving with nausea. Mrs. Veale, the mother of my employee Scott, brought some pie and banana pudding; neighbor Kathy Siles is bringing the rest of supper. I do not know what I would do without our food angels!

Sunday, June 6, 1998

5:30 p.m.

A glimmer of hope! I looked over and saw Miriam snoozing in her chair! While it is not unusual to see her lying there with the leg propped up on a pile of pillows, it is unusual these days to see her feet interlocked, almost like normal! I will take a victory, no matter how small or insignificant. Progress at any level is a boost to my sagging morale.

The next morning the tranquility of morning coffee and newspaper was interrupted for most of an hour by Miriam's nausea. It came quickly, hung around, made a big mess, created chaos and agony, then mercifully left. I am glad I was here; I don't know what she'd have done if I hadn't been. Whenever I leave the house, a multitude of "what ifs" go with me.

Saturday, June 20, 1998

What a difference the last three days have made. Miriam has returned to the land of the coherent and sober, where lucid thought prevails. She has "come down" off of the more powerful and intoxicating pain medications. Her pain has diminished to the point where she feels much better. Therapy yesterday went well. Miriam indicated that she was showing progress with diminished levels of pain. This morning she was up and around enough to help Matthew fold laundry. We spent

23

the night together in the same bed for the first time in over a month and probably only the second time in over a year.

July 5, 1998

It is a comfortable Sunday morning, five weeks and two days after surgery. About 10 days ago, Miriam suddenly felt better. She is off the worst of the pain meds and has been walking using her Protonics brace. Since the new graft is supposed to be weakening and stretching slightly until the sixth week, I encourage her to use crutches or a cane for additional support and protection.

She has been to the plant twice this week and once the previous week. A whole day really wears her out. We park within 40 feet of the door, and I carry everything she needs, but sitting up all day without having the leg elevated eventually causes pain and fatigue.

Our life is beginning to return to a semblance of normalcy. Miriam is able once again to help with meal preparation, which her husband and son greatly appreciate.

August 15, 1998

A blanket of clouds hides the sun on a rather gloomy Saturday morning. Miriam is at physical therapy; Matthew and I will soon take his new puppy to the vet for a first visit. Our life continues to stabilize with Miriam's steady improvement. She still has tremendous limitations for us to deal with, but she is now able to care for herself (and us) with our assistance.

Matthew starts school on Monday, which will allow her to spend more time at the plant. Goodness knows we need her! She is a breath of fresh air wherever she goes. One of her strengths is organization; one of my weaknesses is organization. Sometimes I wonder if she didn't marry me just to have a challenge. Miriam is sleeping better now, only having a bad night on occasion. This week, she started taking a pain pill and a sleeping pill before bed, and this seems to be working.

This coming week, a large trade show for woodworking professionals is coming to Atlanta. Miriam wants to go (and I want to take her), but she would give out walking from the car to the first exhibit hall. I guess we will have to take the wheelchair, or it will be a miserable day for both of us. So many things we used to do as a couple or as a family are either not possible or are a big deal to pull off. Our evening walks around the neighborhood are finally back up to the entire four-driveway cul-de-sac after a 10-month suspension. Last weekend, we went to visit my brother in Dalton. The guest room is on the second floor, so Miriam went up and down the stairs on her bottom. They have invited us back in two weeks to attend a minor league baseball game with them in Chattanooga. Perhaps by then, she will be able to handle all the walking that will be required.

Sunday, November 15, 1998

More than a year has passed since Miriam's accident and more than five months since her last surgery. A strength test, performed during physical therapy this week, quantified what I already suspected—her left leg is 61% weaker than her right.

Some fast-moving weather fronts reminded us this week how little progress there really has been. The changing weather caused one nearly sleepless night and two more very painful days. Pain pills and the TENS unit are again very much a part of her regular routine.

CHAPTER 4
1999

January 3, 1999

The holidays are over, and a new year has begun. 1999 is starting much like 1998 on the knee front: a lot of pain and more surgery on the horizon. It reminds me of the Bill Murray movie *Groundhog Day*, where Murray's character keeps waking up and reliving the same day over and over again.

Things are deteriorating rapidly inside the knee and with our quality of life. Last week, while sitting in her chair without any weight on her legs, the act of rotating her torso to put something down on one side and then turning the other way to pick something up, caused a "pop," a lock-up, and a blood-curdling scream of pain. Our son raced out to the office and informed me that mom needed me NOW! I ended my business call and ran in to find my bride hollering for help with tears streaming down her cheeks. I took hold of her foot and straightened her leg, which seemed to give her some relief.

At varying but lower numbers on the "crisis meter," this scenario was repeated countless times over the weekend. Getting on or off the toilet, into or out of the car, up or down steps, even sitting still and moving her toes could cause another "catch." As far as we know, she has not fallen, stumbled, jammed, or twisted the knee to cause this. She says it feels as if something is loose and floating around inside that gets caught on things.

The intensity of her pain has jumped dramatically, and her mobility is substantially diminished. This past weekend, she wore the Protonics brace exclusively because it gives her more support. In short, she is now regressing quite rapidly. She is having to keep some pain medication in her most of the time now, where Motrin had been enough to keep her comfortable.

Needless to say, we are discouraged. She has worked hard and spent hundreds of hours of pain-filled effort both at P.T. and in the pool at the Y, trying to strengthen her leg. Today her leg is smaller than it was four months ago; her pain is more intense than it was five months ago, and she wears the bigger, heavier brace more than she has since her last surgery! Tonight, I helped her into bed at 8:00.

April 22, 1999

12:45 p.m.

She was in surgery for about an hour and three-quarters. Round five so far has been as smooth as any of the others. What led to this surgery, you ask? She was experiencing nerve pain behind the knee as if a nerve were being "plucked" by something. The purpose of the surgery is exploratory in nature.

Pastor Ray was here when we arrived this morning. He stayed with me until almost noon, after she had been brought to room 3283.

She continues to approach these procedures with bravery and without much apparent anxiety. If the pain of recovering from surgery is the price required to return to the track of sustained progress, she is ready to have her ticket punched. A few days ago, she told me that she could understand why someone would commit suicide to get relief from constant, intense pain when there's no relief in sight!

Dr. Hayes dropped by a while ago and we discussed the surgery. He said everything went well, but he did not find the expected cyst. Instead, he "found a bone, called a Fabella, that some people have, and some don't. He cut some tissue from around the nerve, he explained, but didn't remove the bone because he wasn't sure how this would benefit her." He also removed some scar tissue from under the fat pad and tightened the ACL. After he departed, I was left to explain to my terribly upset wife how she was going to "get better if the bone was not removed." She was discouraged and more than a little distressed.

Once again, our collective schedules are revolving around "the knee." Matthew will miss participating in the fourth-grade play tonight, because he is at his grandparents' house, while his mom and dad are in the hospital. Instead, he "had" to go fishing with grandpa, so it did not take long for him to get over missing the play. Miriam and I were not available for our respective duties at the plant today and probably not tomorrow. This is the smoothest hospital visit to date. When spasms are not occurring, the pain is steady but tolerable. "Only a three or four on a scale of one to ten," she answers when asked.

April 23, 1999

A new day and a new outlook. The night went better than any of the other "first nights" following surgery. She has been pretty blitzed since about seven last evening. The anesthesiologist came in and removed the epidural about eight this morning. It is 10 now and she is slowly sobering up. We will know shortly how she is really doing.

This morning she has had a good bit of nausea and has not been able to keep any food down. The physical therapist came in and tried to get her up for the first time since the surgery. Because she was catheterized in the OR and had benefit of the epidural following surgery, she has not needed to move much, which has contributed greatly to her level of comfort. The attempt at walking ended with a fit of nausea just on the other side of the threshold! It is 10:45 now, and she is back in bed, sleeping off fresh shots of nausea medication.

Long-time friend Chris Fanin came by this morning for a visit. We discussed Y2K and the pending demise of my flooring business and bankruptcy filing. It was a good distraction, a reminder that a real, more normal world continues to function beyond the walls of our hospital room and crisis.

Since starting the flooring plant in 1997, I've been running, or trying to run, two separate enterprises. For many years prior to starting the flooring business, I made a line of outdoor furniture of my own design. The flooring business was officially started July 1, 1997, but we really did not begin production until September. A month later Miriam slipped on the fresh laid floor wax. In November the first surgery was performed; April and May of 1998 brought surgeries two and three; January, and now April of 1999 surgeries four and five. Between the surgeries, recovery times, doctor visits and therapy, a lot of time away from a fledgling business was required by the president and the office staff. This missed time and resulting distraction has been a contributing factor for the financial mess we are in now. Without all these "higher priority" crises, I am confident some of our problems would have been identified and fixed before it was too late to do so. The furniture business, too, has suffered, because the time I've been able to work was largely spent putting out fires in the flooring business, as a result the furniture side has been largely neglected. Mental energy required for both enterprises had been focused on Miriam and her care. It was getting difficult to find something in my life I was doing right, since everywhere I turned it looked like the walls were closing in and I couldn't find an exit. If you want to feel sorry for something, pity my keyboard; I've been taking out a lot of frustrations on it.

9:30 p.m.

We were released from the hospital about four this afternoon. Miriam has not thrown up since arriving home, in spite of two attempts. She ate some Jell-O fruit salad our friend Nancy Parks brought as well as a slice of bread and butter. Other than eating and taking two bathroom breaks, she has slept the entire time we have been home. My parents came over and Mom cooked the fish Matthew and Dad caught last night. Tomorrow, Dad and I are going to the plant to work on furniture. Miriam's sister Debra will come stay with Miriam in the morning and neighbor Julie will stay with her in the afternoon.

There are many questions about this ordeal that we may not have answers to for many years, if ever.

If they are able to fix the knee and successfully rehab it, how fragile will it be? Will all the damage and surgery bring on arthritis prematurely? If an artificial joint is needed 10 to 20 years in the future, who will pay for it? For the last 18 months, her right leg has had to carry more than its share of the workload; will this have future repercussions? Much uncertainty and anxiety center around our future and this knee.

April 24, 1999

We had a good night! Her leg has stayed in the immobilizer since we left the hospital. Dr. Hayes did not send us home with a CPM machine, which makes caring for Miriam much simpler. I am so thrilled that she has not been moaning and wincing with pain. She has been sleeping most of the time and quite peacefully, too.

She really is not that highly medicated. I haven't had an opportunity to get the latest round of prescriptions filled, so we have been using our existing inventory. I called one of the many pharmacists with whom we are now on a first name basis and got advice about which medications we had on hand could be safely combined to give her the relief she needed, without using the higher-powered stuff. It worked, and she slept well even without a sleeping pill. The chemicals are helpful, but we are trying to use only what is necessary.

It occurs to me that some would view or dismiss this level of documentation as the complaints of a "whiner." In fact, I would take issue with such an accusation. Considering what this incident has cost us individually and as a family, I've actually only written about things that come to mind when I have time and an opportunity to write. This knee has affected not only our immediate family, but the extended family, the neighbors, my business partner, our employees, my businesses, as well as a host of other friends and acquaintances who have lent a helping hand when called upon. There is a lot of collateral damage in cases like this that every victim must find a way to bear. We are thankful! We are so fortunate to have a supporting family and community surrounding us; not everyone is so fortunate.

As I was assisting Miriam in and out of the shower a while ago, I was reminded about the increased danger this ordeal has put her and those around her in. For the next week, we will have to wrap the knee with Saran Wrap and tape to keep it dry while bathing. I will have to get the shower head down for her and try to hold her steady while she "hops" into the shower on her good leg, positions her left foot onto an upturned wastebasket for support, and then sits on the seat in the corner of the shower. Driving while taking pain medication is something she probably should not be doing, but it is that or not drive at all. Since her doctor hasn't specifically forbidden it, we assume it's ok. Of course, we haven't asked him about driving either.

Getting around on crutches following five surgeries was risky, as is the risk of getting bumped by the dog or a child and falling down. There is the inherent danger associated with negotiating steps of any kind, walking with poor balance, and always trying to compensate for pain. There is additional driving because she is required to go to therapy and doctor appointments. What if there was a fire at home, the plant, or even in the van; could she get out? So far, we have been fortunate, but the increased risks directly related to this injury are everywhere.

May 1, 1999

This Saturday morning brought the first sunshine this area has seen in several days. We laid in our respective beds longer than usual, needing a respite from a difficult week. A court appearance and filing bankruptcy were among the highlights that provided diversions from a week of rocky recovery on the knee front. The extra special and apparently rather rare bone that was not removed during the recent surgery, seems to be causing problems. Miriam claims the bump was not present prior to her accident. Perhaps the bone was present but the inflammation causing the bump was not? A new problem has surfaced, suddenly the top of her left foot is hurting and burning. Dr. Hayes indicated that the nerve they worked around controlled the top of the foot.

May 5, 1999

Miriam had therapy today and then a follow-up appointment with Dr. Hayes. He is pleased with her progress, apparently. He told her that her foot might hurt another two and a half months and that she could start driving as soon as she could sober up, and her pain didn't cause her to lose concentration and cause an accident. Bolts of pain have caused more than one close call. He also gave her only a small supply of pain medication. I should take her to his house one day or night when she is in severe agony, it would not take him long to get something in her that would ease her pain.

May 8, 1999

It is Saturday. Sleeping in an extra hour, sipping a cup of coffee while watching the birds and fish, and reading a newspaper—all little pleasures that are savored like an oasis in a desert.

The muted moans, whimpers, and groans from the chair next to mine bring me quickly back to reality. The last three days have been very tough for Miriam. Perhaps the weather and changing barometric pressure are to blame, but this woman has not had anything but an occasional moment without pain. It goes on and on. We have not slept in the same bed all week.

She has been trying since her surgery to get an additional set of leads and more rechargeable batteries for the TENS unit. An additional set of leads would allow her to use both channels on the TENS unit, which would support four pads and provide additional relief. Mediquip will not send them without the doctor's approval, and that apparently has not been forthcoming. Once again, it seems like her agony is not anyone else's concern.

Sure, a bum knee creates a host of mobility related challenges, but this is merely inconvenient. It is the ever-present pain that has stripped her of the joy of living! My once gregarious, always happy, seldom complained about anything, never wasted time attending her own pity party, always wants to join in, loving, and affectionate wife has been reduced to a pain filled, shell of a woman living in a drug induced haze. This is a woman who once received much pleasure from caring for her immediate family and those around her.

Miriam has always accomplished more in a day than some people get done in a week. She took great pride in her technical expertise and the life and death drama that is part of the hospital scene. After our son was born, she cut her hours to 32, so she could spend more time with her family. When his health problems demanded around-the-clock parental care, she started working nights on weekends. She often would come home drained from a tough night of having to match and prepare blood for a surgery or trauma patient whose life was hanging by a mere thread. Now, she is reduced to watching medical dramas on television.

The transformation from asset and hub-of-the-wheel to liability and observer-of-life has been the most difficult. We would both give almost anything to be able to turn the clock back and have the custodians put up signs around the area where ty were waxing the floor that fateful night.

This is Mother's Day weekend. At noon today, we went to Miriam's sister Debra's place, where we enjoyed steaks with Miriam's mother and father. Matthew wanted to go fishing in their pond this afternoon, which we did. Fishing has been our harbor from life's storms this spring. Several Saturdays have come and gone since we have been able to go fishing. When Miriam heard Matthew's idea, she quickly turned her sad, puppy-dog-like brown eyes in my direction and asked if she could go fishing with us. Her dad drove her to the edge of the pond, and I assisted her to a folding chair. She promptly skewered a hapless cricket and proceeded to catch fish. I enjoyed hearing her laugh and giggle with delight as she landed one victim after another.

I asked her what she wanted for Mother's Day. Her reply: "Two dwarf frogs for the aquarium so I can watch them from my chair." Miriam has never been what I would classify as high maintenance, but two little frogs? Needless to say, we came home by way of Baxter Street and Animal Kingdom. The aquarium has given us so much pleasure and has been cheap, effective therapy during the several weeks she has been confined to her chair following each surgery.

May 9, 1999

To commemorate Mother's Day, Matthew fixed his mother breakfast in bed (which is really her recliner) this morning, which consisted of scrambled eggs, toast, and coffee. We gave her cards and, of course, her frogs. Her low expectations are appreciated by her husband.

Miriam slept well last night, but by nine this morning was already trying to take a nap. The painkillers numb the pain along with a lot of other things. In spite of the painkillers, she hurts. Her once bright, sparkling eyes now reflect pain and a drug-induced glaze. At times, her countenance is almost hopeful — hopeful that we will wait for her to get better, so she can rejoin us in our pilgrimage through life. She need not worry; we are not going anywhere.

May 15, 1999

This is another rather blissful Saturday morning. None of us stirred until at least an hour after we should have been up.

My bride's existence can be summed up in one word: pain. I see it in her eyes, it is reflected on her face. I hear it in her voice. Nagging, almost constant pain at varying levels of intensity. There is top-of-the-knee pain, behind-the-knee pain, pain radiating from the end of the nerve on top of her foot. Now we have "old pain" and "new pain." Yesterday, while she was at P.T., an assistant set up the range of motion bike with the wrong settings for her stage of progress. The result was searing, ripping, tear producing, pain seasoned with spontaneous waves of nausea radiating from a new spot on the knee, that here-to-for, had been giving no problems. The rest of the session was spent alternating between ultrasound and ice therapies, while listening to the apologies of the horrified assistant. Miriam was sent home with a bag of ice on her knee. She had to drive herself because she was unable to find anyone to come get her! Upon arriving home, she collapsed in her chair. Yet another incompetent or distracted technician causes unnecessary problems.

The bit of progress we had been savoring was swept away (at least temporarily) by this lapse of competence. Thursday night, she even joined me in bed for the first time since her latest round under the knife. Last night, however, she stayed in her chair, not wanting to move.

May 20, 1999

Thursday Morning:

A chorus of birds ushers in the new day at the first hint of daylight.

There is progress to report and celebrate! It appears at this point that the screw-up by the assistant on Friday did not cause any permanent structural damage, just a new type of excruciating pain to help take her mind off of the normal pain for a day or two. Wanda is Miriam's younger sister. Her father-in-law lost his battle with throat cancer on Monday, and Miriam kept nephew Jake for several hours yesterday. Apparently, they walked a couple of laps around the cul-de-sac early in the afternoon. Later she took Matthew to Kmart and walked around the store. In the evening, Matthew wanted us to take a family walk with the dogs— something we did nearly every evening pre-accident. He so much wants his family back to normal. We walked less than a quarter of a mile, which took nearly 20 minutes, but we walked! A few hours later Miriam is paying for it with added discomfort.

May 22, 1999

It is another beautiful Saturday morning. Once again, I awoke to a chorus of happy birds welcoming the new day. Their enthusiasm is very cathartic.

The knee continues to show some improvement, but the red tape with doctors and workman's comp has not. Four weeks after they were requested, she still has not received the leads for the TENS unit! She went Thursday to get fitted for another brace and was informed that W/C may not pay for it! These braces were apparently not intended to be worn this long. In her case, it is not the wear but the size that is causing the problem. Her leg is a mere shadow of what it once was (due to atrophy). She cannot walk across the room now without the brace ending up on the floor! It will take months of intense exercise and therapy to grow back into the brace she has now. Dr. Robel assured us that she would be fitted for a new brace soon after this latest surgery. Now, four weeks later, they are not sure it will be paid for because "It is a duplication!"

Our dream and long-term goal was for my new flooring business to get strong enough to allow Miriam to quit her job at the hospital and come to work with me, but we were a long way from being able to do this. Her weekend night work schedule at the hospital gave us a slice of both worlds: on one hand, we got to work together three days a week, and on the other, the family benefitted from her income and benefits.

Having her resign from her job created several problems and, in hindsight, was a foolish thing to do. As it turned out, four more surgeries were waiting just over the horizon but the agony of physically getting to and from her "light duty" job was now over. Another big advantage to not having obligations at the hospital is that I could take her to the plant with me, care for her, and accomplish something useful, too. She could rest when the need arose and do as much or as little as she was able. There was a convenient bathroom and a sofa when they were needed.

May 23, 1999

This is a sun-drenched Sunday morning with only a thin layer of translucent cirrus clouds, giving a creamy hue to an otherwise blue sky. Yesterday we attended the Athens Air Show. According to Matthew, this is a tradition that must be maintained. We had a good time. This was the second year in a row Miriam viewed the goings-on from a wheelchair. I am sure it was more comfortable than the folding chair I sat in, but it is impossible to go through any of the planes on display in a wheelchair. The wheelchair saves her pain and increases her ability to tolerate a longer outing.

Wheelchairs, crutches, canes, and an assortment of different types of knee braces, each suited for a specific aspect of progress or activity, have become an integral part of our family's life. I bought the wheelchair, a four-legged cane, and a walker at an estate auction I attended shortly after her accident. The walker has been used some, but not nearly as much as the cane and the wheelchair. Even with a brace and a cane, a trip across a parking lot can exhaust her. These items have especially been helpful immediately following surgeries when we wanted to take extra care of the fragile leg. When I bid on them at the auction, I had no idea how useful they would become.

June 4, 1999

Night and day are the differences between yesterday and today, last weekend and this one.

Miriam has been doing so well of late. Last weekend we went to Dalton for the Memorial Day weekend. She was feeling better than at any time since her accident. She was able to help in the kitchen, she assisted with the baby, went fishing (standing up for the entire two hours), and generally had a relatively pain-free, almost normal weekend. We slept in their upstairs guest room and Miriam even carried baby Nathan up and down stairs more than once during the long weekend.

Progress has been steady in all areas: less pain, greater strength, and more mobility, until yesterday. All of a sudden it was like she hit a wall. That same invisible threshold of progress she has not been able to traverse after any of her prior surgeries, once again tripped her up. Her left knee started locking up again. Yesterday it happened while she was driving the van and thankfully, somehow, she missed the fellow blowing his horn at her. This morning, she was sitting beside me in her chair. She had just come from the kitchen with her plate of breakfast and was getting situated in her chair when it locked. I had to take hold of her leg and extend it. When I heard and felt the pop, the lock up was over; the pain and tears of frustration had only begun. The knee locked up again when Miriam was sitting at the kitchen table mid-morning. This time it was Matthew's turn to straighten it until it unlocked. He heard and felt the definite "pop" too.

Tonight, we are in familiar territory, a land of TENS units, pain pills, and involuntary yelps of pain, anguish and tears. She is understandably very discouraged. After this length of time and enduring five surgeries and recoveries and starting over with rehab six times (the first was immediately after the injury), to finally be making progress, only to suddenly fall again into a pit of uncertainty. She is demoralized. She is also again racked with pain. Her whole leg is upset. From the bottom

37

of her foot to the top of her foot and especially all around the knee.

She had a scheduled appointment with Dr. Robel today. Both he and Dr. Hayes examined and discussed the knee. She tried to get it to lock up but was unsuccessful. They told her to put it back in the immobilizer for a week to get things settled back down.

Journal: June 12, 1999

TGIF!

The problems continue after a week in the immobilizer. The pain and hindered movement remain, but thankfully the lockups have been far fewer. The swelling has diminished, and things appear to be settling down, though we are a long way from regaining the ground lost since Thursday a week ago.

I wrote Dr. Robel a letter begging for quick movement toward diagnosis and treatment. He called me Wednesday and asked me to come by yesterday morning to talk and to pick up a different type of immobilizer for her to try. He also asked me to have Miriam call that afternoon to see when he was able to schedule an appointment where doctors Hayes, himself, and Mayes were available to examine the knee and consult with each other about the problems and potential treatment. He said he may send her to see another "knee guy" for another opinion.

While I had him on the phone, I took the opportunity to ask some questions: "the movement you observed during her visit on Friday that you asked her to stop doing because it made you "sick," whose responsibility is it to prevent that?"

His answer: "The ACL."

My next question: "Is it possible that the thermal tightening procedure Dr. Hayes performed during the last surgery worked but has taken this long to stretch back out?"

Answer: "I don't know that much about the thermal plastic procedure, but it may be possible."

He continued: "It will not do any good to cut again until we have some confidence we are heading in the right direction."

Journal: Tuesday, June 15, 1999

Doctors Mayes, Robel and Hayes took turns examining Miriam's knee yesterday. I left the plant at 12:30 so I could be there to "pick their brains." I am glad I was there, but I missed a lot back at the plant. The soon-to-be new owners came to "draw a line in the sand" between the new flooring company and my defunct one. They talked to the employees, as well as to my partner. The general manager of a gated lake community came for the second time and brought one of the development's owners to look at our line of outdoor furniture. While all of this activity critically important to my businesses, career and future was taking place in my absence, I was sitting in the waiting room of yet another Doctor's office.

The consensus among the three orthopedic surgeons, who probably have close to eight decades of practice experience between them, was that there is looseness in the back corner of her knee, in addition to the ACL. If further surgery is required, it will be performed in Birmingham or Vail! They explained that the additional reconstructive procedure that may be required, "is rare, and has not been done around here."

It is safe to say that Miriam is very distraught over this news. The prospect of having to travel for treatment opens several cans of worms we have not had to deal with before now. Questions immediately arose, such as What will we do with Matthew? Will workman's comp pay all the travel expenses? Will they pay for me to go with her? Even if they do, can I afford the time away from the plant?

I am glad they are not simply throwing medicine at her to try to shut us up! We only want additional surgery if there are clear objectives and genuine benefits to be gained from it. At the same time, to hear three of the best bone tappers in the area exclaim that this "is a tough knee" is not very comforting. For the time being, we will proceed one day at a time.

June 25, 1999

Our lives are again on hold while awaiting surgery. Although the doctors have not made this official, the telltale symptoms we were told to look for prior to submitting to additional surgery are all present. Dr. Robel asked Miriam to keep a log of sorts, documenting for him the daily pain, problems, medications taken, as well as related information that might help pinpoint the source of the problems. She is doing so and is regularly faxing it to his office. Hopefully, one day soon, he will look at it and give us a call. Physical therapist Henry has told her that rehab will once again start over after surgery and that there is nothing they can do in the meantime to strengthen the muscles enough to eliminate the need for additional surgery.

Now that she has recovered from the initial shock, as with every other time, her attitude is: "let's get on with it, so I can begin to get well and get my life back!"

The prospect of having to travel out of town will complicate things tremendously. Arrangements will have to be made for Matthew, and what about my work? Miriam will not, cannot, go off on her own; someone will have to go with her and take care of all the things the medical types overlook, forget, or ignore. As her husband, I am the logical one for the job. Meanwhile, Miriam continues to take painkillers and sleep with the TENS unit to subdue the agony. The knee is locking up almost daily now, and she has done so at least four times while driving. So far, she has been able to pull off the road. When Matthew is with her, he jumps out, runs around to the driver's door, grabs Mom's leg, and unlocks it. The numerous hazards this thing poses to her and those around her is scary. For two years, she has often functioned in a drug-induced haze while on crutches, often trying to negotiate wet floors, steps, or uneven terrain. I've often caught myself nodding off while driving to or from the plant, mostly because it is hard to get a restful night's sleep when someone next to you cries out several times in the night or whimpers every time I roll over!

CHAPTER 5
Birmingham

By now, we've learned that just because a doctor writes a script for something, it does not mean the Workman's Comp system will fill it in a timely manner, or possibly ever. This is true for little things like a new set of leads for a TENS unit, or for surgery in a distant city. A few dollars, or many, it seemed we often had to fight for everything Miriam needed.

Letter written by Miriam to Dr. Robel

July 1, 1999

I understand you have referred me on to Birmingham. I've been told authorization has been delayed, so I called Kelly at FG Servicing Agency to see what the delay was about. They need to know the anticipated procedure, so that, in their words, "they could find out who can do this procedure."

I told them what you and Dr Hayes had said about Birmingham, Vail, or New York. But they need the exact doctor's names, etc. PLEASE get this information ASAP. The level of pain this week has been increasing and lasts longer when my knee locks up.

Thank you for your attention to this matter.

Sincerely,

Miriam Johnson

Journal

July 3, 1999

I feel so helpless. This morning I heard her cry out in anguish, ran toward the noise, and found her stuck halfway between the toilet seat and standing up. She could not move. I helped her return to the seat and unlocked her knee, then helped her to her feet. On more than one occasion, our 10-year-old son has had to assist his mother in this maneuver.

We visited Dr. Robel yesterday. He took some X-rays that were quite revealing. According to Dr. Robel, one side of her left knee had no gap between the bones, an indication that the cartilage is wearing terribly. This absence of space may also explain why things have gotten so loose. He went on to proclaim that this was "Out of his league!"

I understand we are now in the middle of the summer vacation season, but the knee is not aware and does not care that this is not a good time to be deteriorating by the day. Besides, it would be good to get surgery done as soon as possible, because Matthew is home this summer to help with the recovery, as is the long-suffering neighbor across the street (I think I saw them leafing through a real-estate magazine the other day. Who would blame them?). Once school resumes, care will not be nearly as convenient. The thought of going through surgery and recovery for a sixth time really angers me. The burden of dealing with this the first time is still fresh on my mind, and the rest kind of run together. The ACLs stand out, however, and according to Dr. Robel, the next, or third ACL reconstruction, a.k.a. surgery #6, will be more extensive than any of those; I can hardly wait!

Dr. Robel ordered her to return to the immobilizer and crutches to prevent further damage prior to surgery. This was not welcome news and put her in a funk for the rest of yesterday. This morning, in true Miriam fashion, her determination has returned, and she is trying to find a way to keep the immobilizer from slipping down and pressing on her kneecap. In other words, she is actively trying to solve problems.

Journal

Saturday morning, July 10, 1999

It is hard to imagine how much we look forward to more surgery. Potential progress and hope for the future cause us to eagerly anticipate yet another surgery; give this woman a pin prick of light in the otherwise dark tunnel, and she will focus on the light! One thing we know for sure: Miriam apparently will not get better without it!

Leaving town naturally causes several challenges: Matthew must have someplace to go; the dogs must be cared for; 17 employees in two businesses need to know in advance what in the world they are supposed to do for an entire week. In the last two years, I have not been away from the plant for more than a few days at a time, never for a whole week.

Dr. Robel's personal appeal was necessary to get the employer/insurer to approve this visit on such short notice, and to get us an appointment this quickly. He must have told them what he told us during the last visit, "This knee is deteriorating rapidly and is sustaining more damage each time it locks up."

We've reserved a room for the week that has a recliner in addition to a bed since Miriam has not slept in a bed for quite some time. It also has a modem jack so we can stay in touch via email. I guess this will be the closest thing to a vacation we get this summer, and we will spend most of the time in separate rooms.

Matthew is 10 years old. He was eight when his mother injured her knee. This will be the second summer of his life that our activity has been hampered by mom's lack of mobility. We can never recover these years of his life! He will never be 10 again! We will never be able to go camping as a family while he is at this stage of his life! More collateral damage from this tragedy, but this one really angers me. Since long before Matthew was born, I have dreamed of the day I would have a 10-year-old. A child old enough to do things with but not old enough to begin pulling away. His tenth year will have been highlighted by at least two knee surgeries, two recoveries, having to unlock mom's knee on a moment's notice, lots of housework, parents preoccupied with a bum knee, a failing business, and financial struggles. This is not what I had hoped for his ninth and tenth years with us!

The part of this trip I am dreading most is getting her back home following surgery. On many occasions, the 10-minute ride from the hospital to the house has been "eventful." The prospects of over four hours of travel with fresh wounds could be over-the-top exciting.

The Knee Gazette
Issue #1

July 13, 1999

It was an inspired idea to put Miriam's recliner in the van! I thought she would not use it until the return trip, but she climbed in it only about 20 miles from Greensboro and rode in it the rest of the trip. "Granny Clampett" was able to issue instructions quite effectively from her perch on her throne. She took a good nap and rested comfortably most of the way.

They have decided on a course of treatment: redo the ACL for the third time and "fix some other stuff." On this occasion, they will take material from the patella tendon on the right leg, so both legs will be involved this go around! They will also replace a damaged ligament on the back of the knee with an Achilles tendon taken from a cadaver. This is new territory and has not been done on previous surgeries. The need for work on the back of the knee may have been discovered earlier if an MRI had been used in the diagnosis process, but until recently, it had not.

A surgical resident informed us, "This will be our big case for the day, and Dr. Cox will need at least two assistants, so we will do it on Monday when we can schedule a large enough block of time."

After two major examinations, Miriam is hurting intensely. Since it is so late and we will have to pay for the room anyhow, we are going to rest and swim this afternoon before returning home in the morning. The good news is that they think the cartilage separating the femur and shin bones is ok! An x-ray taken during her last visit with Dr. Robel led us to believe there may be a problem there, also. If I were arm-chair quarterbacking here, especially with the advantage of looking back after several years, this may have been the fatal flaw in their strategy. Dr. Robel et al. were right — there was a problem in this area.

The Knee Gazette

Sunday July 18, 1999

Matthew is in good hands with brother Bruce and his family. It was hard to leave Dalton this morning, knowing what lies ahead. Jesus' prayer in the garden prior to His betrayal comes to mind. "…let this cup pass from me…" He knew what trials awaited around the next corner; we were speculating about most of ours. We would choose to skip these next few weeks if it were possible. But if this is the price we must pay to get Miriam back on her feet and get our lives back, then we will descend once more into this tortuous pit filled with surgeons, scalpels, and stitches. We are grateful for the support and prayers of so many friends and family. It will be different being this far away from everyone this time around.

We report at 8:30 in the morning, but surgery is not expected until the afternoon. They wanted to "do her last so they would have all the time they needed…" She gets to be their "case of the day tomorrow." Last Tuesday, when she met Dr. Cox and told him her long, sad story, they told us that she won the most interesting story of the day contest. Her case beat out the farmer who kicked his 400 lb. pig in the butt, then got run over by said pig, blowing out his knee.

~ Mark and "Hop-a-long"

The Knee Gazette

Noon, Monday, July 19

Room 442 will become Miriam's home for the next few days. At this writing, surgery is still nearly an hour away. Last evening, we were able to sit in the hot tub then paddle around in the pool before going to IHOP for some apple crisp topped with ice cream. Don't judge us; comfort food was justified!

The facility here is impressive. Their claim to fame includes treating the likes of Michael Jordan, Jane Fonda, a Saudi Prince, Troy Aikman and a host of others, including now, a med-lab tech from Watkinsville, Georgia.

Email is something I am growing to appreciate more and more as I learn how to use it. It is such an effective method of keeping in touch with our friends and family. In the time it would take to address and stamp one envelope (not counting the trip to the mailbox), I can instantly communicate with all of you. I hope you aren't offended by the impersonal format.

The Knee Gazette

4:30 p.m., Monday, July 19, 1999

Dr. Cox and his entourage just left. I am not sure what time they got started, but it may have taken as much as 90 minutes longer than they had planned. He said it would be another hour and a half before she is brought to the room. He said she now has a very tight knee! The repairs went as planned, but they also removed her fabella. She will be pleased to find out that this has been removed. It has been the suspected source of much pain and many problems, although no one could explain why this bone, she was obviously born with, was suddenly causing her problems. No matter, it is gone now. He went on to tell me that there has been a lot of cartilage damage. Only after she is back on her feet will they have any real idea of the prognosis for the future.

6:30 p.m., Monday, July 19

Miriam was returned to "my care" about an hour ago. She is buried under several blankets to minimize the shivering. She said they took her to surgery at 10 minutes till 12, which would mean she was in surgery over four hours!

The left leg is in an immobilizer. The right leg, which donated the center third of its patella tendon for the benefit of the left knee, is simply bandaged up. She is resting comfortably. They have an IV in her hand for fluids and an epidural in her back for pain. This time the epidural medication is on a patient-controlled button that allows her to administer her own pain medication, within reason, of course.

So far, she has eaten a few bites of a roll and sipped some tea. She will do fine if the epidural is not removed too soon. I wonder if I could slip this thing out to the van for the trip home? What if I promised to return it? It would probably require some illegal act on my part to get one out of the building.

~ Mark and "Peg"

The Knee Gazette

8:00 p.m., Monday, July 19, 1999

Well, I have had glimpses of what may be in store for us in the near future and it is not pretty! Being the kind, considerate, thoughtful, and selfish man that I am, I am "helping" her push her button from time to time, doing my part to help prevent the onset of sobriety. My job is much easier when she is snoring. I have heard some groans, moans, and whimpers that remind me of surgeries I'm still trying to forget. One thing I think we (the nurse and myself) will regret before the night is over is their decision not to install a catheter. The simple act of getting on and off a bedpan has caused *waaay* too much discomfort (and related problems) in the past.

Reading, answering, and then reading to Miriam the emails that have come in has helped pass the time today. Miriam's sister has called a couple of times, but other than that, our contact has been through email, which I think is great. The little "ding" that announces incoming email is a far cry from the "RING" of a telephone and does not awaken her.

6:30 a.m., Tuesday, July 20, 1999

Well... the daylight leaking in through the vertical blinds says its morning, but the sandpaper on my eyeballs would beg to differ. The king size bed in our room at La Quinta was traded for a hospital bed, and a roll away and is possibly the source of the sandpaper.

The night could have been worse, and certainly would have been, were it not for the epidural and the occasional dose of nausea medication. Her legs still have almost no feeling in them. The difference between none and almost, has given me a glimpse at the three-headed pain monster lurking just around the corner.

3 p.m., Tuesday July 20, 1999

Prayers are being answered! This day is progressing better than I had feared.

Miriam is in a lot of pain, she is fidgety, she is not a happy camper, and she has not forgotten how to tell me what she needs, or how quickly she needs it. The wonderful thing is that in spite of several waves of nausea, she has not vomited.

The "Fraulein," (she must be a Fraulein, normal sweet southern girls couldn't treat people so heartlessly) from Physical Therapy took her to the dungeon they call Physical Therapy twice today. Miriam even propelled herself (walking with crutches) all the way to and from the dungeon this afternoon!

I escaped for a couple of hours, returned to the hotel room, gazed at the king size bed and took a shower. I may not look better, but I feel better and since the flies have moved on, I must have a different aroma about my person.

Unless something changes, I expect her to be released from the hospital tomorrow. *She is receiving good care here. It was not easy for this Georgia boy to bring his bride to Alabama for medical treatment. Why, in these here parts, they think a bulldog belongs on a leash or in a cage. Here they worship something called a Crimson Tide, and their mascot is an elephant of all things. It's just not easy carryin' on a 'teligent conversation with folks that have such views. "Fraulein therapist," exposed her true roots when she asked me if I would like some "pop." I knew she weren't no propper raised Southern girl, or she would have asked if I wanted a Coke.*

I plan to send this, then leave for a few more hours and possibly even take a nap. Then I hope to eat a meal at some place that does not consider ketchup an entrée, before returning to the hospital for the night.

~ **Mark and "Happy"**

The Knee Gazette

Tuesday, July 20, 1999, 9 p.m.

Miriam is not feeling like running any races, I'll tell you that. She is hurting in earnest now. I think the button did not get pushed often enough this afternoon when she was feeling better, so the level of medicine in her system declined somewhat. It will have to happen sooner or later, but neither of us is looking forward to tomorrow when they remove the epidural and take her button away.

She ate a big lunch and supper today and has kept it all down. I am proud of her and am thrilled with the progress. While I was gone, she watched *E.R., Trauma,* and *Dr. Quinn!* You would think she would be weary of medical stuff by now. After 16 years of marriage, she can still amaze me from time to time.

I talked for a while with Dr. Cox this afternoon. She will probably be discharged late tomorrow if she does well once they remove the epidural. If this occurs, we will stay in town tomorrow night and try to go home on Thursday. All this optimistic speculation may be a bit premature, however. After all, she is only about 30 hours post-surgery.

One thing all our time spent in hospitals in the last 10 years has shown us time and time again, is the importance of someone's presence with the patient. The hospital staff is either too busy tending to other patients or doesn't care enough to provide the care a person needs. This evening for example, while I was gone, it took the nurse 55 minutes to get around to taking her to the bathroom! This is relatively minor. Over the years, on more than one occasion, we've caught someone preparing to administer to her or Matthew another patient's medications!

Right now, the nurse claims that according to the chart, pain medication was administered that Miriam claims she never received. Of course, since I was not here, I don't know. Miriam is probably right. Little things like applying lotion to an itchy back, getting drinks when they are needed, adjusting pillows, and keeping a bucket on "ready alert" can add a great deal of comfort to a patient's hospital stay that staff just hasn't got time to take care of. Besides, when I personally make a trip to the nurse's station to suggest that someone should come to see her or bring some pain medication or something, it almost never takes more than a few minutes for them to address the need. Perhaps I represent a greater threat than a bedridden patient pushing a call button every few minutes; it is probably more likely that my pleasant smile and engaging personality inspire people to respond.

~ **Mark and "Marathon Woman"**

The Knee Gazette

Wednesday, July 21, 1999, 7:30 a.m.

Dawn is clear but hazy outside; cautious optimism gently blows through room 442 on the inside.

The night went well. I think I slept better than Miriam, because every time I turned over, she asked me if I was okay. Personally, I don't think the people that designed that roll away bed ever slept on one.

The nausea monster is in the room, but so far has not taken control. He mostly circles and hovers, looking for an opportunity to strike. The bucket is still empty and clean in spite of many close calls.

We will get her cleaned up in preparation for "Helga's" arrival about mid-morning. After this physical therapy session, the epidural will be removed. How she responds after this will have a lot to do with when she is released and we come home. Right now, they are not planning to release her prior to tomorrow morning.

Keep the emails coming; they bring familiarity into a place without much.

~ **Mark and "Skippy"**

The Knee Gazette

3:30 p.m., Wednesday

If I caused Miriam half the pain that "Helga" does, I would be incarcerated and possibly lynched. She made it through the morning session okay, but the afternoon one was rough! She walked part of the way to the morning session, but this afternoon she rode almost the entire way to and from "the dungeon" in a wheelchair.

The epidural was pulled out late this morning. The pain has begun in earnest now, overpowering some serious oral medication. So far, though, the bucket is still empty and clean...

Miriam is beginning to understand the cliché about "not having a leg to stand on."

She is pitiful; trying to do something as simple as getting into the bathroom is an ordeal.

Miriam thinks the whole concept of sobriety is way oversold. I never thought the day would come when I could be called a "pusher" and my bride a "user," but the evidence is overwhelmingly against us.

I escaped for a few hours to "freshen up," do some useful work on the telephone and on the computer, before communing with the king-size bed back in the hotel room. I returned once again from my micro sabbatical feeling better than when I left.

Pray on, please!

~ **Mark and "Moans-When-She-Moves"**

The Knee Gazette

8 p.m., Wednesday, July 21, 1999

The plan presently in place, but subject to change, has us leaving the hospital and Birmingham in the morning. If everything goes according to this loosely defined schedule, we will arrive home sometime around midafternoon tomorrow. In spite of repeated attempts to locate volunteers to take my place, no one has stepped forward. This is probably because the mother-in-law was scheduled to visit, or a tooth needed pulling, or a prior appointment with the proctologist took precedence, or, you know, something more important. I am certain all my friends and relatives had very legitimate reasons why they were not able to make the trip.

Miriam is still a pain. Uh, I mean, she is in *pain*. Thankfully, the intense agony still has not resulted in a soiling of *le* bucket. She often resorts to breathing exercises we learned way back in Lamaze class to help with bolts of pain.

Since she is doing so well and I am so selfish, we (mostly me) have decided that I should sleep on the king-size bed in the hotel room tonight instead of on the cot ideally suited for a 120 pound person about four feet eight inches tall. Of course, this is to help me get a good night's rest in preparation for the drive home tomorrow. Considerate of me, right?

~ **Mark and "Moans Without Ceasing"**

The Knee Gazette

Thursday Morning, July 22, 1999

I am basking in the joy of having enjoyed a night of uninterrupted sleep on a bed big enough to rest my whole body all at the same time.

Miriam looks good. She had a good night, sleeping, she says, until the pain meds were close to running out. *Le* bucket is still clean! You cannot begin to imagine what a difference that is contributing to her overall comfort.

The van is all loaded; I've checked out of the hotel, and now we are waiting for the doctor to make rounds and discharge her.

The next hurdle I'm dreading is getting her into the van and then into her chair. Once we figure that one out, I think we will be in good shape, at least until she has to "go." By now, you have probably figured out that writing is therapeutic for me. Sure, it serves a useful purpose, but for me, it is also a way to vent. To release some of the frustration over circumstances that have hog-tied our lives for so much of the last 10 years. This is also a way to keep in touch with the real world out there, where people are dealing with normal things like taking the dog to the vet, changing the oil in the car, and trying to figure out where to go for vacation.

Thank you for indulging me and praying for us during this phase of our ordeal. The next six to eight weeks will still be challenging. It will be three weeks before Miriam can drive and six weeks before she can come out of the immobilizer and walk with only a brace.

"Helga" just stopped by to see if Miriam wanted to go to the dungeon this morning before we go, or if we wanted to do the "routine" after arriving home. I assured her that we would inflict a substantial amount of pain upon arriving home.

CHAPTER 6
Another Recovery

The Knee Gazette

Thursday 9 p.m., July 22, 1999

By the Grace of God, we are home. We arrived this afternoon with the help of lots of painkillers, two TENS units, an ice bag, and the recliner installed in the van. Our trusty van did a fine job, but Miriam still felt every bump, crack, seam, pothole, joint, and patch in the road, then felt compelled to report its severity with a moan, yelp, or scream. She was careful, I noticed, to never whinny. You know what they do to lame horses…

I apologize to those of you who had to read about my pity party earlier in the day. We really do have a lot to be thankful for! After all, it is only because of divine providence that we are not wandering around the streets of Mogadishu searching for scraps of food. Even with all there is to be thankful for, at times, I can't help but feel a bit overwhelmed.

Now that she is home, I'm trying to figure out what I'm going to do with her. Matthew is a huge help, but at present he is in Dalton until I figure out how to get him home. People in our church are rallying around yet again and are going to help transport her to and from therapy and bring in some meals. Our neighbor has been extremely helpful, too. Miriam's sister is going to spend some time here this weekend, so people are really stepping forward to help and for that I am very grateful. I only hope their energy holds up until Miriam can get back on her feet, because I still have a compelling need to work.

~ Mark and Miriam

Letter to Dr. Robel

Friday Morning, July 23, 1999

We've returned home from Birmingham.

Is it possible for you to write a prescription for some kind of home health assistance? If all they did was show up for an hour every day for the next three weeks to help her get a bath and ice down her knees, it would be a big help.

I am open to suggestions, but I need some help.

Mark

The Knee Gazette

Saturday, July 24, 1999

Another pair of food angels just departed after leaving enough food for a much larger family than ours. I'm sure I've never given anyone the impression that I/we are underfed (with Matthew being the possible exception). This is such a blessing to us, and a comfort to Miriam. Bringing food to families during difficult times serves many purposes. Perhaps one of the most important is the simple act of giving people an excuse to stop by for a visit that might not normally do so. It also reassures the family in crisis that people care about them at a time when it sometimes feels like they are all alone. In our case, it also gives me one less chore to accomplish, as well as assuring Miriam that her family is getting healthy meals.

Miriam hurts! She told me yesterday that she only thought she was in pain during the other two ACLs... I feel so useless. There is so little I can do for her beyond making her as comfortable as possible. If I could transfer some of her pain to me for a while every day, I'm sure I would, uh, at least consider it...? Truth is, I'm probably not strong enough to handle it, even for a short while! Despite some more close calls and extended periods when she feels like the room is spinning, *le* bucket is still clean, hallelujah!

She can put on such a brave face. It is almost comical to watch her talk on the phone. Only a video phone would tell the truth. Whoever she is talking with may hear laughter in her voice, but if they could see her, they might see tears running down her cheeks. There are times when things settle down to dull aches (plural, remember she had both knees cut on), but there are other times when the searing pain brings her bottom out of her chair.

My brother brought Matthew home early this morning. We were glad to see each other. He has been worried about his mother. It sounds like he had a great week. Bruce and his family attend the church in Dalton that was putting on a kid's camp near Knoxville. Before summer ever arrived, Matthew informed us that he wanted to go to a camp this summer. Since Bruce, his wife Sandy, and their three boys were all going, we thought this was the perfect opportunity for Matthew's first camp experience. Of course, it was just "coincidence" that Miriam had her surgery that same week, so we didn't have to make additional arrangements to accomplish this for him.

One of the things Matthew and I tackled after he got home was our "dead sock basket." For over-organized people out there who don't understand what I am talking about, this paragraph will go right over your head. The "dead sock basket" is where all the "single" socks are stored until a suitable mate, not always the one it was purchased with, is located, and a complete pair can be deposited into the appropriate sock drawer. How a family of three can fill a bushel basket with orphaned socks several times a year is a mystery. In our case, it may have something to do with the fact that our 10-year-old has been largely responsible for the laundry for much of the past year and a half. This was time well spent because not only did several pairs of socks get reconciled or "newly married," but I got to hear all about the fishing pond, the helicopter ride, the hayride, and the horseback ride that occupied our boy this week.

~ **Mark and She-who-prays-for-the-Rapture**

Journal

Sunday, July 25, 1999

Last night was the worst since surgery by a long shot. Waves of nausea slammed against my poor wife and crested into the ever-present, but until yesterday afternoon, clean bucket. This only compounds her already intense misery and contributes nothing to our respective night's sleep.

She says her pain is gaining in intensity. This may be the cause of the vomiting, or we may have monkeyed too much with her medications yesterday. I did add another pain medication from our well-stocked arsenal that our pharmacist said was compatible with what she was already taking, but in an attempt to eliminate the medication causing the problem, we will try to back up to where we were before the problem started.

Once again, Sunday has arrived, and we are not able to attend worship services together because of her knee. Also, I have missed another seven days of work, have had to ship Matthew off to the care of others, and cannot even work effectively at home because my wife requires almost constant attention.

Miriam's research on the internet yielded the following information: damage to the back corner of the knee is difficult to diagnose but often is accomplished with the help of an MRI.

One question that is eating at us: if Miriam had either had an MRI performed, or seen Dr. Cox after the first ACL failed, could at least four of the six surgeries have been eliminated? This possibility is great enough to cause an unhealthy amount of anger and frustration.

For a while at night and early this morning, I emptied one bucket while she filled another. It was obvious that much of what she ate yesterday was not digested. She has been consuming a good bit of yogurt in an attempt to coat and calm her stomach. She wanted to get in the shower this morning, mostly because she hasn't been able to wash her hair for a week. It took some time and some doin', but we got it done. The ordeal exhausted both of us. Thankfully she is sleeping now.

I have warmed up some of the "Manna from Heaven" the Food Angels brought yesterday, so Matthew and I will have a good lunch when he gets home from church.

Tuesday, July 27, 1999

I am dressed in long sleeves and slacks on what is to be a 100-degree day! This time of year, weddings, funerals, and church are the only occasions that get me out of short sleeves and shorts. But this time it is for a meeting with a judge. I have a meeting in Augusta, Georgia, to discuss the future of my now-defunct flooring enterprise. We will negotiate a mutually acceptable agreement, or I will close the doors. At this point, I'm trying to save the jobs of 20 or so employees and unload one of the pumpkin-sized knots I've been carrying around in my stomach for nearly two years.

In order to get to the plant in decent time to get work done and then get to Augusta by 10, I will leave Miriam in Matthew's hands. An 11-year-old child should have things on his mind besides taking care of his mother. At present, she is asleep. Last night was the second night in a row we all slept well. Sunday night, however, she slept so well that she failed to wake up and take more pain meds. She paid for it yesterday. Three times she called me at the plant, wanting to know what else she could take; she was talking through sobs of agony. I had no option this day, I had a court date, so she would somehow have to make through the day without me.

Last evening was no better. I was sitting in the chair next to hers, and her tears had made large wet spots on her shirt where they rolled off her cheeks.

The back of her left leg is very black and blue. Last evening, she complained that her left foot was asleep.

The Knee Gazette

Saturday, July 31, 1999

The week really got away from me. I am sorry for the lack of communication. There is much happening on the knee and business fronts; by the time I get home, the heat and the trials of the day have caused my brain to congeal, placing coherent sentences beyond my reach.

In a nutshell, Miriam is in lots of pain. It has not been an easy week for her. She called Birmingham one day to find out when the pain and swelling would subside. The good doctor's nurse told her it could be two to three more weeks! This did little for her spirits and caused a new cloud to form around her demeanor.

Her right leg, where they "borrowed" parts for the left, is doing well. The left leg is showing little progress. The pain continues to be rather intense, highlighted by periods of downright unbearable.

~ Mark and "Will Whine, But Won't Whinny"

The Knee Gazette

Saturday afternoon, July 31, 1999

According to the Weather Channel, it is 102 outside! This is far and away our hottest day of the summer. Naturally, the A/C in the van quit working late yesterday. Fortunately, we don't have to go anywhere today.

This afternoon seemed like a good time to take naps and watch a "Herbie" movie. Last night "Dennis The Menace" was our entertainment. On weekends, we often get several videos. This is something we can do together as a family. Movies don't cost much money, and it helps distract Miriam from her knee. Suggestions for our "film festivals" are welcomed. "Our" video store (Kroger) quit renting videos this week. We will miss the "3 for $3" deal we took advantage of there. Since we are so far behind in our movies, we don't need to rent the new releases to have something new to watch.

When it is not this hot and not the middle of summer, and Miriam is somewhat mobile, our preferred Saturday family activity is fishing. Mom usually catches more than Matthew and I put together, but we enjoy eating her fish as much as those we catch ourselves. We are hoping that we can do some fishing again this fall. By the middle to the end of September, Miriam should be getting around at least as well as any time since this nightmare began. We are desperate to know there is blue sky and sunshine somewhere on our horizon. Small, incremental glimpses of progress will buoy our spirits and keep hope alive.

It has been a tough week. Something "popped" Thursday evening while Miriam's sisters were helping her get a shower. Since she was sitting down with the leg propped up at the time, we hope it was nothing serious. If you had been standing near the house at the time, you would testify in court that something dreadful was being done to someone on the inside.

"No, your honor, I did not do anything to hurt her," said the large man on the witness stand with one hand on a Bible!

Aside from some swelling and a small knot on the back of the knee, things appear "normal." We hope it was only an adhesion tearing loose. She does not think the pop, or the pain, originated from within the joint itself.

Some of the prescription bottles contain a warning that alcohol consumption may intensify the effect of the medication. These warnings give her ideas. She has talked often in the last two years of taking up drinking (for medicinal purposes of course). I have been considering it simply to help me forget present reality. It is probably good the "joy juice" stores are so far from our home. By the time I get in a vehicle and get halfway to town my better judgment takes over and turns me around.

Last night was tough because she was recovering from yesterday's session of physical therapy. Did you know Birmingham "Helga" has a "brother?" He lives in the Athens area and works in the physical therapy department at Altma Hospital. His name is Henry. Henry has been torturing my bride since her injury. We are way too well acquainted with Henry. Miriam and Henry have spent way too much time together in the last two years. Henry won't allow Miriam to talk with any of his other patients he is preparing for ACL surgery. He is afraid they will turn tail and hobble away after talking with Miriam; he's probably right.

~ **Mark, Matthew and "The Agony of the Knees"**

The Knee Gazette

Monday, August 2, 1999

Miriam's wounds were examined by Dr. Robel today, and he declared, "All looked well." The "pop" she had a couple of days ago did not concern him. He thought it was a ruptured blood vessel or a stitch near the surface that came loose or something. He couldn't resist manipulating it to see how tight it felt; he was impressed.

I admit it. I am a lousy wife and mother. Fortunately for Matthew and me, our Creator recognized this and sentenced Miriam to life at my side. Evidently, the entertainment in Heaven must have gotten a little dry a couple of years ago, so they decided "just for giggles" to incapacitate Miriam and see how I coped. I'm sure, at times, they have nearly fallen off their golden stools with laughter. No one who knows me would accuse me of being a neat nick. Left to my own devices, "clean clutter" would probably best describe my abode. But since I'm not left to my own devices, I have been making a real effort to keep the kitchen clean and the living spaces ordered. This is no small task with people coming and going, bringing food or transporting Miriam to some place, or just dropping by for a visit. This effort is assisted once a week by a lady who comes by to attempt to restore genuine order to the house. How embarrassing would it be having the health department come by for an inspection? In my defense, no one in our home has gotten food poisoning from my kitchen or cooking!

A couple of days last week probably had the heavenly pranksters quite amused. I cleaned up the kitchen by wiping down the counters and loading the dishwasher before leaving for the plant. In my eyes, since you couldn't see dishes in the sink while driving by at 40 mph and the countertops were not completely green, it qualified as a fairly clean kitchen. Our pastor's wonderful wife, Sandra, came for a visit and asked Miriam if she could clean the kitchen while she was there. Miriam, who was stuck to her chair and not able to see what kind of disaster I may have left, asked if it needed it. The answer was an eye-rolling nod.

Another afternoon, the lady came to clean. Upon opening the microwave, she made some comment like: "This is scary." Naturally, my bride took great delight in relating these events to me. She didn't buy my assertion that it was an effort to make her feel needed.

~ **Mark the Emasculated and Miriam Sits A lot**

The Knee Gazette

August 7, 1999

Miriam has made some great progress in the last week. Her pain is less raw because healing is taking place. This has allowed her to reduce the pain medications, to sober up some and actually perform useful work on the computer. She is still not mobile, but she is more comfortable most of the time, which makes it much easier for Matthew and me to share her abode. All that hollerin', cryin', and slurred speech was getting old.

On Monday, she will be three weeks post-surgery. Her right leg is getting stronger, which allows her to function better with her crutches. Today she made one lap inside the house and although she was breaking out in a sweat (excuse me, ...beginning to "glow"), she made it, and did well. Rather than becoming drenched with "glow" (remember, horses sweat, men perspire and women glow), she rested after one lap and allowed her "glow" to evaporate. She spent the rest of the evening watching the toes on her left foot, to see if she could make them move. It doesn't take much to entertain someone in a drug-induced fog.

Perhaps in another six weeks, she will feel strong enough to walk to the edge of a pond and threaten its occupants with her deadly hook. One thing is obvious: she won't be driving nearly as soon as I had hoped, I am guessing it will be another two to three weeks at least! Fortunately, our neighbor, my parents, and our church family continue taking turns transporting her and Matthew to where they need to go. It will probably be after our return trip to Birmingham at the end of the month before she can function safely behind the wheel.

I took the van to the shop for repairs on Tuesday and picked it up $700 and 30 hours later. It ran fine all the way home, where it spent Thursday in the garage. On Friday when Kay Shepherd came to take Miriam to physical therapy, the van ran fine for three of the seven miles to the hospital. The message I received from the answering machine was from Matthew, it went something like: "Dad, the van broke down it is at the Milledge Avenue Baptist Church. Come get us."

Naturally, lots of pictures suddenly appeared on my cranial screen, but none of them were pleasant. One of them was of a wheelchair being pushed along the shoulder of the road...since some time had passed since the message was left, I did the only thing I knew to do — I waited for the phone to ring so I could find out how they got out of this mess.

Fortunately, they were in capable hands. Not only did she get to and from physical therapy, but somehow Kay Shepherd managed to get the van back to the house too. After receiving her call and hearing about their adventure, I went home and took the van back to the shop. The least I could do was try to get it fixed for next week.

Of course, the hesitation, coughing, lack of power, and backfiring that had not been present in the more than 60,000 miles we've driven since owning the van was not related to the tune-up and induction service they had just performed. "Another hundred dollars will replace the faulty sensor in the exhaust system." I was almost too livid to speak. This poor fellow sensed that this seriously oversized ugly man was not happy! He probably hoped I would not begin throwing things (like him) around the service area. I did my best to keep my cool and not disgrace "The Kingdom."

"They would try to make the repair yet that afternoon." Wanting to accomplish something for my trip and lost time at the plant, and knowing I really had little choice, I authorized the repair. Besides, 100-dollar bills grow from little plastic cards, right? You would think so, judging by the number I had pulled from mine this week for the benefit of one blue van. I suspect they got paid for finishing the job they did not complete two days earlier but trying to prove it is another matter. But, after all, it's only time and money, right? It is so convenient that we have a tree in our yard that produces both time and money!

Besides the film festival, our other entertainment comes from the aquarium and bird feeders. This morning we've been entertained by cardinals, goldfinches, tit mouses, house finches, hummingbirds, brown-capped chickadees, and some others we cannot identify. The fish remind me of cows in the pasture watching the pickup trucks go by, wondering anxiously which one is bringing them more hay. Every time someone moves near their glass house, the fish line up to watch and see if the lid opens and food falls in. Miriam has spent enough time studying our finned friends that she knows which ones are playmates and which are rivals; what patterns they swim in and who they swim with; which ones are pregnant and, since she probably watched them mate, she knows who the daddy is.

Providing you with more information than you ever wanted to know.

~ **Mark, Matthew, and "Toes Won't Wiggle"**

The Knee Gazette

Saturday, August 14, 1999

Birds are fighting over food outside my window. I am sipping coffee from my favorite mug and, so far at least, Miriam is having a good morning (she has been awake for all of nine minutes). How much better could life get? We are not unlike the birds outside and the fish in the aquarium; nice people bring us food too. I hope the neighbors don't catch us with our noses pressed to the windows eagerly anticipating the arrival of our next meal.

We are overwhelmed by the outpouring of help from those around us. Monday will be day 28 since Miriam's latest knee surgery, and Matthew and I have not had to cook a meal yet! Although in many ways this has been a humbling experience, we've learned much from and about our extended family. Miriam and I have used the meals as object lessons about God taking care of His people. "Matthew, do you know what manna is?" It has been wonderful to have so many people stop by for a visit, which is much more intimate than stealing a 20-second-long whispered conversation over the back of a pew on Sunday morning. These visits have been very encouraging to all of us, but for Miriam, they provide a badly needed distraction from life in her recliner.

"Food from strangers" has also exposed Matthew to cuisines he may not have been familiar with. He has learned that just because a dish has a familiar name does not mean it will resemble something he recognizes. "Son, are you grumbling about your manna?" is a phrase he has been assaulted with on more than one occasion. My not having to prepare meals has lightened my load considerably.

We are also benefitting from a steady barrage of prayer. There is no other explanation for the source of strength to keep trying and not sit down in a puddle of tears and quit. Since I have known her, I have admired Miriam's nerves of steel when dealing with adversity, but this nagging, ongoing, painful ordeal has used up her natural strength. She has been operating on prayer for some time now. Believe me, we all have!

Miriam continues to show progress. Her bad days now are equal to the good days of only a couple of weeks ago. Although there are moments when things seem to be spinning out of control, they are fortunately relatively short lived, like a fast-moving squall line that blows, soaks, frightens, then leaves. We had one of those last evening. We had eaten a wonderful meal of "manna" and were settling in for another distraction to "life in the chair" (a video), when stomach cramps caused us to quickly get her to the bathroom, where Miriam screamed from knee pain and moaned with stomach cramps. As if that weren't enough, she was assaulted by gusts of nausea that kept Matthew scurrying for clean buckets while I dealt with the "soiled" ones.

Fortunately, this was a fast-moving storm that left as quickly as it arrived. We were then able to settle down and watch Robert Redford fly WWI-era airplanes in "The Great Waldo Pepper." Waldo helped all of us forget about the storm and gave us something else to think and talk about.

This has been the wonderful thing about our family "film festivals." Watching videos is something we can do together that does not require Miriam to be completely "sober." In other films that we watched in the last week, we've seen horses shot because of broken legs, a cow shot to keep it from suffering after complications from giving birth, and a pilot hit over the head to spare him from the pain of being burned alive. Miriam has been very adamant about the fact that she has not whinnied or mooed, but when Waldo smashed his friend's head to keep him from suffering, the color drained from her face when we exchanged glances.

I think our fortunes are about to improve. The highlight of my week was watching five bluebirds bathe in our birdbath at the same time. Surely one of them was the "bluebird of happiness?"

~ **Mark, Matthew, and "My Toes Wiggle a Little"**

The Knee Gazette

August 21 & 22, 1999

Coffee tastes better when there is time to savor it. That is what weekends provide us. A hundred years ago, when life revolved around an agricultural economy, I imagine Saturdays were merely an extension of the rest of the week. Sundays were held apart, except for chores, which never took a day off. Life had a steady rhythm that was structured and well defined. While our ancestors may have waltzed gracefully to Beethoven or Mozart, we are trying to gyrate to electronic pulses coming at us in random patterns. Since as a culture, none of us sow, harvest or milk according to nature's rhythms, we must find and make our own. Weekends are our reprieve from these gyrations, and they are so very welcome.

Miriam is ever so slowly improving. She has been moving around some with the help of a walker. Although it is painful to watch, it is better than seeing her sit in her chair unable to move. Saturday morning, she "walked" all the way to the kitchen and opened the refrigerator– big mistake! Let's be kind and admit it has been without "momma's influence" for a period of time now...

She began opening drawers and talking with someone (me, I guess) who began providing involuntary answers to what sounded like rhetorical questions. I heard a conversation that went something like this: Miriam was standing behind her walker, leaning on it with one arm, while holding up a pizza box whose contents were several days beyond any help a microwave could provide.

"How long has that been in there?"

The voice, possibly mine, answered: "Only since the preacher came by a couple of Sunday nights ago."

Upon opening what was advertised in the literature to be the "crisper," it now resembled a biology lab (the contents were weeks beyond crisp), and she really went off. "I don't think those are any good," she exclaimed while pointing to some red lumps that may have been tomatoes.

Then I heard a rather timid voice that sounded a lot like me, answer her questions with questions: "A zucchini? An onion? Is this a riddle? I give up." I took command and in the name of "You really should get off your feet," insisted that she return to her chair while I cleaned out the biology lab. My "plan" was working. She felt needed.

Saturday afternoon I took Miriam to her sister's pool. Once we got her in, it was great. She wrapped a couple of foam noodles around her and then kind of hung there with her feet suspended above the bottom of the pool. At this point, she was able to kick as much or as little as she felt like it without bearing any weight. This probably is as close to a no impact workout as one can find.

Miriam is still on enough pain medication that she has shown no interest in reading. Reading has always been her passion. She is one of those people who can consume several hundred pages per day; she is the kind of reader libraries were designed for. It would take a big budget to purchase all of her reading material. She often refuses to keep books in the house, just so she can concentrate on her "duties." This time of convalescing is ideal for reading, but her mind has not been clear enough yet. As wonderful and helpful as all these drugs are, they do have their downside.

Next Sunday we'll travel back to Birmingham for a Monday morning follow-up visit with Dr. Cox. Hopefully he will answer some nagging questions. I/we are real concerned about her left foot. The wearier she becomes, the more it wants to turn out and drag. It turns out so far sometimes, it is almost pointing backward! This may be nerve related and something that time will heal, but in the interim, it is bothersome.

Since I have probably crossed the threshold between interesting information and excessive detail long ago, I will sign off for now.

~ Mark, "Wants to Walk," and Matthew

The Knee Gazette

Sunday August 29, 1999

Greetings from B'Ham, Alabama. We departed W'Kinville this morning to the tune of "Hi Ho, Hi Ho, to Another Doctor We Go." Our trusty van delivered us safely about three this afternoon "here" time.

There was measurable progress this week! Miriam actually walked with the help of only a cane. Not around the block or anything, but hey, across the room is far enough to give us hope. She is feeling good enough that she is looking for ways to contribute to the household chores that are within reach. There is a good laundry story to be told, but it will have to wait 'till another day.

This evening we dined on seafood and then Miriam wanted to see a movie, in a theater! *Runaway Bride* had been recommended by some of our "critical" acquaintances, so we did a dinner and a movie thing, almost like a real date, kind of similar to what normal people, living regular lives, do (so we've been told). It was kind of nice! Of course, Miriam sat in the wheelchair, which does have an effect on the movie-theater-cuddle thing, but we enjoyed the desirable seating location instead.

~ Mark and "Walks a Little"

The Knee Gazette

August 30, 1999

Dr. Cox gave us some good news but did not give Miriam all the answers she was hoping for. The pains in her foot, the limited mobility of her toes, the turned-out foot, the pain and the popping noises in the knee apparently bother us more than him. He examined her knee and declared it structurally sound. He wanted her to come out of the immobilizer and begin walking in a brace. This will help to strengthen the muscles, which he thinks will begin to solve some of the other problems too, time will tell. We hope he is right.

~ Mark and "More Mobile than She Was

Letter to Dr. Robel

Monday evening, September 6, 1999

Miriam is making progress! She is slowly beginning to walk short distances without the assistance of crutches, a walker, or a cane. This is encouraging.

Last night, however, we hit a bump that we need your help to get over. About an hour after taking a Loratab and retiring for the night, Miriam had violent stomach cramps with explosive diarrhea and vomiting (it had been about five hrs since she had eaten and then it was only a cheese quesadilla.) At the same time, she broke out in whelps which covered most of her body. I scrambled for some Benadryl and eventually got her calmed down, and we went to sleep.

I assume she has developed an allergy to Loratab that is similar to the one she developed for Tylox? If I am right, we need another pain medication ASAP. She has physical therapy with Henry at 9:45 in the morning if you need to see or talk with her. For about the last week, she has needed Loratab mainly on

*physical therapy days, along with some evenings, to
get the pain under control. Otherwise, Ultram and
Motrin 800 are able to keep her somewhat
comfortable.*

Thanks for your help,

Mark

Journal

Thursday, September 9, 1999

Once again, Matthew and I had to ignore mom's muted sobs in order
to fall asleep. Both of her legs are getting stronger, and her mobility is
slowly returning. Since her allergic reaction the other night, she has had
to deal with additional pain rather than numb it. We've been trying to
get a hold of Dr. Robel for two days to get some other pain medication,
but he has returned neither phone calls or faxed messages. In the
meantime, she suffers. At least three times yesterday she called me
while I was working at the plant, and I had to listen to her try to talk
through her tears. Maybe this helped her feel better? It helped me feel
even more impotent, because once again I couldn't fix her pain.

Physical therapy is consuming two days a week since the last surgery;
next week it goes to three times per week. These sessions are tough
and wipe her out for 24 -36 hours afterward. The net result, however,
is that she has begun to walk with only a brace and cane, which is better
than she has done for the last two months!

September 4, 1999

Labor Day weekend finds us in Dalton at brother Bruce's house. We
visited them over Memorial Day weekend and then again when we
dropped Matthew off for camp, while we were "on our way" to
Birmingham, prior to Miriam's last surgery.

Traveling beyond the county line these days is an adventure.
Attempting to avoid a miserable wife while en route, I put her chair in
the van once again. I figure the pain of getting it in and out of the
house and in and out of the van is less than the pain of listening to her
moan and groan for six hours this weekend (my motives sound selfish,

don't they?). In addition to the recliner, we have the wheelchair, a pair of crutches, a four-legged cane, a knee brace, and four pillows.

Miriam continues to progress ever so slowly. She started driving some this week. On Tuesday she was determined to walk into and out of physical therapy. I am so weary of watching my wife suffer. At times I try to ignore her or forget about our plight for a while, but a yelp, shriek, or groan, usually ends my trip to "fantasy land" after only a few moments.

We attended a minor league baseball game in Chattanooga earlier this evening. The Chattanooga Lookouts (AAA affiliate of the Cincinnati Reds) were facing the Greenville Braves. The star attraction, however, was the San Diego Chicken — the mascot of the Padres. He puts on a good show as he "hexes" the visiting team and humiliates the umpires. One of the few advantages to Miriam's affliction is that she (and I) get good seats and great parking when we go somewhere. At this event, her wheelchair was perched behind the backstop only one tier of seats away from home plate. The rest of our party languished in the cheap seats, dutifully carrying on a family tradition that is several generations old. Being able to actually view the action at an event is a refreshing change and not something we were usually able to do when we attended sporting events with our father. Most of the time it was BYOO (bring your own oxygen). Our dad was great about taking us lots of places but spending money for the really good seats was not part of the adventure. Now that it's my money to spend on frivolous seating, I get it! The tradition is safe with me.

The Knee Gazette

Sunday, September 5, 1999

Miriam's therapist (remember "Helga's brother" Henry?), wants her to practice lifting her leg like she is stepping up on a step. I requested that this maneuver not be performed in public, near a fire hydrant, because passers-by might not understand what kind of therapy she needs.

Our sanity requires that we look for things to chuckle about; this helps take our minds off the things we are tempted to cry over.

Please keep praying for us.

~ Mark, Matthew and "See, I Can Move My Toes Some"

The Knee Gazette

Monday, September 13, 1999

Steady progress and baby steps sum up the last week.

I returned the portable toilet to its rightful owner today, and the walker was put in the storage room. Miriam went to the plant with me on Friday and helped restore order to my chaos there. The employees were so glad to see her that they bought her a plant. Hurting for most of the night was the price she paid for being on her feet all day. She was grinning from ear to ear while fighting back tears. She felt great about plugging in and doing something truly useful.

When I returned from running errands Saturday morning, the kitchen looked like Miriam had returned from a very long trip and had gone to "work." Evidence that she is feeling better is everywhere.

She is steadier on her feet today than she was a week ago. The muscles in her legs are gaining strength, so there is less wobbling than only a short while ago. She is getting by with fewer pain pills, so it is easier to carry on a conversation with her. She is eight weeks post-surgery, and for the first time in six operations, she has gotten this far without a major setback.

I am still hopeful that by Christmas, she can get around almost normally with only the help of a brace. Her left foot is beginning to point in the direction she is trying to walk, as the muscles gain strength and the nerves recover from being messed with during surgery.

Thank you for your continued prayers and interest in our saga.

~ Mark, Matthew and "She Who Walks on Both Feet"

The Knee Gazette

Saturday, September 25, 1999

What a gorgeous morning in North Georgia! The Braves moved closer to clinching their division last night and UGA's Dawgs play this afternoon. The sky is haze–free blue, the air has a fresh fall edge, and the pace of our lives has downshifted from a week-day rat race into a weekend-mellow. This is the kind of day that is wonderful for most anything; chances are good that we won't enjoy this kind of weather next weekend when a Boy Scout camp-out is scheduled.

The birds are hoping that filling their feeders is on my very short agenda for the day. They emptied them several days ago, and the loss of easy foraging is quite offensive to them. The hummingbirds will peck on the windows if I allow their food to run out! The entertainment value they provide, however, makes the line item in the family budget for bird food well worth it. At times, the traffic is so high near Miriam's window that I feel compelled to provide air traffic control services. So far, however, they have not understood or appreciated the value of the fool waving funny colored flags around their feeders.

Miriam's steady and encouraging progress has possibly hit a snag. Hopefully, time will prove it to be merely an inconvenient bump on her road to recovery, but at present, we are discouraged, to say the least. On Friday, while at physical therapy, she was working on a machine designed to work the muscles used in walking when her knee "popped," and she was once again racked with pain. Her therapist was there and was able to feel a knot that should not have been where it was.

She hopes to see the Dr. on Monday. Please pray for us. A seventh surgery would be bitter medicine at this point. Miriam is tough and gritty, but we all have our limits. There have been many days I thought we were teetering on the edge of the special pit set aside for the justifiably insane…

~ **Mark, Matthew, and She Who Can't Lose the Catch in Her Get-a-Long**

Letter to Dr. Robel

Sunday evening, September 26, 1999

The problem that reared its ugly head on Friday while she was under Henry's care has resurfaced at least three times this weekend without bearing weight when it occurred!

The good news is that so far, I think this is different than the other walls we've encountered a few weeks post-surgery. For example, I am not aware of any locking or real instability. There is a lot of pain and some swelling.

Our concern is finding out what is causing this problem and getting it fixed quickly. With this goal in mind, please move quickly with whatever diagnostic procedures are needed: x-rays; ultrasound, or even MRI. If she needs to return to Birmingham, please get us an appointment ASAP. It is my desire that whatever problem exists gets fixed before the grafts are compromised if this is possible.

Journal

October 10, 1999

It's a rainy Sunday evening. Matthew is reading on the love seat, Miriam is reading while whimpering in the chair, while I have been catching up on my Reader's Digests. Our reading is interrupted several times a minute by muted moans from Miriam. Every now and again the sound is less muted and a yelp and even an occasional shriek slips out. How are we supposed to concentrate on our reading with all that racket going on?

She has been in almost constant pain for nearly a month now. While visiting Dr Robel a couple of weeks ago, some x-rays were taken, and a nerve test scheduled for later this month.

"The results had to be given to Dr. Robel, and she could not hand deliver them to him." On Friday afternoon Dr. Robel's nurse told Miriam, that they had not seen the results yet and that she would try to get them faxed prior to Dr. Robel's departure for the Tennessee vs. Georgia football game. Several agonizing days later, we've heard nothing.

It seems to us as though she is supposed to quietly endure her slice of hell until one day it magically disappears, something this nightmare has shown no signs of doing.

Last weekend Matthew's scout troop had a family camping trip at Ft. Yargo State Park in Winder, Georgia. Matthew and I had a great time, and Miriam would normally have gone with us, if she was able to get down and then back up off an air mattress on the ground.

Dr. Robel (and Miriam) do not think the present problems are structural, as the integrity of the joint seems to be solid, but at present, an explanation for the on-going agony eludes us. The nerve test is supposed to reveal the presence of a growth on the nerve (a possible result of it having been messed with so much this year). Where this could lead, we can only speculate.

Miriam has started stuffing a blanket in her mouth when intense pain awakens her in the wee hours of the morning. This is an attempt to prevent her screams from waking me and ruining additional nights of sleep for me. For the most part, it is working, when she gets the blanket in soon enough. I have joked that I am toast if she forgets to take the blanket out sometime. No jury in the world would ever believe she stuffed a blanket in her own mouth herself.

Every morning that I am awakened from a deep sleep by a shrieking wife about 4 a.m., I cannot go back to sleep. Therefore, I drive to and from the plant sleepier than I would have been with a full night's sleep, and often have a hard time concentrating on my work by midafternoon of the following day.

Letter to Dr. Cox

October 23, 1999

Miriam's progress since you reconstructed her knee on July 19, 1999, has ground to an abrupt end. Although her knee is not shifting like it was prior to surgery, intense pain has returned.

This problem began on September 24 during a physical therapy session and refuses to simply go away. The pain is at the back lateral corner of the knee, along the line of the peroneal nerve. The MRI revealed: "A grade 3 meniscal signal seen in the posterior horn of the lateral meniscus. Impression is lateral meniscal tear with associated meniscal cyst."

We have an appointment with you on Tuesday morning at 8:30. We are bringing letters from the physical therapist, Dr. Max Robel, and a report on the results of a NCV, EMG, and an MRI, along with the films.

I hope you are able to restore her to the road of progress quickly.

Letter to Dr. Cox

November 3, 1999

On Tuesday, October 26, you examined Miriam's knee regarding ongoing problems she has experienced since her reconstruction in July. You indicated that she had a torn gastroc and that it should heal, but if it is not better in three weeks, you will "go in and have a look."

*The fabella was not discussed at this examination, but the area of her pain is **the same area from where you removed her fabella in July**. This has been a consistent center of pain for most of the last two years until it was removed. Could complications be developing from this procedure? I recall you mentioning how large the fabella was during our post-op discussion.*

*In the week and a day that has elapsed since your examination, **her pain is only growing more intense**. This is not related to use or motion– she hurts as much at three in the morning while lying in bed as she does at three in the afternoon after being on it for a few hours. **During her physical therapy session this morning, her therapist was alarmed at how swollen the area was around her lateral scar.***

I am concerned for her sanity if someone does not relieve her pain very soon! She is not sleeping well, despite taking a pain pill and a sleep aid. Often, I am awakened from her cries of pain or the shuddering from her sobbing. She is growing ever more desperate for relief from the constant and intense pain.

Journal

Wednesday, November 3, 1999

It's Matthew's birthday. He's the embodiment of a person who drinks life in large gulps and is enthusiastic about most everything. His excitement is contagious and refreshing. When Matthew is enjoying himself, everyone knows it. This birthday is an event that will stretch over several days, and we've been reminded of this on several occasions.

Miriam's desire to give him a special day causes her to will herself out of bed after a nearly sleepless night, in time to fix him orange rolls for breakfast. Miriam will put on a brave smile and refuse to allow her pain to affect her son's special day. Her desire to be his mother has kept her fighting for two years instead of simply giving up and ending the pain somehow. Being a mom was a goal long before he arrived and is a passion that has never wavered. Even though her limitations restrain her, she will do her best to hide her agony to give to him what she can. It is a performance I admire, even though I am fearful of the price that may be paid that night or the next day. There are no freebies or gimmies with her condition. It seems she must pay dearly for every moment of joy or happiness.

She usually goes to bed when Matthew does, so he comes and gets her and takes Mom to bed in the evening. It is a touching sight watching him help her out of her chair, then steady her as she leans on him, and they head toward the back of the house arm in arm. At 11, Matthew has had a less-than-normal childhood (if there is such a thing). The first eight years of his life were spent fighting for his life, and the last two have been spent playing nurse and servant to his mother. He does not complain; he understands that for many years it was her playing nurse to him. Neither would be alive today if it weren't for the other. There is a pretty strong glue bonding those two together! I am proud of them both for the way they support each other through almost never–ending amounts of adversity. As a family, we do our best to lift each other up and keep the blues at bay. The hope that one day things will get better keeps us plodding forward.

Journal

Saturday, November 6, 1999

Miriam is again so plastered by pain medication that she stumbles to bed fairly early most nights. She took Dr. Robel's new prescription yesterday and slept better than she has in a while. The new drug is Elavil, a tricyclic antidepressant that is supposed to help her sleep. From her career as a med lab tech, she knows she could be charged with DUI if she has too much in her system and gets stopped by law enforcement or is involved in an accident.

Miriam nor I have ever used recreational drugs or consumed more than an occasional glass of wine. This "impaired" state she has been living in for much of the last two years and all of the last couple of weeks is new and not desirable for us. I worry about her driving or even simply trying to walk across the room. Stumbling and falling would not be a good thing at this point.

Today, I am taking the Boy Scout troop on a tour of the flooring plant, then on to Skull Shoals along the Oconee River. Miriam is going to go but is not looking forward to bouncing along 10 miles of gravel road leading us to and from our picnic lunch and hike. Each bump gets transported electrically to her brain, where it is converted to agony. She is weary of simply observing life and wants desperately to participate in it whenever she can, often at great personal sacrifice.

Sunday, November 7, 1999

What extraordinary weather we are enjoying this weekend! Yesterday was no exception. The Boy Scout outing went very well. Miriam put a pillow under her leg to help absorb the jarring effect of the gravel road. She still paid a high price (in personal discomfort) to be with us, but, nevertheless, enjoyed the outing. While we explored Skull Shoals, identified trees, and studied the archeological site, she napped in the van.

She took another nap before we left and another after we returned home. The naps are the result of not sleeping well at night and the drugs that have her so fogged in.

I asked Dr. Robel (once again) about amputating the leg at the knee, hoping to also cut off the pain. This is often something she has begged me to do, knowing the vast array of sawing equipment in my possession. He said that amputation would open a new can of worms with a whole new set of problems, so it really is not an option.

People have knee surgery every day and are eventually able to return to some normal measure of activity in a relatively short period of time, but not Miriam. Some athletes can even return to their sport in less than a year. Miriam cannot sit in a chair two years after her first surgery without pain! Elderly patients with arthritis can arrive for two total knee replacements in a wheelchair and walk out after surgery; Miriam cannot walk across her kitchen without the help of a brace and a lot of pain, some four months after her sixth operation! It is easy to see why we are discouraged.

Thursday, November 11, 1999

This morning we are visiting Dr. Robel and have an appointment with an attorney to discuss our pending personal bankruptcy. On Monday, we will be back in Birmingham again, trying to get Miriam some relief from this unbelievable pain she is in. Yesterday afternoon, after she returned home from physical therapy, she called me at the plant to tell me about her session. She could hardly talk because of the pain.

We both slept quite well. Miriam used the TENS and heating pad all night; you might say my wife is "wired." She started hurting again around four in the morning. I found a conductor pad from the TENS unit that had come off and stuck to the sheets. After I fixed that problem and reconnected another wire that had come loose, then replaced the dying battery, she went back to sleep. After she called me yesterday afternoon while I was at work, I tried to get a hold of Dr. Robel. Naturally, when he returned my call, I was out in the plant, and all he could do was leave a message. On the message, he wanted us to come in first thing this morning. We'll see what he does.

Saturday, November 13, 1999

Rather than force sagging eyelids to remain open until a normal bedtime, I / we crashed early last night. It is so helpful that Miriam is sleeping better since she began taking Elavil almost a week ago. We've even cut her Elavil pills in half, and she is still sleeping! This lower dosage is helpful in the morning when it is time to "sober up."

Dr. Robel spent a good bit of time with us Thursday morning. He declared that she had the most difficult knee he has dealt with in his 18 years of medicine. He said she will also require a total knee replacement probably within 10 years, due to the degeneration and arthritis that has accompanied the trauma suffered by this joint. He was going to try to talk with Dr. Cox again and urge him to inject cortisone into the knee during our visit on Monday. During their last conversation, they agreed that going back into the joint must be avoided if possible. The cortisone may help break up the scar tissue. Dr. Robel made Miriam an appointment with a pain management clinic to see if they can help get her some relief.

From there, we met with an attorney concerning our personal bankruptcy cases. We talked for over three hours. The item of greatest concern was the future of our house.

He was also quite interested in "the knee." He was going to consult with another associate better versed in workman's comp to find out about the possibility of going after her back pay, which would go a long way toward helping to bail our house out of harm's way. Although we were current on the mortgage, the house is collateral for the SBA loan we are defaulting on.

The Knee Gazette

Monday, November 15, 1999

This dawn finds us once again in Birmingham, Alabama, for an appointment with Dr. Cox. Once again, we are desperately searching for a solution to Miriam's agonizing pain and increasing instability. Dr. Robel has talked with him on at least two occasions, and they both agree that they don't want to "go back into the knee unless there is no other treatment option," which is fine with us IF they can find another "treatment option" that works. He may inject the area where most of the pain is located with cortisone, which is supposed to help break up the scar tissue that they think is causing most of her discomfort. Dr. Robel didn't want to inject it because of the risk of hitting the peroneal nerve, which might possibly take the lid off of a new and different can of "pain worms" we would prefer not to deal with.

Miriam hurts almost continuously now. I feel so helpless. I often write in the journal or *Knee Gazette* for my own therapy. My very patient

78

readers may soon begin billing me for their time. I simply don't know what else to do. Often, she goes to bed with a heating pad and pillow between her knees and has wired the knee with four leads from the TENS unit, has taken two pain pills, and still hurts. This combination at least is helping her sleep most nights.

~ Mark and Miriam — In Need of a Miracle!

The Knee Gazette

Monday evening, November 15, 1999

We went. Dr. Cox came. He saw, he twisted, he pulled, he x-rayed, and then he injected Miriam's left knee with cortisone. We left his office, checked out of the room, and drove home.

Mark's homespun thought for the day: "Things would be much worse if we lived in Mogadishu!"

Journal

Thursday, November 18, 1999

Even with the injection, she still hurts! Dr. Cox's theory is that the gastroc (what, you've never heard of the gastroc? Me either.) is fired up due to trauma from instability. A fancy way of admitting this knee is once again loosening up! Muscle tone cannot be regained until the pain subsides; the pain won't subside until it quits slipping; it won't quit slipping until there is more muscle tone... anyone else hear the Lambchop song in their head?

On Monday, she will return to Dr. Robel for another cortisone shot and to get fitted for a different kind of brace. She will then be off to the pain management doctor- yea, one more doctor to work into the schedule. We hope that a different type of brace will give the joint more support and prevent the shifting she is experiencing several times a day these days.

Caring for this damn knee is pretty much a full-time, all-consuming job all by itself. As far as revenue-producing employment, she comes down to the plant twice a week for half of a day — not because the work is all done, but because she is in such agony by then that all she can do is drive home, take drugs, and sit in her chair. This latest round of setbacks that began two months ago has once again caused her leg to shrink. Our goal of building muscle mass to add support to the beleaguered ligaments is ever more elusive.

Sunday, November 28, 1999

This Thanksgiving was dramatically different from three years ago, when my family last congregated in Pigeon Forge/Gatlinburg for a holiday together. Three years ago, was before Miriam's accident, so she was a participant rather than a mere observer of the activities of the rest of us. She did most of the shopping for that trip and her share of the pre-trip and during-trip cooking and kitchen work.

This year there was a collective chorus of voices encouraging Miriam to sit down, but evidently the pain of not participating is greater than the pain caused by being on it. Three years ago, we spent lots of time taking walks. We walked around the community where we stayed; we spent a lot of time walking around downtown Gatlinburg and cruising through the small, unique shops that add so much charm to the area. This year we tried twice, but even with Miriam riding in a wheelchair, the pain caused from all of the cobblestones, joints in the concrete, and rough road crossings was too great for her to bear. Taking the wheelchair into the cramped and crowded shops was out of the question, and she didn't feel up to walking, so these excursions mostly ended in frustration.

Miriam did spend time every day soaking in the hot tub, something that she finds very soothing on her knee.

Some other ways our trip this year was affected by the knee include sleeping accommodations. My parents surrendered the ground-floor master bedroom to Miriam and me, despite footing the bill for the entire house. Three years ago, we all paid our share of the expenses; this year, due to our pending bankruptcy, we were reduced to being freeloaders.

Tuesday, November 30, 1999

Yesterday was full of knee-related appointments that Miriam had to attend by herself, since I cannot afford to miss more work. By early last evening, she was in a lot of pain. The simple act of transporting herself from the van to the various appointments saps her of energy, and the required walking fires up the nerve endings, causing even more discomfort. Last night, she melted into a puddle of tears for the first time in a couple of weeks. I helped her to bed early.

Dr. Robel gave her another cortisone injection and had her fitted with a new brace she is using on a trial basis. Henry declined to administer any treatment since she had just gotten the cortisone shot, so the "stroll" into and out of the hospital for physical therapy was for naught. Yesterday was her first visit to see a pain management specialist. He changed her medications and told her of some other injectable options besides cortisone that may be employed in the near future. He and Henry are searching for a portable interfential machine that can deliver the same type of relief she gets at physical therapy.

Today, she is going to the plant. Although she is needed all day, she usually cannot stay much past lunch because she needs to be sober enough to drive home. Once back home, she collapses into her chair with a pain pill. This is usually where her son finds her when he arrives home from school. On days when intense pain has caused her to employ a strong pain reliever, she has a difficult time helping Matthew with homework.

Sunday, December 5, 1999

We had a better week than we've had in a long time. The new pain medication is allowing her to sleep soundly, something that has not happened much in two years! The dark circles around her eyes have diminished considerably with the additional sleep. The downside of this medication is that she is dizzy for a while first thing in the morning, but this passes after she is up for a couple of hours.

Adjustments to her brace have also been helpful, resulting in far less shifting and less pain. Physical therapy this week once again included strengthening exercises and not simply pain mitigation. More restful nights also lead to more stamina during the day. Overall, the news is much better for a change. We will miss our goal of having her walk pain free without a brace by Christmas, but we can be patient if we are at least moving in the right direction.

The Knee Gazette

Sunday, December 19, 1999

The holiday season on the "knee front" is less than merry and jolly for the third straight year. Progress has once again come to a halt, and Miriam has slipped into a muddled haze of drugs, pain, frustration, and decreased mobility. Apparently, the effects of the cortisone shots have worn off because her agony is similar to what it was prior to her first injection in mid-November. She has once again exchanged our bed (and me) for her recliner as her preferred place of rest, something she has not done in quite some time.

The pain control doctor has put her on some medication that helps deliver a restful night's sleep, but it also leaves her quite woozy first thing in the morning. Watching her wobble from the bed to the shower is a scary sight, even though the trip is less than 15 feet and there is a door frame, a dresser, and a vanity to provide support.

"How am I doing?" is an often-asked question. Although I am still thrilled that we do not live in Mogadishu, I am feeling guilty for the anger that is building inside of me. I do not understand why this knee cannot seem to heal or even improve. Our modest goal of having Miriam recover to the point where she could function relatively pain-free and possibly even walk brace-free by Christmas has been pushed back indefinitely. We do not know where to turn or what to do, so we find ourselves in an ever-advancing state of despair.

We continue to covet your prayers as we continue our pilgrimage through this period of trial and tribulation. God is good and is supplying our needs, which we are thankful for, but there are times when our burdens cloud our view of the horizon and any measure of hope.

We hope you have a joyous holiday season.

~ Mark, Matthew, and "Sober Sometimes"

Journal

Christmas Day, 1999

When asked what we most wanted to find under the tree this year, the answer, once again (for the third straight year), was a healthy left knee for Miriam.

Pain and fatigue are the dominant features on my wife's face. Although she slept well last night, it was the first in several nights. Thursday night she started out in our bed but was up a couple of times and was sobbing because of the pain, so at about 2:30 a.m., I helped her to her chair. I lay in our bed on the other side of the wall listening to her cry for nearly two hours before I took her interferential unit to her and helped hook it up. This seemed to give her enough relief to at least slip into a fitful sleep, which allowed me to also sleep. Needless to say, neither of us were much good on Friday! She said the pain was deep-down pain in the bone like someone was running a jackhammer on her shin bone that radiated all the way to her foot.

A passing weather system could have been operating the "hammer," but we may never know for sure. The net result is that because of the pain, neither of us got much sleep.

This is also her 40th birthday. As has become our custom, extended family will gather at our house this afternoon for a small celebration. Miriam's sister will pick up a cake so at least she won't have to bake it herself.

The gifts I gave her, once again, were knee centered. Exciting things like hot packs, cold packs, and a portable folding chair we can easily transport in the van to various outdoor activities. Of course, because of our desperate financial difficulties, more emphasis was placed on traditions than gifts.

December 31, 1999

It is Friday morning, the last dawn of 1999. The calendar flips to a new millennium tonight, but I am painfully reminded how frozen in time our lives have become.

A lot of year-end stuff needed doing at the plant yesterday, so she put in a full day. Even in this controlled low-impact environment, it was an extremely difficult day. By the time we got home, she collapsed in her chair with an agonizing grimace on her once pleasant face.

Journal

January 23, 2000

It's a beautiful Sunday morning. As I compose these thoughts, I am watching a legion of birds feeding at the buffet of seeds spread among an assortment of feeders. There is ice hanging from every limb, branch, and needle within sight, and it continues to rain. The electricity went off about 30 minutes ago; I thought I would get as far as I could before my battery gives out on the laptop. The view outside is the only thing left that works.

Miriam's knee continues to slide steadily downhill. We are so discouraged. A good night's sleep seems once again to be harder and harder to get. Nausea has returned, just to add a little seasoning to her bolts of pain. For some reason, it seems worse when we are trying to go to sleep. Twice in the last week, my pending slumber was interrupted because I needed to help my gagging wife stagger to the bathroom. That is a sound that is not easy to sleep through!

Dr. Robel is confident that her discomfort now is primarily nerve-related rather than structural. This is small comfort since the net result is the same. The next thing on "the list" is to discuss the possibility of a nerve block with Dr. Edwards, the pain guy. During my conversation with Dr. Robel this week, I tried to make it clear that we can deal with limited mobility IF they can do something about the pain. He walked out of the exam room when I once again brought up the subject of amputating the left leg. I don't think anyone understands how desperate we are. I understand his position, but we are truly at our wit's end and not beyond grasping at straws.

I am trying to maintain as normal of a childhood as possible for Matthew, and at times I must sacrifice Miriam's care to do so. She is forced to watch instead of participating (as she longs to do) as Matthew and I get more and more involved in Scouting.

Letter to Dr. Robel

Thursday, January 26, 2000

Miriam invented a new pain yesterday that does not seem to be nerve-related. She complained several times of excruciating pain emanating from under her kneecap. It was tender enough that she would not allow me to feel it. However, she is convinced it is not connected to the nerve pain she has been experiencing.

She said her knee shifted back on her while she was getting out of the shower yesterday morning. Perhaps this was aggravated then? While in bed and in the shower are the only periods of any day that she is without her brace. Could her joint be continuing to loosen once again, or is this the result of her inability to exercise and build any muscle tone in and around the joint?

Letter to Dr. Robel

Tuesday, February 1, 2000

Yesterday afternoon, I went with Miriam to visit Dr. Edwards. He now has a better understanding of the road we've traveled and our level of desperation.

We have a better understanding of the "weapons" in his arsenal and his planned course of action. In a nutshell, he made the following points:

- *A surgical solution is our only hope of a permanent fix. He shares your opinion that the nerve is encased in scar tissue and that surgery is risky.*

- *There is a window of opportunity beyond which surgery may not be affective. He is not sure if we are still within this window.*

- *He will attempt one type of nerve block on Thursday. If this is an almost immediate failure, he will vote for surgery now rather than delay any further.*

Dr. Edwards is also altering Miriam's medications. The goal is to get her out of the drug-induced fog.

The Knee Gazette

Saturday, February 5, 2000

It has been nearly seven weeks since I've written about "*le* knee." Somehow, this seems an appropriate time to submit a "State of the Knee" report. Since nothing good or positive is developing on this front, I've chosen silence rather than risk whining too loudly or too often. In an attempt to include more distractions in our family life, we've been in hot pursuit of a few slices of normalcy.

Matthew got a rocket kit for Christmas that we've enjoyed building and flying. So much so, that we bought another bigger and more challenging rocket that we hope to soon fly. "Normal activities" have been an elusive goal for us. We're trying to do as much normal stuff as possible, like flying rockets and getting involved in Boy Scouts. This is the only crack we'll ever have at this parenting thing, and since we only have the one child, it's not like we will get another opportunity to do better with a younger sibling in a few years; regardless of that, this will be his only childhood, so we must do the best we can for him.

Miriam is beginning to feel like a volleyball. Doctors on both sides of the net, representing a variety of specialties, are batting her back and forth, each hoping someone else will find a solution for her problem. None want her to hit the ground at their feet, lest she become their responsibility. In the interim, while she waits patiently for the next appointment and shred of hope, she is in ever-increasing pain and discomfort. There is a consensus of sorts about what is causing her trouble, but each one hopes the other will fix it.

"The peroneal nerve seems to be entrapped or encased in scar tissue" remains the prevailing theory for the present. However, since x-rays, ultrasounds, or MRIs are apparently useless in confirming this, Exploratory surgery with a microscope offers the only real hope of confirmation and/or a potential fix. Because of the potential complications, no one is eager to start scrubbing for surgery either. Right now, Miriam is in the hands of a Dr. Edwards, who specializes in pain management. He is attempting a nerve block that will hopefully not interrupt the motor function of the leg while successfully deadening the sensory perception of the nerve. Attempt number one took place Thursday and lasted all of two hours; Miriam was neither impressed nor happy with the results! A second attempt is scheduled to take place next Thursday. What's another week of suffering for this poor woman? I think sometimes appointments and procedures are spread so far apart, hoping the body will heal itself. While I understand that for many patients and maladies, this is a legitimate course of "treatment," this patient, with her assorted disorders, left that camp long ago in this layman's humble opinion.

Her pain continues to worsen, which has once again turned rehab into an exercise in pain mitigation. The joint needs muscle mass to lend strength, stability, and support, but the intense pain prohibits the exercises that will build it. This makes for a vicious cycle that has no exit.

At times, we feel like we're trying to swim out of a rip tide of self-pity, gloom, and doom and trying to keep from getting completely overwhelmed and drowned in a sea of our own despair. I find myself wondering if the "Lifeguard" is paying any attention to our plight or, worse, if he doesn't care. Of course, most of the time, a more rational view prevails, and I understand that we are not entitled to an easier pilgrimage than our brethren in any third-world country. They may be wondering where the next meal is coming from or have no access to medical care. When one becomes this self-focused, it is easy to forget that the Son is shining above our clouds of despair and that one day we will arrive at the "Celestial City" and be able to **walk** victoriously through the pearly gates!

~ **Mark, Matthew, and "Laughs too Little"**

Letter to Dr. Robel

Tuesday, February 8, 2000

Dr. Edwards has altered her medication some, so you may think she is not quite so depressed when you see her again. She is sleeping better and is not nearly so loopy, However, she is experiencing some tingling on her fingertips now.

Her knee continues to shift; three times so far today!

The Knee Gazette

February 23, 2000

"Take two orthotics and come back in three months." This was Dr. Cox's "prescription" after our most recent visit to his Birmingham clinic.

This latest of our pilgrimages to the "Steel City" mercifully ended late this afternoon.

Recent regression on the knee front compelled us to make a sooner-than-scheduled return to Birmingham to see "His Eminence." Once again, I loaded a recliner into our van, steered it onto I–20, and drove toward the sunset. I tried a new tactic this time. I declared the van to be a "no moan zone." This creative comment did little to suppress the noise emanating from the recliner but did succeed in getting me one of those looks that you wives reserve for those occasions when we husbands ask for something you have no interest in delivering.

The above "prescription" was delivered after an examination of the knee and observing her limp across the floor several times. Dr. Cox thinks that her gait (and flat feet) are putting too much pressure, stress, and wear on the outside of the joint. He hopes the new inserts in her shoes will help relieve this stress and possibly allow the nerve reporting all the pain to calm down. He says it will take another three months for us to determine whether or not the nerve is done regenerating itself. Interesting, I think, that it took two and a half years and countless visits to some of the finest orthopedic physicians in the region for someone to mention that she has flat feet, and that they are suddenly a problem! It sounds to this know nothing that someone is grasping at straws…

The wrong action taken too soon could cause more problems than are solved- Mark's lay interpretation of what he said. When He first waltzed into the exam room/altar, he mentioned something about having brought a chainsaw. Finally, we were going to get some action, I thought. Need I describe my disappointment (and Miriam's relief) when it became apparent that the chainsaw was his attempt at humor on a mortal level? Miriam's relief was short-lived; when he mentioned waiting another three months to decide what to do next, I think the chainsaw idea was beginning to look more appealing to her!

We are way beyond our "wit's end" and slipped off of "the end of our rope" quite some time ago. We can probably be best described as free-falling in a numb trance of some sort. Often, we pinch each other, hoping one of us will wake up and this nightmare will be over.

As I have related to her caregivers the last two days, my goals for treatment can be summarized in three "simple" steps that I have conveniently listed in their order of priority:

- Stop the pain.

- Get her off the drugs. This will hopefully cut down on the frequency of her "blond moments," as she describes her periods of drug–induced lapses of cognitive activity.

- Fix the structural problems if possible.

~ Mark, Matthew, and "She who violates the Moan Free Zone"

Journal

April 22, 2000

I envision Workman's Comp people (the employer/insurer, AKA E/I) gathered around a conference table discussing the financial impact of Miriam's care on their budget. I would like to have an opportunity to explain to them how fortunate they are that the impact upon them is limited to money. I would welcome the opportunity to send her home with one of them for a weekend! It could even be a weekend after she had had a nerve block. One weekend would dispel any doubts about the level of her suffering and what an impact this is on those of us that provide her care. If they could observe the difference a 20-minute soak in a spa makes, they would waste little time writing a check for one of those.

How about some good news? About six weeks ago, I realized that whenever her knee locked up, her foot was turned way out. This observation (which had been passed on to the professional caregivers in her life and received only a scratch on the chin and possibly a note in the chart) led this simpleton to devise a mechanical restraint that tied her shoe to her brace and prevented the foot from rotating out. I hatched the idea; she immediately implemented it (not wanting to wait for me to get inspired to do so), and Henry refined it. The net result is that her knee has not locked up in six weeks while the restraint is in use! This has reduced the trauma to the nerve and reduced her pain to a more manageable level. She has been able to substantially cut her drug intake and function more normally. (I am speaking in relative terms here!) And it has been several weeks since one of the doctors or attorneys has suggested she get some psychiatric care, because she does not look nearly so "wasted."

Letter to Dr. Robel

Monday, May 1, 2000

Summary: Patient's condition is deteriorating again. Why is it that good news and glimmers of hope are so hard to hang on to? It's like trying to catch a refreshing breeze in a paper sack and save it for another day—simply impossible.

Miriam is once again sliding down a greased pole. The intensity and frequency of her pain seem to be growing with each passing week. This is, once again, preventing her from sleeping, which creates more negative repercussions.

Please review Dr. Neyland's report on the latest NCV/EMG tests. Does this provide proof that will make an impression on "His Greatness" in Birmingham? If so, perhaps the two of you can talk and plan the next course of action. You asked me to remind you to request the involvement of a neurosurgeon during your next conversation with Dr. Cox concerning our upcoming visit to Birmingham.

Our next scheduled appointment is on the 22nd, which is an awful lot of sleepless nights from now.

Her pain was so intense yesterday that she could not pull in a fish that had taken her bait. Normally, she laughs and cries at the same time, but pulls in the fish! In other words, the knot she has been clinging to at the end of her rope is slipping from her grasp.

Letter to Attorney Fred Hill

May 8, 2000

During Miriam's visit with Dr. Edwards on Thursday, the nurse/secretary reported no more problems with Altma Hospital concerning payment for Miriam's nerve blocks. She said Dr. Edwards got more involved, and since then, workman's compensation has not given them any additional trouble.

It is almost a foregone conclusion that additional surgery is pending; it is the ability of the one holding the knife that I am interested in! Also, when a neurosurgeon is working on the problem, Dr. Cox should also be working on structural problems.

Dr. Edwards (who is treating her for pain) is concerned that she may be showing the early signs of a neurological condition called Reflex Sympathetic Dystrophy, or RSD. This causes the sensory nerves to try their hand at motor function, because the nerves intended to control motor function have been damaged. In Miriam's case, this would be from her multiple surgeries. Dr. Robel thinks differently, and I hope he is right. Based on our internet research, this is not an adversary which we care to tangle with. This is one reason I want any additional surgical procedures performed at the same time. This will also prevent this poor woman from having to start over at zero more times than is necessary.

Letter to Dr. Robel

Tuesday, May 15, 2000

We met with Dr. Cook today. Thank you for helping to make those arrangements. I was impressed with the man, even though the visit was far from encouraging. Dr. Cook has basically returned this ball to the court of you Orthopedic guys to "solve the cause of the ongoing trauma to the peroneal nerve." Dr. Cook said he thought he could perform surgery that may provide her with up to eight weeks of pain relief but that if the structural problems were not addressed, it would be only a temporary solution.

While this is being composed, Javy Lopez, himself the recipient of a new ACL not so long ago, is squatting behind home plate at Turner Field. Meanwhile, my wife, now the proud owner of not one but three new ACLs, is not able to read a novel without involuntary expressions of discomfort while just sitting in her chair.

If you are right and "Dr. Birmingham" does not want to touch it, what are we to do? Dr. Cook did give us the name of a specialist at Emory, if we want to seek a second opinion concerning the nerve, but we are not at this point yet.

Assuming Dr. Cox offers to do nothing, and you were in my shoes, what direction would you next turn? I realize I am wallowing in hypotheticals at this point, but a week from now this may be where we find ourselves.

Letter to Dr. Cox

Monday, May 22, 2000

We have an appointment at 10:30 this morning. I wanted to provide a firsthand layman's perspective on Miriam's present condition.

Her condition can be summed up in two words: **INTENSE PAIN**! Although her mobility is severely restricted, the pain is a far greater hindrance to a reasonable quality of life by far than her inability to walk normally.

Her condition today has not improved since you saw her last fall and diagnosed a torn gastroc. Evidently, the passage of time and intense wishing on my part is not by itself going to improve her condition. This is a pattern I have watched occur after three different surgeons performed reconstructive procedures on this knee in less than three years. **I accept Dr. Robel's explanation that this has something to do with her unique collagen makeup and is not a reflection of surgical skill.**

- *What options do we have left?*

- *Can the ligaments be augmented with artificial material that won't be as likely to stretch?*

- *Is there such a thing as a total knee complete with ligaments?*

- *Would new, thicker cartilages tighten up the existing ligaments enough to take out the "Slop?"*

- *Can the peroneal nerve be moved to a location where it will be less likely to be continually traumatized?*

- *Would a post-surgical cast be of any help in allowing her knee to heal without any stress?*

As you can probably tell, we are desperate. I ask you to apply your vast array of skills and experience to come up with a course of action that can give this woman her life back.

~ Mark Johnson, Husband and Round-the-Clock Caregiver

The Knee Gazette

End of May 2000

Miriam is a special person! Maybe it was her uniqueness that I found so attractive 17 springs ago, when I continued to ask for a date, in spite of her repeated rejections. Only recently have I discovered that her "special and unique" qualities extend all the way to the connective tissues knitting her bones together!

Our saga with the knee is way too much like a daytime television drama to suit me. Given a choice, I could have been very happy with a one–episode sitcom, but nooooo, our "show" must include more hospital scenes than Marcus Welby, more courtroom scenes than Perry Mason and enough comical situations to put Gilligan in stitches!

This weekend past was a good example. On Sunday, we returned to Birmingham for another follow–up visit with Dr. Cox. In spite of having a recliner to sit in, Interstate 20 was bouncing Miriam's sensitive knee around a lot. Several times on the way over, she burst into tears because of the pain. One special thing about Miriam I've learned during our 31-month ordeal is that extreme pain makes her nauseous. On Sunday, her pain was extreme enough that I found myself on an I-20 exit ramp with a full bucket in my hand. Let's hope the vegetation is hardy and hungry because it was fed the contents of Miriam's stomach!

We left Sunday morning for our Monday morning appointment so that we could relax that afternoon and evening at the hotel and especially so she could enjoy a good soak in the spa, which really seemed to give Miriam some blessed relief from her agony. As our luck would have it, the spa went out of commission sometime between when we booked the room and when we wanted to use it! Instead of the spa soaking, we took much needed naps and did some reading.

Monday morning, we found Dr. Cox with a meeker and humbler demeanor than we were accustomed to seeing on him.

Evidently, Miriam's "specialness" reminded him that maybe he was not the Creator and that even he is fallible (on rare occasions, of course.) He had spoken earlier in the day with Dr. Robel, so he was already aware of her ongoing problems. Dr. Cox gave her a quick examination and wrote a referral to apparently the only guy in the country with more experience with Miriam's type of knee trouble than himself. Dr. Richard Ware is the Chief of Special Surgery at the Hospital for Special Surgery in New York City. This is part of the Cornell University Medical Center. See how "special" she is?

We received the news in stunned silence. We were disappointed that Dr. Cox thought he could do nothing else for her, but as the news began to sink in, suddenly, an avalanche of questions cascaded through our minds. Is this good news, or will we have to travel farther for another, more heartbreaking disappointment? I must admit to being somewhat overwhelmed by the logistics of making such a long trip with Miriam (the exit ramp scene keeps replaying in my mind). I keep wondering what it will be like to fly with her while she is folded into a coach seat on a commercial airplane for several hours. As bad as that vision is, what about the flight home after surgery?

Dr. Cox does not know what, if anything, Dr. Ware can do for her. His referral includes a consultation with a hand surgeon at the same hospital, who is accustomed to performing delicate microscopic work on nerves.

Before we can pack for a trip to the Big Apple, however, Workman's Comp must approve of such an "extravagant" expenditure. This may be where the courts will become involved, although we are probably headed there anyway to force them to buy the hot tub prescribed six months ago and to try to get some back-wage benefits. Nothing is as simple as "We are sorry we caused your injury Mrs. Johnson, now we will take care of you."

Once again, the script for our "serial" must add drama by pouring salt on an open wound; if she had been a visitor to the hospital instead of an employee, she would be able to collect compensation for her pain and suffering (by now, this should be worth several cups of spilled coffee at McDonalds!), but since this is a Workman's Comp case, this is not possible. On the other hand, the same injury could have occurred in our own kitchen or in an automobile accident, in which case we would be fighting with a health insurance company for basic medical treatment. Even though things could be much worse, it is difficult some days to retain a spirit of gratitude. Besides, gratitude is not a welcomed guest when we get our minds prepared for a good, old-fashioned, self-centered pity party!

CHAPTER 7
He Left Me

Journal

May 28, 2000

A gray Sunday sky, boasting of a chance of rain, brings cooler temperatures to the region for a pleasant change. A pleasant change, however, eludes us on the knee front. After nearly three months, I put out a new *"Knee Gazette"* yesterday. How many times and how many different ways can you tell people that she still hurts like hell and that she's getting worse AGAIN? People get tired of hearing only bad news, and I get tired of relaying it. So, believe it or not, I tend to keep quiet unless pressed for information. In this fallen world full of death, sickness and despair, we all need good news now and then to cling to and give us hope. Take away all our hope, and we descend into a cycle of pity and hopelessness that swallows us like a dark cave. Since most people have plenty of those already, I'd rather not pour more fuel on anyone's smoldering embers of unhappiness.

I thought Miriam handled Dr. Cox's news quite well. She/we have been biding time waiting for Dr. Cox to make a decision about what to do. When he finally did, we were stunned. He had done all he could do, so like Dr. Robel before him, he referred her to someone else. Unlike Dr. Robel, who found someone only five hours from home, Dr. Cox directed us to New York City. I/we began thinking the same questions I was sure the Employer/Insurer would be asking out loud: "New York City? Do you know how many hospitals full of orthopedic surgeons there are between Athens, Georgia and New York City?" Yeah, we were pretty rattled by the news.

Miriam was in near constant pain, so after a few days, as with every other time hope had been snuffed out, her attitude and determination rose from the ashes of despair and somehow galvanized into stoic determination. Her I-don't-quit determination kept her focused on the goal of one day getting her life back, which probably kept many pity parties at bay. This also served as armor for the battle that would have to be waged with the E/I to get approved for treatment in such a distant city.

There is obviously a psychological component caused by the on-going drama. On the way home from Birmingham on Monday, with the overwhelming news weighing heavily on our minds, we pulled off of I-20 and stopped for a late lunch at a Cracker Barrel. Following the meal, Miriam went to the restroom. When she returned to the parking lot and didn't see the van where she thought we had left it, she decided the prospects of surgery in New York had finally pushed me over the edge and that I had left her! I thought she might have taken Dr. Cox's news about not being able to do anything for her harder, but I wasn't expecting her to begin jumping to dramatic conclusions in the Cracker Barrel parking lot. She really thought I would/could leave her at a restaurant along the interstate? That I would drive off in the little minivan, and she would never see me again? Did she think I'd be able to 'splain her absence to our son, not to mention a host of family and friends? I learned all of this once I had been found in a parking spot closer and more convenient for her. Had she just turned her head in the other direction, she would have spotted me. Maybe she is more fragile than I thought.

We are now 11 months post-surgery, and only now has Dr. Cox decided it is time to punt. It is as if progress freezes in our presence. Doctors, lawyers, and the hospital are all playing wait and see, hoping something will develop, Miriam will die, or someone else will hatch a plan they can observe from a safe distance. Meanwhile, Miriam suffers pain that is so intense it's inconceivable. Dr. Edwards is perhaps the one professional in our life who is doing something on a weekly basis to give her relief. He has proven to be a good listener and has gotten involved with the Workman's Comp folks when Miriam's weekly sessions of relief were in jeopardy. He has also written letters to help keep her treatment moving forward.

Journal

Tuesday, June 6, 2000

Last Thursday, while ascending three steps to enter my sister's home for our niece's birthday celebration, Miriam's right knee became aggravated. This is the leg where the tendon was harvested for the ACL graft on the left knee last July. Why we ever let them cut on her good knee, I'll never know. It will require about a month for the right knee to settle down again. In the meantime, it, too, will rejoin the pain parade. Why is it so important that she not get a break?

She went to the plant with me yesterday morning. I help her get in the building and get situated in front of the computer, but she is up and down all day tending to office machines, going to the bathroom, etc. She made it all the way to 10 before melting into tears for the first time of the young day! Although there are no steps or long halls, simply "functioning" at as minimal level as possible, causes excruciating pain and this was only the first of several "puddles" before I finally insist that we leave about 5:30. When she is present and able, she is responsible for timecards, inventory, preparing shipping documents and maintaining the database. On this day, the "Augusta office" (new owners) decided they need to reconcile their records with our database, so the added phone work prevented her from getting finished in time to leave by 3:30, when the first ride heads for Watkinsville.

By the time we arrive home, "zingers" are zipping down her left leg and exploding between her toes. At one point during the trip home, I thought I would need to pull over so she could vomit.

After putting leftovers on to warm, I begin calling friends and family members in search of an available hot tub for her to soak in for a few minutes. The one at the Y is out of commission; the owners of two others are not home. Her sister had one a year ago, but it was a cheap model and quite expensive to operate, so it wasn't always in service when Miriam needed it. They have since sold it with the house, but even it was a 20-minute drive from our home! By 9 p.m., one of my desperate messages received a reply and I loaded her in the van for the eight-minute drive toward some potential relief.

The effect is dramatic and nearly instant. In only a few minutes, her pained expression is replaced by the pleasant, smiling demeanor that captured my heart all those years ago. This was a small tub that required some contortions on Miriam's part to apply the jet action to the offending pain, but the results were truly remarkable. Too bad it wore off by two in the morning! Were there a hot tub sitting on our deck, she would have been back in for another soak and enough relief to perhaps allow her to sleep the rest of the night.

Tuesday, June 6, 2000, 10 p.m.

I've just helped my sobbing wife to bed. She has been in tears most of the last two hours because of the pains shooting down her left leg and into her foot. This appears to be rapidly getting worse! Dr. Edward's RSD theory may prove to be correct, but I still hope not.

She took Dilauded, a drug seven times stronger than Morphine, about 30 minutes ago. I rubbed her leg for about 20 minutes and seemed to get it quieted down, but when the rubbing stopped, the pain returned. When I put her to bed, I wrapped the shin portion of her leg with a heating pad, attempting to find something that gives her some relief.

Wednesday, June 7, 2000

It is early morning after another long night. I finally had to go to bed out of concern for today. My night was only interrupted once by her bell. She needed to go to the bathroom. When I got to her chair, her bucket was in her lap, her cheeks were wet with tears, and she was writhing from a nearly continuous assault of "zingers." A mercy killing would stop her pain but would also "kill" our son, as his family unit would slip from the face of this earth when the prison doors clanged shut behind me. He needs whatever family unit we can still provide.

As far as I am concerned, she has just gone on full and total disability. She will not go to the plant today. Too much activity could be adding to her deteriorating condition. Monday, she spent 10 hours with me at the plant; yesterday, she went to physical therapy and then walked around Kroger. "She was feeling fine and didn't see a need to ride in the electric cart they provide patrons with mobility issues," she replied indignantly to my question. When I am with her, she rides in a wheelchair when we are in a large store. It is senseless for us to maintain an appearance of normalcy (via her working part-time) if it only succeeds in A) easing the E/I's financial pain, while B) adding to her already intense physical suffering.

3

Letter to Fred Hill

June 8, 2000

Miriam has an appointment this morning with Dr. Edwards for another nerve block. He will insert a long-term epidural if we will not be going to New York in the next 30 days. Do you have any idea what kind of timetable is likely to unfold before us? We meet with Dr. Robel tomorrow and I am confident we will have his referral letter at that time if not before.

Upon reading Dr. Cox's letter of referral, I can see why the E/I turned it down. It appears to have been transcribed by an elementary school dropout. This letter gives the impression that we requested the referral to Dr. Ware. I can assure you that: A) We did not know of Dr. Ware until Dr. Cox mentioned his name and B) We arrived in Birmingham fully expecting to be scheduled for surgery there. C) We were dumbstruck when Dr. Cox announced we were going to New York! Do I need to try to get this letter reworded, or will Dr. Robel's letter be sufficient?

This clinic in Birmingham is something to behold. The facility is state of the art; the walls of every exam room are covered with sports memorabilia from former patients. The physicians themselves are surrounded by graduate physicians on orthopedic fellowships. The "fellows" handle most of the details upon Dr. Cox's instructions. My point? This referral letter is not correct in the information it conveys for perhaps a variety of reasons.

Letter to Dr. Edwards and Dr. Robel

Sunday, June 18, 2000

The effectiveness of the spinal cord stimulator trial **is very impressive!** *One look at Miriam's face tells most of the story. Her pain has been greatly diminished, allowing her to sleep better and function with the help of almost no drugs!*

For example, we took our son to a camp in South Carolina on Saturday. Miriam was able to ride in the van without her recliner, walk around the camp and examine her son's accommodations for the coming week, and then felt good enough that we took the rest of the day and drove into the mountains! **Without the stimulator, the trip to and from camp would have been an agonizing test of her drug-hazed endurance.** *She would have sat in the van while at the camp, and we would have come directly home, where she would have spent the rest of the afternoon and a rough night, paying for and recovering from the lapse in judgment that allowed her to go on the journey to start with!*

This piece of hardware has allowed her to reach out and touch life again instead of simply observing it through a window of constant pain! We are already dreading Thursday when this apparatus is scheduled for removal. **Is there any way possible it can stay in until the permanent version is installed?** *I know this is out of the ordinary, but the results of this trial are dramatic and indisputable.*

Do you want an idea of how much pain she has been in? The technician who initially adjusted this unit after Dr. Edwards installed it, provided a graphic indication: the stimulator has a range of settings from one to ten, ten being the highest level of electrical charge possible. Miriam was told that most people for whom this technician has set up stimulators, can only tolerate level two or three on the machine, and that this level covers the pain, and they are not able to tolerate a higher intensity of electrical energy from the unit. Miriam did not get comfortable until level seven! At level eight, her lower extremities begin to convulse uncontrollably. She used level eight for example, to cover the pain of walking up a short but steep incline during our outing yesterday in the mountains. She was laughing at the odd movements of her legs, but the pain was kept to a manageable level! Evidently the demon living in her leg can be thwarted by electrical impulses applied in the right dose at the right location.

The Knee Gazette

Sunday, June 25, 2000

Altma Hospital, Miriam's employer at the time of her accident (and signatory on all checks made payable for the medical expenses of repairing her knee), A.K.A. the E/I, has decided that they would "rather not buy her a spa." They have also determined that they would prefer not to send her to the specialist to whom she has been referred in New York. They have, however, agreed to pay for the permanent installation of a spinal cord stimulator, for which Miriam successfully completed a one-week trial this past Thursday. This is largely due, I'm certain, in no small part to the fact that they have been shelling out $300 to $500 per week for nerve blocks. Clearly, this was a decision based on compassion for Miriam's condition and had nothing to do with possibly saving money in the long run. Perhaps the permanent installation of the spinal cord stimulator will remove the need for further surgery or a spa. It would be great if this is the case; time will tell. Another riveting game of "Wait and See" has begun.

Miriam has gotten some relief on her worst nights recently by imposing on the generosity of some kind folks at church who have made their spa available for her use. It is amazing how quickly and how completely it works its magic on her ailing knee. Another family has offered the use of a spa they no longer use. We are in the process of getting it moved, repaired and set up; perhaps she will have something soon that we don't have to drive across the county to use.

I will get her into a spa this afternoon to try to calm the spasms that caused us to unceremoniously leave church early this morning. What a difference a week can make. Last Sunday, during the trial of her spinal cord stimulator, she attended her Sunday school class for the first time in months, and people nearly climbed out of the woodwork to tell me how good she looked; today, she had to leave the service early with tears streaming down her pain–contorted face. I brought her home and propped her up in her recliner with a bag of ice water wrapped around the knee. It was probably better to bring her home than risk having visitors wonder if this church accepted moaning, groaning, writhing on the floor, and spontaneous vomiting as a normal part of worship.

There is some hope on the horizon. The relief provided by the temporary spinal cord stimulator was remarkable. The permanent version of this electronic miracle will be surgically implanted beneath the skin similar to a pacemaker. It will have leads attached to her spinal cord that will create "noise" in the nervous system that helps prevent her brain from receiving the pain signals coming from her knee. The battery pack will be installed in a cave carved into one of her buttocks. Although this machine really cures nothing, it should be a tremendous help with masking the pain. She will have a controller that she can hold up to the implanted unit in her fanny and make any adjustments that are needed. I keep telling her that I will have every husband's dream: a remote control for the wife! She says it won't work from across the room, but I assure her that after a couple of trips to Radio Shack, I will be able to make one that will, especially since she will already be wired for it. "I wonder if I'll be able to add any extra buttons?" She replied with "one of those looks."

~ **Exit Ramp Terror**

Journal

Monday, July 3, 2000

I feel almost zombie-like. I may look human, but no one is home. The lack of sleep the last three nights is really taking its toll. Miriam's leg "feels like a mouse is running around under her skin." I began the night on the sofa to keep mutual disruption to a minimum. This plan worked until my deep slumber was interrupted by Miriam's pleading sobs, calling to me from the dining area. She needed help getting back into the make-shift loaner spa so she could hopefully get her leg to settle down. Although it was a loaner spa, we were thankful to have it to use.

We had only been asleep 90 minutes. I could tell this was going to be a rough night. I was glad that I was there. Sunday morning, I helped get Matthew's scout troop to Rainey Mountain. For a week of camp. I had originally planned to stay with the troop for a night or two but did not want to leave Miriam by herself. What a difference between Scout camp and Awana camp. The two camps were only a couple weeks apart, but during the stimulator trial, she not only went along but felt like taking an adventure, too! This time she stayed home and tried to catch up on sleep.

After the spa, I went to bed with her. Throughout the night, her sobbing awakened me; she needed her foot rubbed; she wanted to be held; she was so very miserable. I woke up feeling as though I had not slept.

The gifted spa still does not heat. Hopefully, the "spa man" will stop by this afternoon and solve that problem. In the meantime, it is more of an "ambient air temperature tub" than a hot tub. Since it is summer and the air temperature is high, it's not too cold to be of benefit. The massaging effect of the water is still helpful despite the coolish temperature. Between Wednesday and Thursday, she spent about four hours in it!

I brought Miriam to the plant today for the first time since she left the payroll. She is here so I can work and still tend to her care. It doesn't take long for her to bring order to my world simply by sitting in a chair. A large part of the day is spent lying on the sofa, occasionally napping. Fortunately, I work for an understanding employer who doesn't mind her presence.

The Knee Gazette

Tuesday, July 4, 2000

A day off! We slept last night with only minimal interruptions. This means the world looks different this morning. The spinal cord stimulator gets implanted in 10 days; keeping the "misery index" at a tolerable level until then will, I think, be quite a challenge if the last few days are any indication. I hope she receives immediate relief once it is implanted. She cannot live in this constant state of intense misery for much longer without a death in the family, either from suicide or from a mercy killing. One of the medications she is on now is a narcotic used a lot for cancer patients to help with their chronic pain. It seems to be providing some relief.

The heater still is not working in the spa, but that has not kept Miriam from using it. She spent over an hour in it this afternoon and is preparing to get in again. It is especially helpful before bedtime. The spa allows her to take a very relaxed body and leg and quietly lay it in the bed.

A short while ago, her knee locked up. This is the first time it has done this while the foot restraining strap was in use. I emptied her supper from the trash can where it was deposited when the bolt of pain hit her, cleaned her up, and helped her into the not-quite-warm-enough spa, which is the closest thing to relief I can get for her short of a bullet in the head. This is our life. I write about it because this is the only way anyone will know how bad this hell really is. My parents, her sisters, the neighbors, our fellow parishioners, co-workers, even our own son, do not see how bad things get sometimes. They are not here in the middle of the night. While helping her out of the spa tonight her knee locked up once again. No one heard her screams or saw her tears but me.

My frustration with the employer/insurer who refuses to buy her a spa that works, or to send her to see "the only Dr. in the country who, according to Dr. Cox, might be able to fix her knee," is pretty intense. I hope I can keep her alive until the 14th, when the spinal cord stimulator is scheduled to be installed. I just hope it works as well as the trial version and gives her some relief. We wait, we wait, and we wait some more, hoping and praying God in Heaven will have mercy on us.

The chiming clock has summoned a new day and reminded me how far past my bedtime it really is. However, there are details recorded for posterity that would have been lost if they hadn't been written while fresh on my mind. This time, with my keyboard-shaped therapist, may help me to sleep in the near term and ultimately keep me out of the funny farm.

Journal

Friday, July 7, 2000

My beloved uncle Frank passed away yesterday morning. I quickly made other arrangements for Miriam and my scout duties and am traveling with my parents to Indiana for the funeral. Events like this remind me that normal life and the circle of life still exist outside of our bubble of crisis. Beyond the sadness, it will be good to see extended family and take my mind off our travails. We will laugh, cry, hug and remember one of my father's dear brothers.

The Knee Gazette

Friday, July 14, 2000

The much-anticipated day has finally arrived. Miriam had surgery today to implant a spinal cord stimulator (SCS). The results are almost immediate.

A friend from Miriam's Sunday school class took her to Winder for the morning surgery. I left work around noon and had just settled into my third Reader's Digest article when they wheeled Miriam into her room in outpatient recovery. She was groggy and miserable. Through her fog, she complained loudly of her knee.

I timidly asked the nurse, "Have they turned on the unit yet?" I was rewarded with the negative response I had hoped for. Soon a representative from the unit's manufacturer appeared with an impressive device she claimed was able to program the box that was now implanted in Miriam's left "cheek," beneath the skin, buried under some stitches and a bunch of tape. After pressing a few buttons, Miriam's agonized expression and vocal complaints faded away, and she drifted into a light snooze.

We arrived home by about five, and as I got her settled into her chair, a familiar routine had officially begun — post-op recovery, round number seven! This one, however, was going to be different. She is not supposed to even sit up except for short periods of time, for several weeks! It will take eight weeks for the leads anchored near her spinal cord to heal into a fixed position, so extreme care must be taken to prevent bending, twisting, or lifting motions that will cause the leads to move and require them to be repositioned.

The post-op recovery instructions caught us off guard. For the trial, the leads were installed in the same area as the permanent leads, and then she enjoyed a very active week; now we learn that for the permanent leads, she must lay flat and be a couch potato for two months. This doesn't make much sense to this humble woodworker. I do know that the pattern for all her major surgeries has been to withhold recovery information until after surgery. Probably because many elective surgeries would not be done if people knew what the recovery would be like. In our case, with me being the primary care provider and still needing to work, the burden of providing her care for the recovery period following her first knee surgery was almost too much to bear.

Once we had entered this "treatment vortex," there was no escape. Had we had any clue about what lay ahead, Miriam would never have gone through the surgery room door the first time. By the time this surgery was performed, the cyclonic pattern of high hopes followed by crushing disappointment was well established. Our reasoning was that if we don't try, it won't get better. Isn't that the same philosophy that keeps compulsive gamblers at the table?

The good news is that the stimulator is doing its job and covering most of the leg pain; the bad news is that the incisions required in her back and bottom to implant the unit are very painful and now are the source of brand-new pain she has to deal with. The stimulator is positioned to work for her legs, so it does nothing for pain "farther north." Once she recovers from the implanting process, she should feel like a new woman, which will hopefully make the present discomfort worthwhile. Is this how a shell-shocked soldier on a battlefield feels? Since I've never been in that situation, I can only speculate. The "bombs" exploding in our lives are thankfully figurative rather than literal, but the numb sensation of hopelessness may be similar.

Saturday, July 15, 2000

What a night! My bride was not happy, not comfortable, and needed everything different than it presently was. From pillows to covers, her head to her feet, it was either too high or too low; not in the right place; too hard or too soft; too hot or too cold; her bladder filled up often, and her stomach cramped. Outside of Matthew's room, little sleep was had in this household. I'm so glad he can sleep.

Matthew has been a great help through our entire ordeal. I worry too much about any negative impact all this adversity may be having on his childhood. He has had to shoulder much more responsibility than most children his age. Perhaps he is developing character traits that will serve him well in the years to come instead of scars that will turn him into a cynical adult one day. We will work on any "needed repairs" after the crisis has passed and we've reached calmer water.

Journal

Sunday, July 16, 2000

Two months have now passed since we were in Dr. Cox's office, and he referred her to Dr. Ware. So far, the employer/insurer has simply said "NO." They also continue to say "NO" more than six months after receiving the prescription for the spa. I suspect in the latter case they are hoping the spinal cord stimulator will resolve her pain issues and a spa will no longer be needed. At least that's the answer I would offer were I in their shoes, but since I'm not in their shoes, as Miriam's primary advocate (somebody needs to be), I'm angry, no, furious at their apparent callousness.

Journal

Saturday, July 22, 2000

Miriam slept in, finally making an appearance at 9:45! She looks good. She has been sleeping better since the SCS was installed, after surviving that first night. She has dutifully spent the week lying on the sofa except for the trip to see Dr. Edwards on Thursday. She is healing well and was given permission to begin taking showers. Hopefully next week she will be able to return to the hot tub.

The SCS is doing a good job with the knee pain, however some of the reflex sympathetic dystrophy–like cramps and zingers in her left foot have broken through the SCS's highest settings. Dr. Edwards perhaps will adjust it in another week or so. His instructions were clear — "Be a couch potato for another five to six weeks to allow the leads to heal in place."

Sunday, July 23, 2000

Miriam's knee locked up this morning as she was getting out of the shower. It has hurt her ever since. The SCS is not covering all of her pain. She does not look nearly as good this morning as yesterday. She slept well, but obvious pain is contorting her face.

We received a certified letter yesterday informing us of an independent medical examination (IME) appointment in Atlanta on Friday. The employer/insurer (E./I/) can send her to as many of these exercises in futility (my opinion) as they are willing to pay for. The fact that I have to take time from work to take her is of no consequence to them.

Journal

Wednesday, July 26, 2000

The E/I really infuriates me. According to attorney Fred, they are now offering a Y membership as a compromise to buying her a spa. They had the nerve to tell him that "if she went at 8 p.m., she probably wouldn't need one at 2 a.m." I guess the rest of our lives are to be spent taking her to the Y every evening before bed to treat the knee that was ruined due to their negligence. By the way, the nearest YWCA is a 15-minute drive from our home. Thirty minutes total travel time, plus at least an hour-long session in the spa before taking her home and tucking her in bed; so the "magic tree" in the back yard that spits out Benjamins whenever we have to pay for something, must now hatch eggs that add ninety minute extensions to my days. There is a consensus of opinion between Dr. Robel and Fred that since they have purchased the SCS, they are even less inclined to buy her a spa. I get it, and I wish my involvement could be so easy.

Fred informed Miriam yesterday that he was filing to get me compensated for providing her "attendant care" on Friday while I took her to Atlanta for the IME. While this is nice, it is almost an insult! What about two Fridays prior when I had to leave work, drive to Winder, take her home following the implanting of the SCS, and not sleep that night because of her need for constant care? Or the hundreds of sleepless nights caused because I was providing the care she needed in the last three years; or, what about the trips to Birmingham when she was in too much pain to do anything but take drugs and sit in her recliner in the back of the van? Was she supposed to deliver herself to Dr. Cox? Yes, I'm venting, but remember, this is my therapy; the dogs are thankful I have a keyboard to hammer on instead of kicking them.

"They" (her former employer) have no clue what Miriam's life has been like since the night she slipped on their pretty, freshly laid wax floor. She worked for Altma Hospital for 20 years! Cindy Harris, the workman's compensation and employee health nurse has called on several occasions as part of her job to help contain the cost of Miriam's care. The callous, insensitive, and demeaning approach she used when talking to Miriam was partly responsible for our seeking an attorney to assist us. She unintentionally convinced us that we had become unwilling participants in a game of "ream Miriam."

The condescending nature of her conversations with Miriam sounded to us as though they didn't think anything was wrong and that Miriam was milking them for all she could get. This may be why no one wanted to "validate" Miriam's injury with displays of kindness and empathy. No matter the reason, the complete silence from the employer to whom she committed 20 years of service with an exemplary record, is like pouring salt into an open wound!

Letter to Attorney Fred Hill

Thursday, July 27, 2000

It was time to adjust it now that Miriam had two weeks to get accustomed to it, so Miriam was returned to Doctor Edwards' office for a follow-up visit with a programming technician. Their conversation went something like this:

Miriam: "You can turn it up, right? There are times when it just doesn't cover the pain in my foot."

Technician: "Uh, it only goes to 10, and you are at 9.9 now! I will adjust the signal width to see if that does a better job of covering your pain, but you know you're going to have to turn this off for at least an hour a day and turn it down to a lower setting so the battery will last a while, don't you?"

She changed the mode to pulse, which should also help cover the pain as well as prolong the life of the battery.

Miriam has had the unit set on the highest possible setting for several days now. It is clear the positioning of the permanent leads is not nearly as effective as the ones for her trial.

She has also healed to the point where she can get in the spa and will do so again tonight. The reflex sympathetic dystrophy (RSD), (no need to sugar-coat the obvious truth any longer, we need to call it what it is; wishing it were not so, will not change the facts), is cramping her left foot and causing a lot of discomfort the spinal cord stimulator is not able to cover.

After spending an hour in the spa last night, the cramping calmed down and she was able to go to bed and sleep. ...take her to the Y, these people must be out of their mind! Just the trip from the building to the car would likely undo the progress made during the soak.

It will probably be a rough trip to Atlanta tomorrow for the I.M.E. By the way, as best we can tell, Dr. Edwards has not officially diagnosed Miriam as having RSD. He instead refers to her pains, cramps, sweats, and localized chilling, as "RSD–like symptoms."

Letter Attorney Fred Hill

Saturday, July 29, 2000

A jury of our peers has returned a verdict. Apparently, they did not need additional time for deliberations (three years was long enough) or feel compelled to involve judges or lawyers in the process. People who know us and something of our collective character have watched Miriam's battle with pain and mobility long enough. This jury cannot believe the hospital's total lack of compassion and action concerning this case. They are equally dismayed at the apparent absence of legal recourse for such a blatantly obvious affliction and resulting complications!

This jury of friends and compassionate acquaintances have generously provided funds to get Miriam a spa that will address her unique needs. Others are helping build a deck to put it on. Other friends and family members continue to help with meals, so I have time to earn a living, be a father, and tend to Miriam's care too.

Perhaps the hospital has won the battle over paying for a spa, but the war won't be over for a long, long time.

Journal

Sunday, August 27, 2000

The recovery has been much more difficult and challenging than we anticipated. She is now six weeks post-SCS implantation. Some developments that need to be recorded before they are forgotten are:

Word has quietly come from two different sources that a trip to New York has been approved. Apparently, it's not official yet, as notice of an appointment time and plane tickets have not arrived.

Her pain is so intense that she keeps the SCS turned up to its highest setting in an attempt to cover it. During a follow-up visit to check the SCS, a technician told her that she would need a new battery "by Christmas!"

The cost of the SCS to Altma Hospital is about $50,000! This knowledge shocked us; we thought the cost was somewhere around $12,000. Soon though, Miriam's dismay gave way to a bought of depression: "If this thing costs this much, and it's only able to help with this much of the pain, what am I going to do?"

She has driven very little since her last surgery since she is supposed to turn the stimulator off before getting behind the wheel, and she can't be "high on drugs" either. Finally, in June of 2000, after I asked him, "Would you want her sharing the road with your loved ones, given her medication regimen?"

Dr. Robel wrote a note that took away her driving privileges. She was not happy but understood. There was a strategic angle to my request. If she could no longer drive herself to her appointments, the E/I would be required to solve the problem. Was it inconvenient? Yes, but I was tired of shouldering all the burden and responsibility for her care and began looking for ways to transfer some of it to the E/I.

Very simple and minor tasks around the house leave her exhausted and, in more pain, than when she started. More and more drugs are required now than when the stimulator was first implanted to keep the pain under control. There is a huge difference between the trial version and her permanent stimulator. The additional pain and recovery from the implantation were just not worth the minuscule benefit it provided. Yet another failed attempt to restore Miriam to living a near normal life.

The nerve malady (RSD) may be affecting the right foot more in the last few days than it has since the stimulator was implanted. She leaves the right leg channel off almost all the time to prolong the life of the battery. We worry that if a new battery is required several years before it is supposed to be, that a fight will be required to get W/C to buy her a new one. We don't understand why the temporary unit worked so much better than the permanent one. This one does not seem to be nearly as powerful as the trial unit. The trial unit, she could turn it up to the point where her leg jumped uncontrollably; this one can't even make it twitch. The answer may be lead positioning. The trial version hit the right spots; the permanent obviously did not.

CHAPTER 8
Road Show

The Knee Gazette

August 29, 2000

Our church family, friends and our family have brought countless meals after each of Miriam's seven surgeries along with untold numbers of visits. These have helped lift sagging spirits more often than anyone will ever know. People have gone shopping for us and have helped take her to a legion of appointments. One dear friend even took her to the hospital for the latest surgery, which enabled me to work a few additional hours! Other friends have allowed her the use of their spa, another loaned us one they were no longer using, while still another purchased one ideally suited to Miriam's needs and gave it to her! Somebody anonymously paid a maid to come clean the house; someone else came and repaired our dryer at no charge. Other dear souls have helped transport Matthew to and from various events and, most recently, to and from his new school. Some men from my parent's church gave their Saturday to help me build a deck able to support the new spa.

This is all in addition to the prayers that have been offered on our behalf. Surely without this support, Miriam would have given up long ago. She has neither taken drastic action to free herself from this bondage of pain nor languished for long in a pit of despair. Somehow, "Thank You" understates what we desire to express, but rest assured our gratitude is heartfelt and genuine.

Miriam's incisions from the SCS have healed nicely, but she is still having trouble adjusting to the foreign object in her fanny. For some reason, the permanent stimulator does not have as much "punch" as the temporary trial unit. A technician has informed her that at the current rate of consumption, she will need a new battery in less than a year; this battery is supposed to last from four to seven years! This is a real indication of the pain she is dealing with, and/or that the position of the leads is not correct. If there was not significant pain to offset the electrical pulses of the stimulator, she could not tolerate the level of electrical energy coursing through her body.

The most disturbing trend I see is the growing effort required to keep her pain at bay. Until June, she was able to function well enough to at least come to the plant with me part time for a couple of days a week. She answered the phone and took care of some paperwork; mostly this helped her feel connected with life instead of just watching it pass by while her nose was pressed against the window. Even this level of marginal activity finally had to be suspended because of the toll it was taking on her. Toward the end, she required two days to recover from "working" one. It was difficult for her to give up this remaining shred of dignity and become wholly dependent (in her eyes). As she struggles to perform the simplest tasks around home, it has become apparent to her just how necessary it was for her to give up working entirely. It is not unusual now for her to keep her stimulator maxed out, spend several hours a day in the spa, take powerful painkillers, and still hurt!

At her lowest moments she sees herself as a millstone around the lives of Matthew and me and wants desperately for us to be able to live our lives free of her problems. These times usually follow a night of little sleep, followed by a day of constant pain, nausea, and the inability to do any of the things she desperately wants to do for us. I try to assure her that Matthew and I would rather have her in her diminished condition than not have her at all. Of course, I don't stop there; in my most thoughtful and caring tone of voice, I tell her that "She deserves a much better man than I and that I would be glad to help her find one!" That is just one more example of how I have her best interests at heart!

~ Mark, Matthew, and "The Electric Woman"

Journal

September 8, 2000

Physical therapist Henry saw Miriam for the first time in nearly eight weeks. She had taken time off to heal from the SCS implantation. He told her she is worse today than at any time since she began seeing him, only a few days post injury. I concur. As far as mobility and pain, she is far worse today than before they began cutting.

The Knee Gazette

September 12, 2000

The good news: a trip to New York City has been approved. The appointment is for 1 p.m. on Friday. She will meet with a subordinate of the man Miriam was supposed to see. It may be like it was in Birmingham, where the physician she was referred to does not see workman's compensation cases. Only one ticket was purchased, so Miriam, by herself, is supposed to get to Atlanta in time to catch an early flight, not to New York, but to Charlotte. You really can't make this stuff up! She is to change planes in Charlotte, arrive at LaGuardia, and make it to Manhattan by the time of her appointment. After she sees the doctor, she is scheduled to return to Atlanta, again with a plane change in Charlotte. She is scheduled to land back in Atlanta at about 10:30 Friday night. This trip is planned for a woman who is unable to walk through a grocery store by herself!

I wrote the attorney this morning and told him "If she was able to make a trip like this, why would she need to see a doctor?"

It is as if the E/I agreed to send her to New York but was determined to make it as miserable as possible. There are an untold number of non-stop flights from Atlanta to LaGuardia every day, but to make it as difficult as possible on her, Miriam is scheduled to go through Charlotte, where she will change planes, BY HERSELF, and then return the same day! I was incredulous; Miriam was nearly inconsolable she was so upset. If that was their goal, they scored!

~ Mark, Matthew, and the "Mom on the Go"

The Knee Gazette

September 17, 2000

The "Mom on the go" has gone and returned. The Broadway play could be titled: "A Knee Over Manhattan." A headline in the New York Post would read: "Manhattan Kneed by Georgia Peach." The *New York Times* article would probably be entitled: "Georgia Woman Sees Doctor Without Delay."

Yes, they did manage to scrounge up a second ticket so I could accompany her. We returned to our humble home at 8:30 on Saturday evening. Miriam was glad to get back to her spa and air bed. Although the trip was difficult for her, it went better than I anticipated. We enjoyed smooth flights, but the take-offs and landings were extremely painful for her. Upon our departure from the plane in Atlanta last evening, I handed the nice lady a carefully closed bag containing Miriam's last meal.

Dr. Wilson and Dr. Ware examined her, took some photos of her legs, shared opinions, discussed options, and gave us some hope! Before he left the room, Dr. Ware shook my hand, looked me in the eye, and told me he would assist Dr. Wilson with the case. This may have been his response to the impassioned plea I made a few days earlier to him via email. He shouldn't post his email address on the hospital's website if he doesn't want people to use it, right?

In my correspondence, I told him of the referral by Dr. Cox and of our three-month-long fight with workman's compensation just to have the opportunity to see him. I may have also mentioned something about what a great personal sacrifice in pain and agony Miriam would have to make just to get there for the appointment, maybe. I was not embellishing, just making sure he understood the nature of the case.

It was so refreshing to have two physicians in the same room, at the same time, examining her, sharing ideas, and then answering questions. They conferred before, during and after the exam, in our presence. This is something we have not witnessed until now. Both men presented humble, down-to-earth demeanors. They were compassionate men who were not afraid to admit it when they did not know something. This sharing of ideas, especially in our presence, was fantastic for me! This is the way problems get solved in every other field, why not medicine?

Their conclusion was that there are two problems to address:

The first was nerve damage, which was probably caused by scar tissue from prior surgeries; the second, and most obvious, was the structural instability of the joint itself. The nerve damage will be addressed by a hand surgeon, who will dissect out the nerve and take measures to prevent future problems.

They have a plan! The nerve surgery will be done first, then the joint will be rebuilt. The structural portion will be a slightly modified repeat of what Dr. Cox did a year ago this past July but will also include the replacement of some cartilage, "which will help hold the tibia in place." If the nerve surgery takes more than two or three hours, the joint surgery will follow six months later. If they can do it all at the same time, they will, but this is yet to be determined.

I anticipate another fight with the employer/insurer to get approval for all of this, but hopefully, we will prevail yet again.

Doctors Warren and Wilson kept us in their office for so long that we missed our scheduled six p.m. flight out of La Guardia. The battery of X-rays was not completed until after 6:30. An MRI was scheduled for noon on Saturday, so we were stuck in Manhattan. I wheeled her in a borrowed wheelchair to a 12th-floor apartment at the "Helmsley," a hotel/residential building attached to New York Presbyterian Hospital. It was only a block from The Hospital for Special Surgery, so it wasn't a long ride for the lady from Georgia.

The apartment was across the street from Sotheby's Auction House. From our room, we could look into a portion of their "attic" where various items of interest were stored on shelves. With twin beds and a TV without a remote, the room was more functional than luxurious. After having her leg manipulated and examined as hard as they did, Miriam would not have slept any better at the Waldorf Astoria. I, on the other hand, was so beat I could have slept just fine on the floor. We were in bed by 10, so much for a night on the town in NYC! How I could ever have driven home from the Atlanta airport after a scheduled 10:30 touchdown Friday night, I don't know. We were already exhausted at the halfway point of the scheduled round-trip marathon. Once we arrived in our room, we left only for nearby food. The rest of the time, we rested and read from the "comfort" of our respective beds.

We left New York with hope — something we haven't had since Dr. Cox's surgery began to unravel.

~ Mark, Miriam, Matthew, and "The Doctor Stalkers from Georgia"

Journal

September 18, 2000

We returned Saturday evening from a trip to NYC to see Dr. Riley Wilson and, as we hoped, Dr. Richard Ware.

When Dr. Wilson entered the exam room, Miriam was sitting on the edge of the exam table. Her brace, shoe and sock were all stored in the corner and her legs dangled off the edge. This is the standard preparation for what now must surely be approaching nearly 100 examinations in the last 36 months. In this position, Miriam's right foot hangs normally, the left droops and rotates out to about a 75-degree angle.

This sight amazes Dr. Wilson. He is a young man, only about eight years out of school. He soon left to go to Dr. Ware's office to get on his afternoon schedule. He returned with Dr. Ware's nurse, who informed us that Dr. Ware would like to see her after he finishes with his last patient of the day. We made it clear that we did not mind waiting, and that making our 6 p.m. flight was not a priority. We were here to see Dr. Ware.

This was the man we had worked so hard to have an opportunity to see. This is who Dr. Cox referred her to; but being the chief Orthopedic Surgeon at a prestigious hospital like The Hospital for Special Surgery, keeps him busy. Like other men who don't want to involve themselves in court battles, he normally does not see Workman's Comp patients. Our appointment was with Dr. Wilson; Dr. Ware was to simply examine her and provide Dr. Wilson with his assessment of her situation.

When Dr. Ware walked into the exam room, Dr. Wilson was with him and acted like an excited child leading mom to a new discovery. Dr. Ware's first words were formed into a question directed at Dr. Wilson.

"Do you have your digital camera?"

They photographed the dangle, then they photographed her trying to walk; then they had her lie down on the bed and relax her legs. Miriam's left foot simply fell over onto the bed, leaving her two feet at nearly right angles to each other. Another picture was taken, and comments of dismay were uttered. Impressing someone of Dr. Ware's stature and experience is probably not a good thing!

Once they were finished twisting and turning Miriam's tender leg, they talked. First, they talked to each other, then to us. The fact that the men were not too proud to be in the same room at the same time, and with the patient present, made quite an impression on me. This is something that just has not happened at any point during the entire ordeal.

Following the exam, we were directed to a hotel/apartment building somehow connected with NY Presbyterian Hospital. We were on the 12th floor in an efficiency apartment. After we "moved" into our room, which involved unpacking one pair of underwear each, it was time to find food. We left home a few minutes after five on Friday morning in order to catch the 7:45 flight to Charlotte. A compassionate attendant upgraded us to First Class, which gave Miriam plenty of leg room and a shorter walk to her seat. On the flight out of Charlotte, Miriam was given a bulkhead seat. I was a row behind her. This provided enough leg room to allow her to extend her leg enough to get comfortable. It had been a long day and we were whipped, but we had to have food.

We ate dinner at an Italian restaurant recommended by Dr. Wilson. We dined on the sidewalk because I could not get her wheelchair up the steps of the restaurant. From our table we watched New York City pass by. There were probably more cabs and buses than there were cars. Lots of pedestrians, a surprising number walking large dogs! This probably surprised us the most; we don't normally associate big cities with big dogs. I expected to see as many large dogs in NY as I do taxis in Watkinsville, Georgia, almost none. But there they were, huge dogs taking their owners for evening walks. I asked the cab driver taking us to the airport on Saturday about where all the dogs take care of their "business?"

He replied, "On the street, but there's a $250 fine if the master fails to clean it up."

Picking up poop after your dog, wow, I really am a country bumpkin! I didn't know it was even a thing. I've kicked it from inconvenient places, and even used a shovel from time to time to clean out a dog pen, but never have I had the pleasure of following my dog with a glove and a bag to pick up fresh deposits. "...Toto, we're not in Kansas anymore..."

Another thing that surprised me was the number of women compared with the number of men. NYC looked like an interesting place to be a single fellow! The streets were clean, and people obviously felt comfortable walking about alone after dark. After dinner we strolled and rolled half a block to a store where we could pick up a few of the necessities we left at home. Nothing major, but clean teeth and combed hair would probably be appreciated come morning. We hoped we would not see anyone on Saturday who might notice we were wearing the same clothes we arrived in on Friday. Too bad if they did, we weren't there to impress anyone.

Saturday morning, we picked up breakfast at a neighborhood deli and returned to our room to eat. The food we found in NY was very reasonably priced. Lunch on Friday was no more expensive than what I am accustomed to paying for lunch at the Ingles Deli in Greensboro, Georgia. In Manhattan, breakfast for two was less than $9!

Overall, the trip went better than I anticipated. The airports provided wheelchairs; we got to see Dr. Ware, and we came home with renewed hope for a better tomorrow.

Letter to Dr. Wilson

September 24, 2000

She has given much thought to your question concerning the point when the latest surgery began to "unravel." Her answer to the question posed in your office was not complete and not clear; but the information was documented on the "Timeline" put together by her physical therapist.

The end officially began with another audible "pop," while she was using the recumbent stepper during a physical therapy session eight to nine weeks after Dr. Cox's surgery. Up to this point, everything had gone well and according to plan. It was shortly after this, during a follow-up visit to Dr. Cox's office to find out why she was having problems, that we were told that she had "torn her gastroc." Miriam thinks some part of the graft failed when the pop occurred.

The Knee Gazette

Saturday, October 14, 2000

Although the time frame is much closer to a few months than the "few days" we were promised during our visit in his Manhattan office, Dr. Wilson has finally outlined a plan for the "Mother of all Knees." The month that has elapsed since our visit has been an emotional roller coaster for Miriam. We returned to Georgia hoping for quick and decisive action that would provide some relief from the shackles of this debilitating pain. Two weeks went by without a word! The anticipation that Miriam was clinging to and that kept her going was rapidly exhausting the optimism that fueled it. It was time for husband to get involved and take some decisive action by "stirring the pot" yet again...

My part in the Broadway comedic tragedy entitled "A Knee Over Manhattan" could be titled: "Have Keyboard, Will Stroke." I sent the good Dr. the following email:

September 28, 2000

To: Dr. Wilson

Tomorrow it will be two weeks since our visit to your office. We left NY with some desperately needed hope and your assurances that we would be hearing from you "next week.

Almost two have passed with no word of a possible itinerary for implementing the plan that was hatched during our visit with you and Dr. Ware. Are there problems or a change of plans that we should be aware of?

Although it is difficult to believe, I swear this knee (and her discomfort) is getting worse by the day.

Please let us know what you are thinking and planning. I beg you to put this case "on a front burner" so she can hopefully get some relief.

Dr. Wilson emailed the following reply:

Mr. Johnson,

I received your fax today. I am understanding and empathic with regard to your situation. However, not having been able to get an MRI to better understand the condition of the cartilage in your wife's knee and the competency of her reconstruction makes things a bit difficult. Remember, with such end-stage knees, I (and my colleagues as well) are very leary of immediately offering yet another surgical solution to a persistent problem. Our plan was to present this case at our educational meeting. Dr. Ware is currently away and wishes to participate. As more information is available, I will certainly keep you aware.

Riley Wilson, MD
Assistant Professor Sports Medicine & Shoulder Service
Hospital for Special Surgery
Cornell University Medical College
New York, New York

Judging by the sobbing coming from the earpiece of my office telephone, my dear wife was unhappy about something, but it took a little while for her to calm down enough to tell me about having received an email. This is a fine example of the author's claim that our genders originated from separate planets (Venice and Mars). I understood the message to say: "We are still thinking about how to address the complicated problems this knee presents." She understood the message to read: "We are not going to do anything."

At this point, she slipped into a state of despair that I could do nothing about. Getting genuinely concerned for her mental well-being (and safety), I again turned to my keyboard. The "plea," which read in part:

October 2, 2000

TO: Dr. Wilson

RE: Miriam Johnson

You are probably already tired of my badgering, but I refuse to apologize until there is progress toward solving this woman's knee. If you lived in our household for only one 24-hour period, you would understand my/our state of desperation. The experience reflected on Dr. Ware's face suggests that he has been repairing joints far longer than MRI machines have been making images of them. The "plan" the two of you "sketched" out for us before we left your office was rational, made sense, and was based upon the fresh examinations and "gut feelings" of two of this country's most skilled minds (and hands) in the orthopedic field. You offered an explanation for each of the failed procedures that made sense to us and increased our level of hope for a solution in the near future. I beg you not to retreat from the confidence you displayed more than two weeks ago.

As women often do, Miriam "read between the lines" in your last email and determined that you now plan to do nothing. You can only imagine the devastating effect this has had on her morale in the last week. I didn't read it that way, and I'm confident that was not the message you intended to convey, but she has been nearly inconsolable since.

As you mentioned during our visit, we are nearing the end of the line with this knee. No matter what is done, I can't imagine it getting worse. Something must be done to address her pain. Life in a wheelchair is still a life; living with this pain for 30 or 40 more years is not an option! At present, the stimulator stays on its highest setting. She is taking enough muscle relaxers and painkillers that her mind stays numb; the gleam has long ago left her eyes. On top of these drastic attempts to kill the pain, she spends several hours a day in a spa soaking in the swirling water to take pressure off the leg and relax the knotted muscles. We desperately need the help we discussed during our visit. Thank you for your attention to this matter,

Mark Johnson, Worried Husband

Thankfully, his reply was prompt (I'm really liking this direct communication with the physician).

"Our mission as a tertiary orthopedic hospital is to provide the best care possible for all types of problems: large and small. Make no mistake, your wife's knee represents a large problem. However, I would urge you to not mistake my caution for an unwillingness to help. Trying to get one surgeon, let alone three, on the same page takes some doing—I am trying. On another note, I still feel that an MRI is necessary, so if I need to speak with someone at Emory or Peachtree Ortho, perhaps (remember Dr. Jon Heard that I mentioned), this might be the best approach. I am to be in touch with Watson this week, and Ware remains away until week's end."

RJW

This time, the voice on the other end of my office phone was much different. Naturally, I "stroked" a note of thanks to Dr. Wilson:

You, sir, are a surgeon with remarkable ability! With only a few keystrokes you managed to excise a depression and replace it with a the-glass-is-indeed-half-full perspective. What a difference; I thank you! Miriam called me immediately upon receiving your email. The tone of her voice had changed dramatically over what I had left when I went to work. The difference? Hope had returned to her outlook. The rest of the day and night went much better. Although she still hurts, now she can look ahead toward what will surely be a better day. Keep us posted and let us know what we can do to keep things moving forward.

Mark

Now that something seems to be happening, Dr. Wilson is using the telephone rather the keyboard. He called Miriam twice this week. On Monday, he told her the nerve and the knee would be repaired at the same time; on Friday he outlined a different approach that once again sent my poor wife into a state of short-term despair.

The most recent "plan" is for Dr. Watson to dissect the nerve and then Dr. Wilson will remove all the hardware from the knee and do some bone grafts on the holes left behind. There is concern about the amount of work having been done on these bones. Each reconstruction has left tunnels and holes that have the potential of affecting the strength of the bones near the joint. The last thing they want to deal with is a broken bone once their work is complete. Of course, this plan also provides for a "recon mission" to have a look at the condition of the cartilages and to see if they can tell exactly why Dr. Cox's surgery failed. Once the bone grafts have healed, probably in the spring, Dr. Ware and Dr. Wilson will "reconstruct the knee joint" with new ligaments and probably also replace some cartilage.

Miriam is to call his office Monday morning and schedule the surgery for "a Thursday." Of course, the good people at Workman's Comp. are probably going to have something to say about all this once they find out.

As you can imagine, Miriam's emotions are pretty frayed right now. I think she will be fine once dates, times, schedules and approvals are all set. Hopefully we will be in NY within the next 30 days.

~ Mark, Matthew, and "Puddles"

Journal

Sunday, October 29, 2000

The best part about Daylight Savings is the morning after resetting the clocks in the fall. For about three days, a person can wake up at "the normal time" and use that extra hour to do productive things like productive people who get up an hour early all year long. In our house, that extra hour will probably disappear into a morning nap.

Miriam is holding on, but I don't know how. There seems to be a direct correlation between her level of activity during the day and how well she sleeps at night. It is nearly impossible to keep her on the couch or in her chair during the daytime. She wants desperately to contribute to the family, so she pushes herself and consistently sacrifices her wellbeing in the process. An admirable attribute until one realizes the price she is paying.

We have begun receiving a weekly check from W/C and some from disability. Although "this never happens," her disability was approved without the help of an attorney or a hearing! This combination is improving our survivability tremendously.

Attorney Fred reports that the employer/insurer wants to assign a "Rehab Specialist" to Miriam's case. We have mixed emotions at this point. Miriam is convinced this is not good, "They haven't given a damn about me thus far, so why now, unless it is to force me back to work before I am able, or to get the weekly checks stopped." She is concerned this person will come to the house on one of her good days, see a clean kitchen and a made bed and declare her fit to return to work. I am trying to convince her that this could be helpful. We have nothing to hide. I have told her that her 20-minute contribution around the house, requiring a two-hour rest period to recuperate, does not qualify her to return to work.

The Knee Gazette

Saturday, November 4, 2000

The script has been written and the cast is now in place for the soon-to-debut Broadway production entitled: *A KNEE LIKE NO OTHER*. This will be a comedic tragedy starring a poor Lab Tech named Miriam who fell down and was not able to get up for a long, long time.

The production will feature two main acts built around scenes involving daily drama. The curtain is scheduled to rise for Act I on November 30; Act II is tentatively planned for some time in the spring of 2001. The setting for both acts will be the Hospital for Special Surgery, located in New York City. The cast of characters includes two orthopedic surgeons and another surgeon who specializes in micro-surgery on hands. All are well-known and regarded within their respective fields. The leading man will be played by the victim's husband. He is somewhat of a concerned buffoon who spends most of the show pacing the hospital corridors and intimidating "caregivers" into delivering care for his wife. His imposing stature and humorous, though somewhat twisted, perspective on things not considered funny by most people are the primary source of levity throughout the production.

Act I will feature the expertise of Dr. Watson, a nationally respected hand surgeon, whose job it will be to free the peroneal nerve from scar tissue that has it bound up and theoretically is causing most of Miriam's agony. Dr. Wilson will participate in both the November and springtime surgeries. His job during the first surgery will be to remove all the hardware installed during previous surgeries and fill the holes with bone grafts as well as to perform an overall reconnaissance mission to assess the condition of the remaining tissues, while trying to determine a cause for the previous failures. The plan for Act II will be finalized once this assessment is complete. In a sense, he will be preparing the knee for the spring procedure, when Dr. Ware will apply his extensive reputation to constructing a functioning joint from a pile of parts that now barely resemble a loose formation.

At this point, the procedure has been approved by Workman's Comp, but the flight arrangements have not yet been made. Hopefully, they will buy both of us a ticket this time. It would be even better if we get a direct flight from Atlanta to NY. Could routing us through Charlotte last time have possibly saved the employer/insurer any money? I suspect it was done out of spite, just because they could.

Among the cast of supporting characters is their son Matthew. This child has just celebrated his 12th birthday; he was eight when he became a primary caregiver to his mother. His duties have included, among other things, washing dishes, cooking, and laundry. He apparently is getting tired. He informed his parents a few weeks ago that for his birthday, he would like to take a Caribbean cruise, by himself! Now you will understand when the curtain rises on Scene I, Act I, and Matthew is sunning himself on the deck of a ship while nursing a tall glass of lemonade. Meanwhile, his parents are dealing with winterish weather in NYC.

It will be fine with us if an encore performance is not required.

~ The Husband, the Son, and the Star

Journal

Friday, November 17, 2000

On Monday we met with a woman named Stacy Casey. This is the medical case manager I mentioned in the previous entry. A medical case manager has a tough, important and sometimes thankless job. They are assigned to difficult cases that take time and effort to resolve.

They are paid by the E/I to oversee the care of an injured worker. They are supposed to be neutral, taking neither the side of the E/I or the patient. If they do their job right, probably neither party is happy with them.

We met at attorney Fred's office. The meeting lasted more than two hours, during which she took pages and pages of notes. We left the meeting cautiously optimistic that perhaps the nature and tone of our experience within the Workman's Comp system of Georgia was about to change for the better. The next day she called Miriam to inform her that the employer/insurer would pay for her recliner, our new bed, the handrails we had put up, as well as the wheelchair I had purchased at an estate auction, but she was now using regularly! I like this woman already.

At this same meeting, Fred handed us the travel arrangements for the November 30th surgery. As expected, they could have been more satisfactory. Fortunately, we had the foresight to buy our own tickets, in case they came up with something ridiculous like seating on the 33rd row on a flight requiring us to get up at three on the morning of our appointment scheduled for 10. They were thoughtful enough to find direct flights this time, but Miriam cannot sit on row 33 before surgery, how could she possibly do it with her leg in a cast post-surgery?

Stacy apologized for not being able to change the travel arrangements. She went on to tell Miriam that "Orders had come from higher-up that these arrangements would not be altered."

My reply: "They will be altered, by us, using our own tickets! These people are beyond comprehension." They may never know how we circumvented the trap of misery they set for us.

So far, the only thing the E/I have yet to agree to pay for is the spa. Stacy said, "Spas are considered to be luxury items, so they are difficult to get approved."

For the record, last night during a 45-degree rain, Miriam used her "luxury item" before going to bed and again in the middle of the night. What a party!

Journal

Sunday, November 19, 2000, 11:15 a.m.

Spasms emanating from behind her left ankle caused us to leave church in the middle of the morning service. Miriam is now sitting in her spa, despite the 35-degree rain trickling off of her shower cap. I will be kind and simply suggest that we do not consider her spa to be a luxury item, instead it's more of a necessity needed for pain mitigation. We are, with funds mostly donated by friends and family, working to enclose the spa so it is more pleasant for her to use in weather like this.

I had high hopes for getting her spa out of the rain yesterday, but sleet forced me to take my big-hearted crew of friends and family off the roof to prevent someone else from suffering a fate similar to Miriam's. We were successful, however, in getting the trusses set in place and getting a few sheets of plywood nailed on before the weather abruptly ended our progress.

We begin preparations for our annual Thanksgiving tradition with mixed emotions. For the first year since Miriam's accident, our destination does not have a spa. The house my parents rented is apparently a tri-level near the beach on Jekyll Island. Arrangements for these accommodations must be made nearly a year in advance of a holiday like Thanksgiving. Each year, we neglect to search for a place ideally suited to Miriam's needs because we prefer to think positively and assume that "Surely this crisis will be over by Thanksgiving." For three years we have been wrong!

Thanksgiving of '97, we went to Carter's Lake in North Georgia. Miriam was recovering from her first ACL surgery, and it was early enough in the process that she was entirely wheelchair-bound and not able to use a spa if we had had access to one. Thanksgiving of '98 we stayed in a house near Helen that had a hot tub. This is really where Miriam first discovered the benefit a spa could provide her. Last Thanksgiving, we rented a house in Pigeon Forge. The benefit of the spa was somewhat mitigated by the flight of stairs that separated it from the living quarters of the house, but she still braved it several times during the weekend. At that time she was far more mobile than she is today.

Upon our return home, we told Dr. Robel about the relief she received from her time in the spas. In early January, with no genuine relief for her pain in sight, he wrote her a prescription for a "whirlpool." This prescription was delivered immediately to Fred and our wait began in earnest. Two months later, after a steady flow of "encouragement" from my fax machine, Fred told us, "Although the E/I had agreed to nothing, they did want to know what would be satisfactory." Fred instructed us to look around and give him a couple of options to present to them.

We did a lot of homework, and within a couple of weeks, I sent Fred a term paper on spas, complete with detailed information on three that Miriam found to be most satisfactory for her knee. We had traveled to dealers, and Miriam had even climbed into them for a proper test.

The result: "We prefer to not buy her a spa." It was at this point our family and friends rallied 'round and made it possible for her to have a spa. This did not keep me from pressing the E/I, however, because in my mind, they should have to bear this cost.

By the end of May, the E/I, through their workman's comp administrator, also declined to honor Dr. Cox's referral to New York to see Dr. Ware. On top of these slaps in the face, Debbie Travis (FG Servicing Agency's representative handling Miriam's case at the time) called attorney Fred and asked him what it would take to "Settle this case!"

I felt completely impotent, powerless to help my bride find relief from her agony. This only added fuel and then further fanned the flames of my fury. I am still seething with rage over the absence of concern demonstrated by FG Servicing Agency with its arbitrary decision concerning the spa. FG Servicing Agency, I should point out, was merely the servicing company for Altma Hospital since they were self-insured (the E/I). It was the E/I pulling the strings and making the decisions. The E/I obviously didn't have to massage the cramping leg and foot, tote barf buckets, or try to function in a near-constant state of sleep deprivation while a loved one was writhing in pain. No, the people who caused her injury simply pretended they had done their part to restore her to health and that it must be her fault if the efforts had failed.

Things happen. I do not blame anyone for Miriam's injury. My anger and bitterness have developed and grown because treatment has been delayed or denied, which could possibly give her relief from the horrible pain and allow her to recover some of her/our lost life. We did not seek legal counsel until A) it became obvious that she was not getting better, and B) we were growing weary of being treated in a demeaning fashion by those in authority making decisions concerning her case. There was also a calendar issue that was mentioned by our bankruptcy attorney. He warned that the statute of limitations could expire, and her case would just end! This is what really inspired us to hire an attorney who specializes in workman's compensation cases.

We are pleased that the "NY plan" was finally approved and are hopeful that by next Thanksgiving she will be able to negotiate stairs and won't need a spa. Probably, in the spirit of wanting to remain optimistic, we won't look for an accessible Thanksgiving gathering place for next year either! Yea, I know, we are slow learners.

CHAPTER 9
To New York

Journal/ *The Knee Gazette*

Tuesday, November 28, 2000

Another surreal odyssey has begun! It is hard to comprehend that I am taking my bride to New York City for the first of two scheduled surgeries on her left knee. True, this is perhaps more believable than when I was taking her to Alabama for "knife work," but it is still a bizarre and out-of-the-ordinary thing to be doing. Things like this are just not what "normal people" do.

We are at cruise altitude courtesy of Delta Airlines. I am wedged into a seat designed by Pygmies for people who are five foot ten feet tall and weigh no more than 170 pounds. Since I am neither, I am not comfortable! From this seat, immediately behind the bulkhead (more legroom for Miriam), I can see around the curtain into the part of the airplane reserved for people with deeper pockets than have I. While those of us sitting behind the bulkhead were handed a brown bag containing our snack when we boarded the plane, the people sitting in front of the bulkhead were settling into seats large enough for some third-world villages, or, in my case, one over-sized American. "The Fortunate Few" have already been served an appetizer and now have linen tablecloths spread out on their little tables! They will be getting a full meal complete with complimentary adult beverages. I have considered taking up drinking on several occasions in the last few years; if I were seated on the other side of the bulkhead, I would probably imbibe.

Back here in "steerage," I am unwrapping the Knots Berry Farm

Shortbread that came in my snack sack. The gentleman two rows ahead of me and across the aisle is sipping white wine from a real glass! His real metal fork clinked when he laid it on his real China plate, so he could sip his wine and then pat the corners of his mouth with his real linen napkin. But on the other hand, he didn't get this nice little bag with handles on it either!

This bag may come in handy before we land. Miriam has begun to writhe in pain from having her leg so cramped. I lost feeling in my legs 30 minutes ago; I cannot imagine what life would be like on row 32, where the thoughtful and compassionate folks who made our travel arrangements at the E/I had scheduled us to sit on a 6:30 flight tomorrow morning. She has the first of three appointments starting at 10. I did not want to risk missing these, so we flew up the night before, even though we had to pay for the plane ticket and the room ourselves. I want to do everything possible to facilitate this treatment and eventual recovery. We learned a lesson from the first trip and got our own tickets, just in case they tried to seat us on row 32 or expect us to change planes in Charlotte again. Can you tell that I am not confident the E/I has our best interest at heart? I am already getting worried about the trip home. Even from this bulkhead seat, there is no room for a leg in a cast! Perhaps for the return trip, we will be on a plane that is newer and larger than this tired, aged 727 we are on now. The fact that this plane has seen better days is evidenced by the "vintage" license tag on the tail.

The prospects of more surgery do not seem to be causing Miriam any real anxiety other than having to leave her son. She wanted me to call him from the airport because she didn't think she could maintain her composure while talking with him. The effect of her condition upon him and his life is among her deepest regrets with the whole ordeal. Matthew worries about mom, too. During our conversation, he insisted that I not tell her about the sore throat and aching shoulders that he has had all day. He didn't want to worry her!

We have arrived at our hotel located near LaGuardia airport. For the same price we paid for a sketchy hotel in NYC, we could have gotten a two-room suite at one of Atlanta's finest hotels. Miriam asked me a few minutes ago if her bed could have bed bugs. I assured her it was probably just dry skin, but I would put on a good dose of the flea powder I had brought before I joined her! As luck would have it, we will be entertained by the sound of airplanes taking off and landing all night. But then, after spending several hours folded into the smallest airplane seat I've ever had the privilege of sitting in, even this room looks big.

The Knee Gazette

Wednesday, November 29, 2000

Although it is only 11 a.m., it has already been an eventful morning. The night's sleep was frequently interrupted by the woman in the bed next to mine, who was having bad dreams caused by her medications. It is not easy to rest when someone near you keeps yelling out in terrified tones about things that make no sense. I have become calloused over the years, and out of self-preservation, have learned to sleep through a lot of stuff, but last night exceeded what I normally ignore. It seemed like every few minutes, she would sit up in bed and scream something unintelligible, then wobble (the drugs really had her looped) to the bathroom. She would return to bed, take a drink of water, and begin the cycle all over again! This morning she asked me why my eyes looked puffy.

The complimentary breakfast served at the hotel reminded me of the snack we enjoyed on the plane last night. In both cases, the items served could just as well have been used for building materials. But since this was free (ok, already paid for), this was what we ate. It really mattered little what we ate, because Miriam lost it during the cab ride into Manhattan. The combination of the rough road, the driver, and the stuffy air inside the cab did her in. This wave of nausea exceeded the ability of the recently acquired wrist stimulator to suppress it. This little gadget is something we recently saw in the newspaper and requested Dr. Robel to prescribe. It arrived just in time for our trip, thanks to Miriam's sister, who picked it up on her lunch hour and delivered it to our house only a couple of hours before our departure. Fortunately, we had borrowed some of the "special bags" from the airplane, just in case the wristband wasn't a complete cure.

This has been a day! We were able to check into the room shortly after one this afternoon, and she has not left it since. I was presumptuous enough to assume that once we got in the room, she would settle in, become more comfortable, and give me some time off to read, nap, and catch up on the writing. She immediately went to bed, and I began to settle into a vegetative state involving a comfortable chair and a newspaper. I made it all the way to the second article when she begged me to go find her some ginger ale to help calm her stomach.

Soon, she was again tucked in bed, this time with a glass of ginger ale at her side, and I once again mistakenly thought I would have some free time. Once again, she had other plans. This time she stood just out of reach of my backhand and asked me to lay down beside her and "breathe so she could time her breathing to mine and go to sleep." Apparently, this is something she has been doing for some time when she is having trouble falling asleep, and I wasn't even aware of it. The next conscious moment I had was more than two hours later when she was standing beside me, telling me she was "hungry."

We called a local restaurant, and 30 minutes later, our supper was delivered to our room. Miriam seems to be feeling better now except for occasional waves of nausea. Hopefully, she can keep this meal down. At lunchtime today, I thought she was going to hurl all over the cashier who was ringing up our sandwiches. I gave her one of those "No, dear, not now, dear, not here, dear" looks, and she somehow kept from spoiling a room full of lunches.

Aside from our appointment with Dr. Watson and a brief conversation with Dr. Wilson, she was put through routine pre-op procedures. Dr. Watson will perform the nerve part of the surgery on Thursday, which is now scheduled for early morning. This was his first opportunity for him to see what he had gotten himself into by agreeing to get involved in this case at the request of Dr. Wilson.

Like everyone else, Dr. Watson was amazed at the amount of drop in her foot and the degree of neurological dysfunction from her knee to her foot. In the last year Miriam has lost the ability to raise her foot or wiggle her toes on the left leg! Although he didn't fetch a camera and start taking pictures like Dr. Ware and Dr. Wilson did back in September, he did ask a resident to "come look at this!" Dr. Watson's comment to us once his examination was complete, was that he "Didn't have much choice but to go free the nerve, but he could not guarantee that this would solve her pain."

Miriam was disappointed at the lack of confidence he displayed, but it would have been irresponsible for him to offer false hope. As I explained to her, these guys have two choices: do nothing, or do the best they can and hope for the best. I am glad they are moving forward.

Dr. Wilson hit us with some information we were surprised to find concerning his portion of the surgery. He will be harvesting bone material from Miriam's hip to use in the grafts for her knee. In September we understood that he would use bone from the tissue bank for this and that it would not come from Miriam.

I am really looking forward to the trip home even more now! If the woman's "sitter" and her "walker" have both just been cut on, how on earth will she be able to ride in a cab or sit in an airplane seat? Grace! We need heaps of grace poured all over us! Lord, are you listening? We sure are going to need your help!

Our hotel room is located in the guest quarters of the hospital. Many of their patients travel from as far away as Europe to benefit from the caliber of the orthopedic care delivered here, so they built a hotel adjacent to the hospital. This room is really more like an apartment than a hotel and is far superior to the room we stayed in last night! We are on the 6th floor and from our windows we can see the East River, even though this is not a waterfront room. We have a bedroom with a king-sized bed and a living, dining and kitchen combination! The living room is equipped with a sleeper sofa and a large, upholstered chair, television, and coffee table. The kitchen has everything our kitchen at home has, except that there is no microwave. Of course, tomorrow Miriam will be assigned a room at the hospital and this will become my personal "retreat" for the duration of our stay here. When I am able to leave her, I will use this room for rest and to clean up.

~ "Sleepy" and "Dopey" Johnson

The Knee Gazette

Thursday, November 30, 2000

This is a day Miriam has looked forward to with anticipation for months now. We both slept well last night, and she was in very good spirits a short while ago when I left her in pre-op. I have returned to our room, choosing to wait here rather than in the waiting room. I am not far away if I am needed.

My mind is cluttered with a flurry of thoughts and emotions as my wife enters the operating room for the eighth time in the last three years. I wonder, are we missing some spiritual truth or lesson that, once we grasp, will allow this trial to end, or is this simply an aspect of life after "The Fall?" I tend to lean toward the latter, but I keep thinking about 'ole Job...

Will we be able to handle the disappointment if, four months from now, she is in as much pain as she is now? The follow-up to this surgery is scheduled to take place in the late spring, but this is the one that should relieve her pain if it is going to happen. Surgery nine is where they will reconstruct the ligaments and rebuild the knee. Even if both procedures go well and are successful, it could be almost a year before she heals and rehabs to the point where life is returning to some form of normalcy. This part of the "trial" we can handle; we have become experts at looking ahead to a better day, especially when the trend is in the right direction. Since this has been described as "the end of the line" for this knee, there is no place else in this temporal world to turn in the event of another surgical failure.

It is 1 p.m. I returned to the waiting room two and a half hours ago; Dr. Wilson has just now come out and talked with me. The surgery lasted four and a half hours! Dr. Wilson reported that the nerve was severely squeezed and constricted by scar tissue. Dr. Watson released the nerve from its bondage and packed fat tissue around it to provide some padding.

The remaining time was spent trying to find all the hardware, removing it and applying bone grafts to the holes left behind. He was very upbeat and remains confident that they are executing a good plan. He could not identify any particular reason for the previous failure (s) but indicated that he will immobilize her leg for perhaps as long as six months following the reconstruction in the spring. He wants to allow for total healing before the new grafts are strained at all. Dr. Wilson described today's procedure as not serious, just time-consuming.

Seven hours after leaving her in pre-op, I was allowed a five-minute visit in recovery. She looked good! She said they "didn't quite have her hip dead enough when they started cutting on it. She graphically described the sound as bone was chipped from her hip for use in the knee. Fortunately, they heeded our advice and our pleas and performed the surgery without general anesthesia. Also, they are planning to install a catheter and leave in the epidural until sometime tomorrow. These last two steps should go a long way toward allowing her to have a good night tonight. Dr. Wilson told me that he will put her on a motion machine to keep her leg moving and try to prevent scar tissue from adhering to the nerve. So far, she has not experienced any nausea...

Thursday evening, November 30, 2000

Miriam was moved into a semi-private room at about three this afternoon. She is exactly one bed and one curtain away from a view of the East River. Initially, she was resting comfortably, but by 5 p.m., this began to change. First, it was her hip, where the bone material was harvested, that was bothering her; once they got that pain calmed down, the incision on the side of her knee was hurting. This may be a longer night for her than I thought. I probably won't be with her the whole night, because there really isn't any place for me to stay.

I am very impressed with the care she is receiving. Her nurses were very attentive and quickly brought in people from other specialties to help them cope with Miriam's pain and nausea. Although she has been nauseated, she hasn't vomited.

Miriam has a brace on her left leg that runs from the ankle to the middle of the thigh. She has a bandage on the left side of her pelvis covering the area where the bone was harvested. Her spinal cord stimulator is on its customary highest setting. She is receiving nausea meds and other fluids I. V. She is connected to a PCA pump for pain; they have her on oxygen, and she is getting her normal dose of Dilaudid. Perhaps the amazing thing to me is that she is even conscious! When by her side, she has kept me busy fetching ice chips, pillows, and chapstick, but unlike many of the past surgeries, I haven't had to demand that she receive care and then watch carefully to be sure the proper medications or doctors' orders have been carried out. These people are making my job a lot easier!

The Knee Gazette

Friday morning, December 1, 2000

My wake-up call came about 5:30. It was Miriam's nurse. She needed some help... I explained that I wasn't much to look at anyway, but that I certainly must shower and then would be right over.

When I walked into Miriam's room, the scene was not encouraging. There were no less than four lab coats, of at least three different colors, all bent over my wife. They cut an exasperated glance in my direction before focusing again on their patient. They were attempting to restart an I.V. and weren't having much success. Her IV had apparently come out during a thrashing episode during the night. Miriam appeared comatose. During her moments of semi-consciousness, her eyes seemed unable to focus, and her arms and legs flailed about as someone having convulsions.

In addition to the four in the room, another was on the phone seeking additional guidance from someone else. This room is full of expertise, and they called me? Maybe they don't know I don't have a lab coat or that I make chairs for a living; the extent of my medical training starts and stops with pulling splinters from my hands. They decided to take her back to recovery, where they could connect her to monitors and be better equipped to handle Miriam's deteriorating condition. This is when I returned to the room and began this "therapy session" with the laptop while awaiting news from the hospital. Venting with a keyboard is probably healthier than shaking my fist at Heaven or throwing heavy objects through windows. Although the laptop could short out and jolt me with a few meager volts, The Guy Upstairs at whom I'd be shaking my fist could hurl a bolt of lightning charged with several million volts at me, the laptop is surely the better choice.

During the night, she apparently slept some, but the slumber was not very quiet or relaxed. I felt sorry for her roommate, who I'm sure was unable to get much rest through it all. According to the nurse, she was fidgety, cried out in pain and was frequently swept by waves of nausea. As far as I know, she has not put anything in the nearby barf basin, she just heaved for a short while until the storm passed.

I was asked to leave last night at about 10. I didn't know how to act! In all of the previous surgeries, I "got" to stay at her side all night. Notice I mentioned nothing about sleeping there. They didn't have to ask twice, and I didn't have to bribe anyone to get them to ask at all! So, I took my guilt-free, but selfish self, back to my sixth-floor suite across the road. It looked like she was in good hands, so I didn't worry. I have learned that about all we can do for these first couple of days after surgery is survive them. Besides, my turn at the "fun and games" will begin on the return flight home, which I am awaiting with eager anticipation!

I got a kick out of looking out of the window and watching the dogs taking their owners for a walk. As soon as "Fido" (I forgot, this is Manhattan, and dogs here probably sport more sophisticated monikers, something like "Felipe"), does his business, the well-trained owner must clean up after said pet, or risk getting slapped by a $250 fine. Shortly after 10, within my very limited range of vision, I counted no less than eight people walking dogs on the street in front of this hotel. Most were large dogs, and some people were walking more than one! Can you imagine how undignified a Black Lab looks when it is riding in an elevator? I swear one looked at me and said: "I should be on a duck hunting boat in a swamp, not cruising in a high-rise elevator."

An hour after leaving the hospital, the phone rang. It was Miriam's nurse. Miriam was having some spasms and needed some of the medication we had in our arsenal, but their pharmacy apparently didn't have. Within a few short minutes I was dressed and back at my miserable bride's side. I felt compassion, but still no guilt, remember, they ASKED me to leave!

~ Guilt-free in Manhattan

Friday Afternoon

Okay, maybe a twinge of guilt this afternoon when I announced that I was leaving for a couple of hours to get something to eat and then to take a nap. The wild-eyed look from my wife said it all– you better come back, buster! Fortunately, the guilt passed as soon as my head hit the pillow...

Her encore performance in recovery this morning lasted five hours, which is longer than most patients spend there during their first appearance. Miriam is just special! When she returned to her room, she looked much better but had no recollection of the events that led to her exile. I'm not sure what happened while she was gone either, as I was not permitted to see her. She has not had a very good day. The nausea has continued to come and go, and she has slept lightly from time to time for short periods. She is miserable and has a hard time being still. This, too, is a vicious cycle. The more she moves around, the more she jeopardizes her IV and risks stirring up a bolt of pain, which causes more nausea, which requires more moving around, etc. I have also learned that it is unwise for me to point this out to her. I keep forgetting that women want empathy, not solutions.

The woman sharing Miriam's room lives only two blocks from the hospital. When her phone is not ringing, people are visiting. At times there have been as many as five visitors at one time! Their laughing and carrying on interfered with Miriam's rest, but I'm sure Miriam's all-night agony interfered with her ability to rest, too. She will be going home tomorrow, and Miriam should get to move to the bed with a view for the remainder of our stay. With luck, there won't be anyone moving into this bed until Monday, when we hope to be gone.

~ Guiltless and Miss Miserable

Saturday, December 2, 2000

A bright sun is trying to undo what the cold air mass accomplished overnight. The tempo of activity here at the hospital has slowed considerably over what we have observed the last couple of days. Apparently, weekends also happen in the big city. The only place where the weekend seems to have had no affect is at the corner deli, where I bought my coffee and "ham-egg-and-cheese-on-a-roll."

When one walks into one of these places, you are supposed to know what you want. They are small, often crowded, and remarkably efficient, and the people work at a furious pace. No time is wasted on smiles, pleasantries, or reading the menu unless you are the fifth or sixth person in line; it is all business. In an attempt to cover my ignorance, I simply ordered the same thing as the guy before me and something I thought was pretty safe: "black coffee." I paid my $5.05 and left with a sack that had something in it. It might have been fun to look into the eyes of the guy who spoke only broken English and in my best Jawja drawl ask for "a biscut w/ sawsage graavy, skrambled eggs, grits and kuntry haam, please." Chances are good that I would have lost my place in line and possibly even been banished from the store! This easily would have exceeded the 3.5 seconds each customer is allotted to interact with the person behind the counter. Since our first breakfast of "building material," I have avoided the doughnut-looking things without any "goodie" on them that some people spread cream cheese upon. I need the little old lady of Wendy's fame to march up to the counter with me and holler, "Where's the taste?"

I sipped my coffee and ate my roll while sitting in the Family Lounge just down the hall from Miriam's room. There is no curtain obstructing my view of the boat traffic on the East River from here.

Miriam is due back in her room shortly. She was returned once again to step-down recovery last night. I wonder if this is some kind of record for the number of times one patient has visited recovery following the same surgery; this was number three for her. They are being very careful with her medications and have refused to give her much of what she is accustomed to in her normal routine. Consequently, Miriam does not benefit of some of the things we have found that work for some of her various maladies. Because of this, she was deteriorating rapidly last night, mostly because she didn't have any of her anti-spasm medication. Before they gave her additional pain, nausea or spasm medication, they wanted to move her back to recovery where she would be much more closely monitored. Without some additional chemical help, I knew it was going to be a very rough night for her. I was encouraged by the fact that she was sleeping for longer periods of time yesterday. Once the pain and swelling from the surgery begin to subside, we will have a better idea whether there has been any real progress on the chronic pain front.

Too early to tell when we will be returning home, but I will be shocked if it is before Monday. I still have no idea what I will do with her on the plane, but I am thankful it will only last a couple of hours...

Saturday Afternoon and Evening

Finally, at nearly noon, Miriam was released from recovery and returned to her room. The good news is that her roommate went home, and I am now enjoying a full-wall-of-windows view of the East River. The barge and boat traffic are fascinating to this life-long landlubber. It apparently is a tidal river because it looks to me like it is now flowing in a different direction than it was this morning. Either that or my memory is in worse shape than I thought.

When Miriam returned to her room, there were three beautiful bouquets of flowers waiting for her. She didn't believe for a minute that I had anything to do with their presence; apparently the big-mouthed roommate had promised to leave them before Miriam was taken to recovery yesterday, so no surprise and no credit for Mark. Perhaps I will get credit for a feeble attempt at being a romantic. Or worse, it will get "tallied" on the same "scorecard" as a comment I made the other day as she was preparing for surgery. After she had removed all her jewelry (it didn't take long to remove the jewelry), I made a crack about "My being free now," when I saw her naked ring finger. She promptly reminded me of the ring I had "through my nose, to which she had a permanent leash attached."

It appears that Miriam is turning the corner. She looks and acts like she is feeling some better. Helga, the physical therapist that cared for Miriam in Birmingham has a sister I'll call Olga. Are all physical therapists descended from German gulags somewhere? Olga is performing similar torture here in the hospital room; in Birmingham, Miriam had to go to the dungeon to receive her therapy treatment. During today's session, her Ivy-League-educated therapist had her walk a few steps before returning her to the bed and installing a CPM machine which makes her leg move. Her hoity-toity education required the assistance of a Texas-educated woodworker to get the IV threaded through the sleeve of the gown in the right direction. As the problem was developing, Olga mentioned that her Ivy League education was deficient in this area. She wasn't kidding! Before I intervened, she had a mess that resembled a snarl of fishing line on a bait-casting reel.

Now for some good news: Miriam thinks she has more control over her foot and toes now than she did prior to the surgery! AND Olga was able to set up the motion machine with the correct settings, so Miriam's fresh surgery was not compromised the way we think happened in Birmingham.

Dr. Wilson is planning to write orders requiring Workman's Comp to buy seats in first class for the flight home! The next loud scream you hear will be when Workman's Comp sees this note. I will believe this is actually going to happen only when the plane is airborne, and we are sitting in front of the bulkhead, clinking our forks on real plates.

To keep from exceeding my daily ration of cyberspace, I will wrap this up and get it on its way.

~ **The Peach and the Cracker Reporting From the Big Apple**

Sunday morning, December 3, 2000

Miriam looks human this morning. The oxygen, epidural, and catheter were all removed yesterday, and the nurse's aide reports that she has done well with the bedpan during the night. Miriam is complaining of a headache and some incision pain this morning, but I am able to see more movement from her left foot than I have seen in nearly a year! She had only minimal spasms in the leg during the night and so far has not had any of the hideous toe-curling cramps that have visited her so frequently in the last six months.

I will go to work this afternoon on the travel arrangements for the trip home. Tomorrow morning Dr. Wilson wants to have her molded for a device to help keep her from dragging her left foot. This apparatus will not be ready until early afternoon, so I will try to schedule a flight for late afternoon.

~ The Morning Report from the "Window over the River East"

Sunday afternoon, December 3, 2000

Miriam continues to remain stable and reasonably comfortable. Twice, I have gotten her up, and she has walked to the bathroom. She has slept a fair amount today, but, when she wakes up, I have to check the email box to see if anyone has written. So far, only once has there been "no messages"; I am overwhelmed by the time people have taken to write. Miriam has always enjoyed getting the mail. I've been told that as a child, she once fell and broke a finger while trying to beat a sibling to the mailbox. Email was made for Miriam because the mailman in cyberspace will deliver whenever there is mail, not just once a day. She/we are receiving much encouragement from your emails, thank you.

Our flight has been changed to 4:30 Monday afternoon. I am glad that I didn't start holding my breath about a seat in first class, because this won't happen, unless the people staffing the gate take pity on her. At least we are on something besides a 727 and have bulkhead seats. Thankfully it is only about a two-hour flight!

It is 3:30 in the afternoon and the sun is already sinking near the horizon. Outside our window, the East River is in the throes of changing its direction of flow. I've enjoyed watching the tugboats pushing barges of different shapes and sizes past our window. Occasionally, a police boat or pleasure boat of some description will speed past. There have also been at least two groups of kayakers that have paddled by. From my perch, I can also see the planes arriving and departing from LaGuardia.

When I am not composing a *Knee Gazette*, I am busy tending to Miriam. Even here, they do not have enough staff to take care of all her needs, wants, and demands. She is better today, but during the first couple of days following surgery, she really keeps me busy. I am amazed how one woman lying in a bed can find so many things that need tending to! Ice needs to be fetched, lotion needs to be spread on the back, Chapstick applied, hair tied back, ginger ale located, iced down, and poured up, pillows need to be rearranged, blankets spread out, etc. Since they do not have popsicles at this hospital, I had to go find her some, along with a timer to remind her when she could push the button on her pain medication. Popsicles seem to help with nausea, so not finding any was not an option. When she is most miserable, she is also fidgety and seldom content. When she is nauseated, this adds excitement to the routine. More than once the laptop has come close to a floor-drop when I had to scramble for the basin. I was amused to find that within a few hours of Miriam coming to her room, someone had seen the wisdom in swapping the little kidney-shaped vomit receptacle for a full-sized basin.

Each day I have managed to shirk my duties to Miriam long enough to take a walk. This is a people-watcher's paradise. On this night, I strolled only a couple of blocks from the hospital to First Street, "The place" we've been told, to find something good to eat. I saved my appetite since breakfast, determined to find a sit-down meal where I would be handed a menu and would not have to speed-read it off the wall before spewing the order to an impatient cashier.

First Street offers a veritable smorgasbord of choices to select from. On Friday night I ate at a genuine NY style pizzeria. The pizza was good, but the entertainment was better. I watched bicycle after bicycle stop in front of the restaurant. Each time a rider would dismount quickly, wrap what resembled a logging chain to something immobile (aka bicycle security system), grab an insulated pouch from the handlebar basket and run inside. Once inside, they would pick up an order, pay for it and quickly leave the store carrying their piping-hot cargo and an address. In some cases, the elapsed time was less than three minutes! None of the bikes were new or fancy, nor did they have any kind of light that would signal their presence to pedestrians or motorists. The bikers I saw were all male and probably under 30 years of age. After watching the "parade" from inside this one establishment, I began to notice them on the streets and sidewalks– they were everywhere! In the time it took me to eat two pieces of pizza, I know there were 20 or more take-outs picked up! Multiply this by who knows how many hundred restaurants that are in Manhattan and who advertise "free delivery" and you end up with a bunch of bikes scurrying about town, ignoring traffic signals and weaving among cars and people. Their living is derived solely from the tips they collect at the destination. Had I understood this scenario better last Wednesday night, I would have tipped the delivery boy more generously!

During Saturday's mini walkabout, I paused in front of a place called The Silver Spoon, entered, and was shown to a seat. Watching and reading people is probably a survival skill developed in the interest of self-preservation in the big city. Soon after my broiled seafood meal was ordered, the waiter, a 40-something man with jet-black hair and an all-business demeanor, asked a question that startled and amused me: "Where are you from? You're not from around here!" Perhaps he noticed that my demeanor lacked the calluses required to live here very long.

While I was savoring my very reasonably priced meal of scallops, shrimp, salmon and filet of sole, the waiter, along with a couple of bus boys, returned to chat. "The stranger" quickly turned the tables and began asking the questions. I asked how long he had lived in New York. He replied: "30 years." He was born in Argentina to a European father and an Argentine mother. When he was 17, his father brought himself and six siblings to Miami to live. He has never married, but he travels to Argentina at least twice a year to visit family. "New York is all business," he began. "This is not a warm, laid-back, family kind of place." He echoed what we've heard from others too. Ironic, I think, that in a place so crowded with people, there is so much isolation and loneliness.

~ **Strangers in a Strange Town**

Monday morning, December 4, 2000

This dawn marks the first of two days I have dreaded since the idea of surgery in NY was conceived, the two days when we travel home. Once I get her on the ground in Atlanta, I will be in familiar territory. The van still has her recliner in it from our Thanksgiving adventure to

Jekyll Island. The trip from the airport to home in the van will be far shorter than the trip from Birmingham after the last surgery; it is the part between this room and the van that has worried me so.

As Miriam was finishing getting cleaned up and dressed, the phone rang. Delta Airlines called to inform me that our flight had been canceled! Remember me mentioning in an earlier issue about our having purchased our own tickets in spite of the ones workman's comp bought? When Miriam bought our tickets, she gave Delta the phone number to the hospital, which allowed them to have a way to get in touch with us. Otherwise, we would not have learned about the cancellation until we arrived at the airport this afternoon.

I told the Delta representative that we were in good shape here and that we could make an earlier flight if one was available. "How about two o'clock?" she asked. I replied that I thought this would work but that arrangements must be made for Miriam's leg. "Coach is full, I'll tell you what I will do. I will put you in first class at no additional charge. Will this be okay?"

I could hardly speak; tears were welling up in my eyes, but I assured her that this would be very helpful. When Miriam came out of the bathroom and tried to confirm the conversation she thought she had just heard, I lost my composure.

When we logged on this morning to check our email, there were nine wonderful messages for me to read to her, more than one concerned prayer about our trip home and specifically that we would get first-class seats! Thank you for your prayers. This will still likely be an "event-filled" trip, but these seats will make the two most worrisome hours much easier. I am thankful our God is not too busy to answer the prayers of a group of caring people who have petitioned Him on behalf of a pair of humble pilgrims from Georgia.

This will be our final report for this trip from Manhattan. I will compose a follow-up from home when time permits.

CHAPTER 10
Recovering Again

The Knee Gazette

Monday afternoon, shortly after take-off

I was just handed a hot towel by the flight attendant. I looked around to be sure I didn't use it for something it wasn't intended. For the first time in its life, the computer is resting comfortably on a white linen tablecloth. Miriam is sitting sideways in her seat, surrounded by most of the pillows in first class. Her left leg has been stretched onto my lap for most of the hour since we boarded. We will soon find out what a snack looks like on the front side of the bulkhead.

As you should expect by now, simple details like leaving a building, getting into a car and going to the airport are something less than routine and mundane for us; when we are involved, these little things become moments of high drama. Today it began with the simple task of getting out of the hospital. The flight had been moved up to 2 p.m., so we scheduled a car to pick us up at 12. By 11, the doctors had all been in, "Olga" had inflicted enough agony necessary to keep her job, and Miriam had even been measured for and fitted with the brace Dr. Wilson had ordered. By 12:10, we were still waiting for someone from transport to come drive the wheelchair to the lobby! The nurse quickly came to understand that I was not about to miss our ride or flight for lack of someone to push a wheelchair and offered to do it herself since the most obvious of the available alternatives would have violated several hospital regulations!

Once in the lobby, it was time to wait for the "car service" we thought we had hired to take us to the airport. By 12:40, I abandoned the search for the "special" car and accosted the first cab who agreed to go to LaGuardia. Of course, I kept Miriam out of sight until after he had agreed to the fare. We've learned that people with mobility problems are "invisible" to cab drivers. Too much work and it slows them down, is probably the reason.

Throughout most of the cab ride, Miriam's face was ashen. She was sitting across the back seat, so I sat up front and tried to ignore her. Every now and again I stole a glance in her direction hoping to see that the little bag we borrowed from Delta on the flight up was still empty. Although this driver tried his best to give her as smooth of a ride as possible, there was only so much he could do given the condition of the roads over which we traveled. Miriam did make it all the way to the airport with an empty bag!

Once we arrived at the airport, I got Miriam settled into a wheelchair and began bouncing her toward the gate. Miriam's pre-flight trauma was not over yet, because the floor of the terminal was made of brick. Miriam felt every mortar line as the wheels bounced over each joint. Once we got onto another type of floor, I realized that the wheels on the chair had flat spots, which only continued to jostle the tender leg. Sometimes it feels like "Murphy" follows us around like a dark cloud.

We boarded the plane almost immediately after checking in. We had been lounging in the mile-wide leather seats about 40 minutes before the plane backed away from the gate. A smiling attendant served refreshments to help pass the time.

The snack that the nice lady spread out on the linen tablecloth consisted of a chicken pasta salad, roll and a brownie. It was very much appreciated, since there hadn't been any time to think about lunch while we were trying to get to the airport. Out of courtesy to the passengers sitting behind the bulkhead, however, I was careful not to clink my flatware on the China.

Once airborne, Miriam did fine until we began to descend into Atlanta. Evidently the pressure changes were reverberating through her fresh wounds. There wasn't much I could do except give her a hand to squeeze, which I quickly regretted. She worked it over pretty good until the wheels hit the runway, then she nearly crushed it. Most of us don't realize how rough take-offs and landings really are until we sit next to a human seismograph.

It is good to be home! My dad and Matthew were at the house waiting for us when we arrived. We are very blessed; I cannot really imagine living in an impersonal place like Manhattan. The love of our family and friends makes us far wealthier than many of the "beautiful people" I have observed in the last week. It was good to see Miriam reunited with her boy this evening. I know he has spent a lot of time thinking about her while we've been gone.

I am not anticipating much obvious progress beyond simply recovering from this surgery, because the "real" surgery won't take place for three to five months, when the ligaments in the knee will be rebuilt. This next surgery, Dr. Wilson promises, will be the really rough one! This will give us something to look forward to.

~ **Mark, Miriam, and Matthew**

The Knee Gazette

Saturday, December 9, 2000

Miriam is now a week and two days post-surgery. As expected, this has not been an easy or comfortable week for her. Once we got home, her knee began to swell. By Tuesday evening it had swelled enough that two stitches had pulled loose. It remains rather grotesque in appearance, similar to a misshapen gourd with a big zipper on one side. The good news is that she continues to have more control over her foot and toes than she had prior to the surgery.

Although Miriam is relatively stable most of the time, she still experiences some periods of spasms and cramping in addition to the incision pain, especially at night. We talked with Dr. Wilson yesterday and he was pleased that she had improved motion this soon after surgery, in spite of the swelling. The swelling didn't seem to concern him much; although he wondered how much of it was due to the flight so soon after surgery. Her stitches are due to come out Monday, perhaps the swelling will subside between now and then.

At this writing, Miriam has not vomited since leaving the hospital! Some of the credit for this may be attributable to an electronic watch-like wristband that has recently been developed to help with post-op nausea. Most patients receive the desired results from little disposable units that last for a couple of days and then get thrown away. For

Miriam, Dr. Robel ordered an industrial version that comes complete with its own power company substation and high-voltage lines connected directly to the wrist. This wristband, in addition to the spinal cord stimulator, will make Miriam a lonely person when lightning is in the area!

Miriam spends her days on the couch with her leg mounted in a machine that slowly flexes it the appropriate amount. The attendant care which Workman's Comp is finally providing is a big help. This lady helps Miriam bathe, prepares breakfast and lunch for her, empties the bedside "chamber pot," and goes with her to therapy and doctor appointments. This has taken a big load off not just me, but many others who would be rearranging schedules to assist with these duties. At night I'm able to have her in the bed beside me, where I am learning to sleep through more and more of her bad nights; but I'm there if she absolutely needs me for something. This arrangement works far better for me than leaving her on the couch. Somehow, when she is in another room, I am not able to ignore her and don't sleep nearly as well as when she is right beside me.

Hopefully by the time two more weeks pass, she will have healed enough to be able to get back into her beloved spa. I changed the water last night and am performing some other needed maintenance, so it will be ready when she is ready. With luck it will also have a roof for the rain and windows for the wind by then, too.

~ **"Sweetheart" and "Yes, Dear"**

The Knee Gazette

Saturday, December 16, 2000

She has had another very difficult week. The swelling has kept her knee looking rather grotesque. The pain has kept her (and me) from sleeping. When she would drop off to sleep, the throbbing in her knee would awaken her. What would awaken me was when the throbbing would give way to something more intense, causing her to spontaneously yell out. When she is assaulted by one of her toe-curling, leg-grabbing spasms, I have to grab her toes and attempt to straighten them while stretching the cramp out of her leg. After a few moments, the "storm" mercifully passes and, usually, doesn't return for at least several hours. By then, any blissful slumber has been chased from the night, and we are left trying to grab any winks of sleep that sneak back into our room. Thankfully, since I am the one who has to drive an hour a day and try to accomplish employable activities, I get more winks than she does. However, the lack of real rest has worn both of us to a frazzle. I know a long day is ahead of me when I find myself falling asleep on the way to the plant in the morning!

Several very kind people have suggested that I should have been a writer. The fact is, without a spell checker and my 9th-grade typing class, I would be a hopeless hack. This pitiful grasp of grammar, syntax, and sentence structure may have been enough to get me through college, but hardly qualifies me as a bonafide wordsmith. Writing has been great therapy during this ordeal and is one of the few "hobbies" I can enjoy while tending to Miriam, even when she is in a hospital room.

Miriam, it turns out, slept so well last night that she didn't wake up to take any medication during the night! This is of course both good and bad. Good because she awoke well rested; bad because there was no pain medication in her system to subdue the rising tide of pain she experienced after getting up and taking her first shower in more than two weeks. The swelling has gone down considerably in the last 24 hours. Dr. Robel told her she could begin taking showers but won't let her get in the spa for another week. There is finally measurable progress, for which I am grateful.

Miriam's sister Debra came today and did some holiday cooking for her. The smells helped usher the holiday spirit into our home. She came before Thanksgiving and helped Matthew and Miriam put up and decorate the tree. Miriam and I have both done a large portion of our Holiday shopping online and through mail-order. She wants me to take her to the musical at church tomorrow night, which I will attempt if she feels up to it.

It is appropriate, especially at this time of year, that I make a list of some of the things I am thankful for. It is easy some days to get so fogged in by our own "challenges" that I cannot see the many things that keep life worth living. In no particular order, here is my list of the top 10 things for which I am thankful this year:

1. I am thankful for the two wreckers and four mechanics from two different garages, located about 60 miles apart, who

worked on our van the day before Thanksgiving and allowed us to reach our family's gathering point for this year's holiday celebration.

2. I am thankful for the multitude of prayer warriors who have supported us throughout our family's crisis.

3. I am thankful we are not dealing with a life and death situation, as many families must.

4. I am thankful for our respective families and the assistance they provide week in and week out, that help us with the details of daily life.

5. I am thankful for the constant support of our church family. They have truly ministered to us during this seemingly endless ordeal.

6. I am thankful for a very helpful 12-year-old, who has put up with tired, cranky, needy parents for much of the last three years (25% of his life!).

7. I am thankful for Boy Scouts, which provides me with a good excuse to shirk my duties to my wife, in the interest of "being a good dad" during our camp-out weekends.

8. I am thankful that Miriam is able to be clear-headed enough to take care of family book-keeping, bill paying and helping Matthew with his schoolwork.

9. I am thankful for the wife I have, but I am also thankful I have but one wife.

10. I am truly thankful that if Miriam had to fall, she did it at work and that we have Workman's Comp to fall back on, scream at, and complain about. This would have been a far greater disaster, I think, if she had fallen in her own kitchen.

I think she is sleeping better and more consistently and continues to have improved mobility in her foot and toes than before the surgery. Whether it is fact or simply wishful thinking on my part, I am convinced that her pain is different now than before November 30. I keep telling her that the pain she is experiencing now is related to the surgery and that it is healing. She "replies" to these comments by pretending that I'm not talking. As far as she is concerned, the net result is what is important– she hurts, she feels nauseous, she is miserable, and nothing I can tell her is making her feel any better.

~ Merry Christmas from Mark, Matthew, and "The Watkinsville Hurler"

Journal

Sunday, December 17, 2000

The dawn brought snow and cold temperatures, which have chased away the night, the balmy temperatures, and the thunderstorms. The wind is really howling, and the sky is clearing. Our birds have left their swinging perches on the bird feeders to wait out the wind where there is more shelter.

Last night, after I got her in bed, Miriam went to sleep but began having bad dreams. She was thrashing about, talking and crying at the same time. I had little choice but to try to awaken her and settle her down. She was dreaming that they were about to cut off her leg and I had told them to do so. How can I defend being a villain in her sleep?

She has been complaining the last two days about her hip hurting where the bone graft material was chipped off. This pain had settled down since we arrived home; I'm not sure why it is paining her again unless the drastic weather changes have something to do with it.

I have been able to keep the kitchen and our living quarters from being condemned by the health department. Our home is really in need of Miriam. Except for one week this summer when the trial stimulator was in place, she has not felt like doing any of the hard cleaning and organizing that she has spoiled us to expect from her. The sole focus of all of us for her is to help her get through another day, which hopefully will bring her one day closer to getting well enough to resume some semblance of a normal life.

The Knee Gazette

January 1, 2001

It is good that everyone now agrees that the next millennium has finally begun. As fifth graders, when the subject of the next century was brought up in class and we did the math, this day was more than an eternity away! What happened, where did the years go? The mid-40s sure doesn't seem as aged as it was back then... Happy New Millennium!

This has been a good holiday season for us, full of rich times spent with our family and friends. Miriam has been frustrated that she has not been able to contribute from the kitchen the way she loves to do. She has managed to fix some soup and warm up a few things. We have a stool on wheels that she can roll around the kitchen that helps keep her off of the leg, but even this allows her only a few minutes at a time in her beloved kitchen before she must retreat to the sofa or recliner.

Christmas Eve was her last really bad day, so there is genuine progress. She has been able to sit up long enough to participate in a few board games and has joined Matthew and me in wasting some time on Matthew's new PlayStation, playing baseball. However, once the leg decides she has spent too much time up and about, it elicits a high price in agony and suffering.

Her routine once again includes her beloved spa.

> Q: What has long dark brown hair and is covered with icicles?

> A: One lame brunette "dashing" from the spa to the bedroom when it is 20 degrees out.

I think I would be homeless if she were required one day to decide between me or the spa. After all, it eases her pain and gives her a lot of pleasure, whereas I mostly do work and just annoy her (I do, however, maintain her spa!) She is cute hunched down in the steaming water with little more than her nose and the top of her head sticking above the water. I am amazed however, how quickly she can cover the eight feet between the spa and the bedroom door. I mostly got her spa accessories for Christmas and her birthday, since this is where she spends so much of her time. Have you ever seen a hammock for a spa? Although it is not yet installed, I found one while shopping online, along with a table that can hold a drink and the super-cheap cordless phone I got for use in and around the spa.

One day before Christmas, all three of us were enjoying some family time in the spa earlier in the evening than usual. Miriam was hurting, I was shivering and Matthew, not wanting to be left out, joined us. We were minding our own business, sitting in the dark, enjoying the hot water massage when we saw headlights turn into our driveway. Matthew "won the election" and had to get out and see who the visitor(s) were. When he didn't return after an appropriate amount of time, I decided to brave the cold and see who it was, who had taken time out of their holiday schedule to drop by for a visit.

As I opened the bedroom door, I heard music. I pulled on something appropriate to cover the swimsuit and found a group of Carolers, dressed in winter finery, singing to a bewildered Matthew. The poor boy was probably trying to come up with a reasonable explanation for where his parents were. This group was from a church in Athens and had come to sing for Miriam! Although I was deeply moved and am sure it would have made the stop quite memorable for everyone involved, I declined to take them around back and have them serenade Miriam while she soaked in the spa.

On this New Year's Day in Georgia, it is snowing and 33 degrees! Miriam is again in the spa; Matthew is unloading the dishwasher, and I am "in therapy" — writing to our friends and watching the birds and squirrels partake of the buffet we have spread before them from eight feeders and a variety of seed and suet. There are often 20 or more birds either feeding or waiting their turn on a nearby limb. This provides a lot of pleasure and entertainment for Miriam and me while we enjoy our morning coffee in the sunroom.

Miriam saw a recipe in Southern Living Magazine for something called Frogmore Stew. After going to Kroger for the ingredients, it is basically a pot of soup costing enough money to choke a frog. I have been through Frogmore, SC, and have arrived at the following conclusion concerning our supper soup and its namesake: it probably required the combined net assets of the entire community to make a pot! Not really, Frogmore is in the Low Country near the coast, so the ingredients are local and readily available for them. For the rest of us, it would taste better if we didn't know how much it cost to make.

I am pleased that Miriam feels good enough to do some cooking. Every now and again I see glimpses of the woman I married, such as when her face erupts into an ear-to-ear smile and her dark brown eyes flash with fire at a joke or snide remark. This is so encouraging after seeing nothing but a dull reflection of pain and misery for so long. Yes, she still hurts; perhaps the intensity has diminished enough that she can once again taste little bites of life seasoned with real chips of joy.

~ **Mark, Matthew, and "Icicle"**

Journal

Wednesday, January 3, 2001

At six in the morning, in Watkinsville, Georgia, the thermometer reads 14 degrees F. This is significant only because it is indicative of the agony Miriam is in. This low temperature did not prevent her from getting into the spa on four different occasions from 9 p.m. to 6 a.m.! She had felt good on Tuesday, did some light housework, and backed off the pain medications. Who knows if it was the combination or one of the individual actions, but the net result robbed both of us of another night of sleep.

Attendant care stopped at the end of the year. This perhaps is why Miriam feels compelled to push herself. It is not easy for her to sit around and not be productive, especially while she sees housework piling up in all directions and her family worn to a frazzle.

Journal

Sunday afternoon, January 14, 2001

Eleven days have elapsed since my last, rather short entry. This is more indicative of the pace of my activity than the absence of material to write about. When the day is finally over, my brain is incapable of coherent thought, so it is good that I do not write in that condition.

Miriam is asleep at present. She slept well last night, got up, took a shower, and got dressed for church, only to have me beg for the morning off. By 11 a.m., however, the good feeling from the night's sleep had been consumed by the energy spent on showering and dressing, and she was sliding into her spa for the first soak of the day, with tears welling up in her eyes, reflecting the fear that this pain will never end. Aside from making her as comfortable as possible, there is little I can do. I am so consumed by her care, however, that I have little time to dwell on this feeling of impotence. I have too little time for my son, my job, or my business because her needs are so pressing.

Professionally, I have a customer in the UK having a problem and would like someone from our organization to pay them a visit. All I would have to do is say the word, and I would be flying across the "pond." Instead, I have made a concerted effort to convince the owners of the plant that one of them must go. I have a furniture customer in California who wants to distribute my line to the "left coast," and I really should go and visit. There's a trade show in Vegas on the first of February that I should attend, as well as one later in the spring in Palm Springs. My income and business will have to continue to suffer; there is no way I could go on any kind of extended business trip at this time.

Attendant care has mercifully been restarted for a few hours per day during the week. As grateful as we are for this help, the rest of the story is that they have annexed all my non-working hours to care for their patient. I get angry if I dwell in this too much. This has made my life much easier and allowed me to concentrate more on work, which has allowed me to spend more hours at the plant, but Miriam's care is never far from my thoughts. Sleepless nights also continue to have an effect on my job performance, but attendant care has allowed Miriam to stay off of the leg more since the surgery, and she has been sleeping better.

This weekend is a representative snapshot of our lives these days. Saturday morning, I was working on the spa room. My father and an old acquaintance who is also a handyman by trade are thankfully here to assist me. We have finished installing the sheathing on the walls and got the windows and door installed. After they go home, I install a hammock in the spa that I got Miriam for Christmas. This will allow her to lay suspended in the swirling water. Miriam is smiling from ear to ear because of the progress.

Last evening, we went with the neighbors to visit our favorite BBQ restaurant. At one time, this was a tradition we enjoyed once a month, but has been reduced for one reason or another, to a two or three times per year event. After we returned home, we visited for a while until Miriam went to the bathroom, vomited her meal and wanted to retire to the spa. The neighbors decided to go home.

It's now 7:40. I just helped Miriam out of the spa for the third time today. She took her assortment of bedtime drugs and is in bed, hopefully to sleep, but we won't know for a couple of hours.

Some observations and questions about the Big Apple from the perspective of a Southern country boy:

What would happen if any of the dogs who were walking their owners past our building were to see a patch of grass? Would they know what it was or what it was good for? A fate worse than death would be to awaken one day and find that you have been turned into a fire hydrant in **NYC!**

Watching these people with their dogs is quite a spectacle! I am speculating there are a bunch of single folks in this town who have substituted a dog for a mate or for the children they don't have. There appears to be an unspoken code of conduct between pet owners that goes something like this: one simply must not walk on by another person walking a dog. No, that would be rude. You must stop, let the dogs "greet" one another, and then "baby talk" to their new friends. It is a bazaar ritual that we noticed during our last visit that continues to make us chuckle. An x-ray technician, upon hearing Miriam's comment about the dogs, confirmed some of our suspicions. He told her that he thinks many people have given up on interpersonal relationships and simply got pets instead...

Beside every elevator in these high-rise buildings is a sign that reads: "In the event of a fire, do not use the elevators." Why don't they go ahead and add another line that reads: "Abandon the invalids?" Am I supposed to walk down 20 flights of stairs with Miriam on my back? Wheelchairs work well in an elevator but are useless around stairs.

People around here must not have much to do. For three days, traffic was grid-locked around Times Square while people strained to look at some idiot who sealed himself inside of a block of ice. Performance art? My low-class education failed to explain to us simpletons that art can come in lots of different forms.

New Yorkers have learned how to get a lot out of a little bit of space. Nearly every block has at least one small hole-in-the-wall deli that serves good food at reasonable prices to an amazing number of people, often from a space smaller than some people's walk-in closet!

Apparently the much-heralded ADA (Americans with Disabilities Act) has an exclusion for NYC. Even the Orthopedic Hospital has hallways that are too narrow for two wheelchairs to pass by one another! During our last visit, we dined beside a restaurant on the sidewalk because there was no ramp for a wheelchair. We then ventured into a grocery store where I had to park Miriam beside the door because there was no hope of getting her wheelchair down the aisles.

NYC likes Christmas! I understand why the brat of "Home Alone" fame, who was so fond of Christmas trees, came to NYC. On the premises of this hospital, to simply walk from one building to another, a person must walk past 28 full-size, lighted Christmas trees! On a street near here, a Christmas tree market has set up shop on the curb. It looks strange to this country boy to see people walking down the sidewalk carrying trees.

In the "learn something new (and useless) everyday category," did you know Delta Airlines has boats? We kept seeing "The Charles Lindbergh" and the "Amelia Earhart" pass by Miriam's window on the river. Finally, one of the nurses explained that this is Delta's shuttle between LaGuardia and Kennedy airports!

We talked with a lot of people who didn't plan to live in "The City" their whole life. Younger people especially declared they wanted to move when it came time to raise children. "New York City is no place to raise children" was an often-repeated phrase.

More than a couple of residents declared NYC to be "all business", a fact they were either proud of or saddened by, I could not tell. This perhaps explains why they are so eager to talk with a stranger who looks willing to listen. From this outsider's perspective, NYC appears to be a place where the people are playing poker; their faces are as void of emotion and expression as four gunslingers sittin' around a table in an old Western. People scurry quickly from place to place, desperately hoping that no one dares call their bluff and force them to reveal their emptiness. The excitement and largeness of a place like NYC make it a fascinating place to visit. I am thankful to live in a place where genuine connections are made with other people. Living as an island in a sea of people all acting like islands would be sad, I think.

CHAPTER 11
Waiting for New York — Take II

The Knee Gazette

Saturday, January 20, 2001

Later today, the highest office in the land will be pried from the grasp of the man who once hailed from Arkansas, but now "stays" in New York because folks from those parts elected his wife and former first lady, to the Senate. The midday ceremony will peacefully transfer power from Mr. Clinton to Mr. Bush, the son of the man Mr. Clinton defeated two terms ago. During the Washington ceremony, there will be a protest in Florida over the outcome of the election. Absent from the protest that he orchestrated, will be the man who counseled our president after he was caught engaging in "unpresidential activity." We learned this week, that while counseling the president, the counselor was apparently engaged in "research" beyond the bounds of his own marriage that his wife did not approve of. Because of this indiscretion, Mr. Jesse Jackson will be begging her forgiveness instead of looking angry in front of the cameras in Tallahassee. This is a lot of drama to squeeze into one day, and a better story than most composers of fiction could dream up!

Meanwhile, back in Watkinsville, Georgia, where our "rubber meets the road," the truth is also stranger and more dramatic than most "story spinners" could contrive. Miriam is finally separated from the blustery wind and cool temperatures, while she soaks in her spa. Last weekend, after my helpers helped finish sheathing the walls and installing the windows, I finally installed the spa hammock I got her for Christmas. As this is being written, she is lying in the hammock, suspended in the warm swirling water, sipping her piping hot, freshly brewed coffee.

The price she has paid for this seat in the "lap of luxury" has been and continues to be extremely high. I can think of only two nights in the last week when she slept well. Although she has not vomited in a week, her comfort level has once again deteriorated since crossing the six-week mark after surgery. This six-week threshold is a hurdle she seems incapable of conquering. For eight procedures now, six weeks post-surgery has marked the pinnacle of her progress. The nerve-related pain in her left leg has been so intense that she emailed her doctor a few days ago about the possibility of severing the nerve! His reply: "This is not an option since it would paralyze her entire leg." Her next surgery is not scheduled until May, but messing with the angry nerve is not on the schedule for this surgery; that was what the last surgery was for. How Miriam has retained her sanity in the face of so much adversity and so many disappointments is amazing to me. I have a front-row seat for this production and still cannot believe how bad it really has been.

Miriam's best days now are probably equal to her bad days two years ago. In other words, there has been a decline in her ability to walk and an increase in her pain with each successive surgery. We continue pursuing a surgical solution because there are no signs that this knee will stabilize, much less improve, if left alone. I don't think the nerves can become less angry until the joint itself is stabilized, so yet again, we pursue surgery. Short of an elusive miracle, surgery appears to be the only possible solution for this poor woman on this side of Paradise.

The rehab specialist managing Miriam's case for Workman's Comp visited our home last week. During her visit, she approved for attendant care to be provided for the rest of the month. The attendant has been a tremendous help to Miriam and has taken a great load of worry off my shoulders. Matthew gets home from school about the time the caregiver leaves, so someone is with her almost around the clock, which is what she really needs. Whether or not it is appropriate for her son to provide care the E/I should be paying for is a discussion for another day. The case manager has expressed dismay at the treatment Miriam has received from the E/I since the accident and has worked hard to help them understand the extent of Miriam's injury and problems. I think they are finally convinced that Miriam's problems are real and not an attempt to get attention and bilk the system.

I know it has been a while since I've written, but I worry about spreading so much disappointing news. Besides, we do not want to whine an inappropriate amount, everyone has trials to deal with. My journal also has large gaps in it. Much of my time is consumed by work, household chores, recovering from lost sleep and working on the spa room; but aside from the time crunch, how many ways can I write about Miriam being in pain and that we are discouraged? After more than three years of this, my well of creative clichés is nearly dry, and I'm completely out of metaphors. We continue to covet your prayers, emails, phone calls and visits. These connections do wonders for both of us, but especially are great for Miriam, who no longer gets out and about as she once did or would like to.

~ "Worn" and "Frazzled"

Journal

Monday evening, January 22, 2001

Miriam has had a terrible day. Yesterday, she felt well enough that we attended the morning worship service at church; today, she did little except sleep and soak in the spa. Her pain was so intense she was not able to read or cross-stitch. Some weeks it seems that she is progressively getting worse by the day, exploring new levels of agony we were certain could not exist.

The constant pain that she is in is, in my opinion, a fate far worse than death! If she had a terminal illness, at least she would be slowly moving toward a release from the agony. In her case, being otherwise healthy and only 41 years of age, she could live/exist another 40 or 50 years in this condition! When considered, those prospects alone are enough to put us in a real funk, so we try to not think about that possibility.

"Super" Sunday, January 28, 2001

This noon Miriam insisted on cooking for her family. She alternately stands on one leg, sits on the stool, and leans on her crutches. Usually, she is moaning, screaming, or crying as she attempts to balance on one leg while holding the other one off the floor. I watch and hope she doesn't trip or stumble and injure something else.

Tonight, however, the across-the-road neighbors, the Adams family, used this as a convenient excuse for a party and invited us to join them for tacos. We stayed until half-time and enjoyed the evening. The not-so-super game ended with the team possessing the greatest number of felons on its roster clobbering their opponents by several touchdowns. I am not a fan of pro football; this game, plus one more, would have made two for the year that I took time to watch.

Sunday, February 4, 2001

Well, it is that time of week again: the coffee-sipping, birdwatching, quiet time while Miriam gets showered and dressed and decides whether she feels able to attend church. For the second week in a row, she made all the preparations and collapsed into a "puddle" of pain, exhaustion, and frustration. At 10:20, she returned to bed for some additional rest and, hopefully, some relief.

I have been fighting a cold since last Sunday and am only now slowly feeling better. Last evening, I was tired, my head felt like it was the size of a prize-winning pumpkin, and there was no hope of breathing through the appendage taking up space between my mustache and eyes. I did not feel like doing anything except vegetating on the sofa and exercising my remote-control finger. But my bride and son had been looking with anticipation toward a trek to Walmart and dining at a Chinese restaurant, so off we went.

After seating us and exchanging pleasantries, a woman with whom Miriam once worked, related a story that fueled anger that had been simmering within Miriam's bosom: It seems that only a few weeks after Miriam's fall, a lady slipped and nearly fell in almost the same location where Miriam shredded her life. This lady promptly turned to a man working nearby with the mop in his hand and berated him for being so careless, reminding him of the recent injury to Miriam. The mop-man's supervisor soon showed up and expressed displeasure over the harsh tone used on his subordinate. He then apparently went on to declare that Miriam's accident was her fault, not theirs!

This only reinforces the prevailing attitude that Miriam has felt from her former employer since the initial fall. Only in the last few months have they acknowledged the seriousness of her condition and become more cooperative in getting her the care she needs.

It is 10:45 and Miriam just traded the bed for the second trip to the spa of the morning. I should add that the acknowledgment mentioned in the prior paragraph has not included an offer to pay for the spa; they are, however, and perhaps begrudgingly, providing attendant care six hours per day, five days a week, as well as transportation to and from her medical appointments. It is up to Matthew and me to cover the remaining 138 hours each week. This week, she was left alone for two hours on Friday night and one hour on Saturday morning while I watched Matthew play in a basketball game. I left her again yesterday afternoon for two hours while we attended a Boy Scout function. Because her leg is so prone to lock up, which requires help to unlock, I do not like leaving her at all; but I/we also have obligations to our son to provide some occasional taste of normalcy. I wonder, though, what care would the E/I have to provide if Miriam had no family? Unable to live alone, she would probably be in a personal care home somewhere.

Thousands of thoughts and ideas careen through my feeble brain every week. The mental energy spent on Miriam, her care, and our future, leaves little for things like earning a living! Miriam's case has been referred to as "end stage" by more than one physician. What does this mean? Will the law allow for a point to be reached where the E/I can declare that nothing else can be done, throw a few dollars at us, and have their obligation to this case come to an end? "Settlement" is a word that keeps cropping up during conversations with attorney Fred and case manager Stacy. The prospect of accepting any amount of money in return for freeing the E/I of future obligations terrifies us. A sentence of poverty resulting from a pitiful settlement would only add insult to the desperate injury and related agony that has befallen us already. Unfortunately, we do not have an "uninterested" third party to whom we can direct our questions. Attorney Fred stands to benefit from 25% of any settlement, so he clearly has an interest in the outcome of the case. Case manager Stacy has been a tremendous source of information the last few months, but I keep reminding Miriam that she was hired by the E/I to manage the case, so she is clearly not independent of an outside agenda either. The truth is that we just do not know who we should listen to, especially since we have no experience with any of this.

Attorney Fred has been a big disappointment! He has been on the case for 13 months, but he has done nearly nothing for Miriam. True, in the middle of the summer, weekly checks began to arrive, but this was far different from the tone and schedule he laid out before us last January, just prior to Miriam signing his agreement. Once she "signed on the dotted line," we were told, before we even left the office that day, "Do not call us; we will call you when we need something!" As we sat in his office, "getting acquainted," we were told to expect to be "in court within six weeks and that checks would start arriving shortly thereafter." It took more than six months and several nasty letters from me before the checks started and the subject of going to court has not been brought up since! I finally quit writing to him because his ability to ignore my pleas for help exceeded my capacity beg him to do something.

Journal

February 21, 2001

Three weeks have passed since Miriam has received a weekly check; we have yet to receive the balance due from a check that paid her only half of what was due more than four months ago. Ninety days post-surgery we have not been reimbursed for the out-of-pocket expenses incurred during her end-of- November trip to NYC for surgery. Today attorney Fred's secretary informs Miriam that "We may not push too hard for this money!"

Fred's lack of concern for Miriam continues to cause us to wonder who his client really is in this case. That may sound harsh, but we are fighting for survival out here and at times nobody seems to care.

Saturday morning, March 3, 2001

On the knee front, little has changed. Miriam has been fitted for a full leg brace which should be ready within the next 10 days. Dr. Robel and Henry hope this will help to straighten her leg and stretch shrunken tissues prior to the next surgery. If it helps to eliminate lockups, it will be worth its weight in gold!

On the legal front, there has also been little change. Miriam finally did receive a check reimbursing expenses from the last surgery. This delay was not entirely their fault, however. We did not get the expenses submitted prior to the first of the year, after which our very diligent attorney promptly allowed it to help hold down his desk for several weeks before getting around to putting it in the mail to the E/I. There has not been a weekly check in more than a month, and there has been no mention of the money still owed from back in October. As frustrating as all of this is, it pales compared to Miriam getting insulted by Fred's staff when she calls to inquire about money needed to pay bills and live off of. On Monday, she was told: "Miriam, you can't count on that money, you will have to make other arrangements."

Miriam was scorched! She put in a call to the State Office for Workman's Comp and was told that a hearing should be requested. They went on to tell her that "If her attorney is too busy to handle her case, she should find another one!"

How bad is Miriam these days? The following is a good indication: I need to go to Dalton to see my brother Bruce. This trip will serve two purposes other than the need for a visit. I have an order of furniture to deliver to that area and it is past time to have my eyes examined by "the family eye doc." Miriam loves to travel and normally would not miss any opportunity to spend time away from home. This time she has begged off, saying she simply cannot make the trip. "Going to Athens wears me out these days." Her sister has been asked to come spend the night with her and Matthew and I will go by ourselves. This is not the way it is supposed to be!

It is the time of year when the fish are starting to bite. This is the season when we go fishing nearly every Saturday. Since Miriam is no longer able to stand on the bank of a pond, I commenced late in the summer to build a boat suited to her needs. The problem is that the deck, spa, and spa room consumed all the boat-building hours, so now it is nearly spring, and we need a better way to enjoy our favorite family pastime. I decided to build a boat mostly for economy's sake but am looking forward to the challenge too. A pontoon boat or deck boat would be the ideal vessel to take her fishing, but budget constraints have precluded any serious thoughts of buying such a boat. I think I can build one if I can spend some time in the shop. But the spa room must be finished first.

The Knee Gazette

Sunday, March 11, 2001

Ten and a half hours in bed, some Ibuprofen, a few aspirin, and two trips to the spa, have eased my agony enough to be able to sit in a recliner and focus my eyes. No, these words are not Miriam's; they are mine. You see, it has been nine years and more than a few pounds since I did any roofing work. I am happy to report this morning that Miriam's spa room has a completed roof. Although it felt like I was alone in the endeavor, I had three good helpers. Doug, Brandon, and Robbie. These precious friends generously gave us their Saturday for Miriam's benefit. After many failed attempts, good weather and a Saturday happened on the same day, and we took advantage of it. Progress on the room has seemed slow, but weekends unencumbered by bad weather, sickness, or Scouting activities provided the only opportunity for progress. Even though entire cities have been built and wars fought in less time than it took me to build a simple room onto the back of our house, perhaps I should not be too hard on myself.

There has not been much to report about Miriam's condition or the cursed knee. She is in a lot of pain, and it is not getting better. We are patiently and hopefully waiting for mid-May when she is scheduled to return to NYC for knee reconstruction. She has not driven since November, so taxi cabs take her to various appointments. Miriam looks good! She had her hair cut recently and this, combined with the success of the "Wince and Purge" diet she has been on for 20-plus pounds now, she really does look good. Too bad she does not feel nearly as good as she looks!

On Friday she was fitted with a new brace that goes from the beginning of her leg to the bottom of her foot. Her leg is not at all pleased with the new confines, and almost continuously voices this displeasure by sending wrinkling and contorting signals to her face and causing way too much air to pass over her vocal cords. Said leg is either growing weary of constantly complaining, or is growing accustomed to the new digs, for she is doing better this morning than this time yesterday. Having just made this upbeat proclamation, an "agony storm" just passed through, that had me ripping off the straps securing her leg to the brace, while number one son dutifully stood by with "special" bucket in hand, just in case Mom's breakfast decided it wanted back out.

The main purpose of this brace is to prevent her foot from rotating out at the almost 90-degree angle that it seems to prefer. Since the connective tissues have gotten progressively used to this position, a lot of stretching will be required to get it to once again point in the direction she is trying to go, instead of permanently signaling for a hard left turn. This new source of discomfort is the leg's way of exacting revenge for making it do something it does not want to do.

Her physical therapist and local orthopedic surgeon got together and decided it would improve the chances for success for the next surgery if this could be addressed beforehand. They may be right, but then they do not have to live with the side effects of their well-intentioned idea either.

Well, the squirrels have almost succeeded in emptying the "Squirrel-proof" feeders hanging only inches from the windows of the house, so I had better fill them before they get hangry.

~ Mark, Matthew, and the Woman with the Angry Leg

Journal

Saturday, March 17, 2001

What a week! It will take a considerable amount of time for us to recover from all the news that washed over us in the last few days. On Monday, Dr. Wilson talked with Miriam and explained the importance of performing the next surgery with "fresh allografts." Translated, this essentially puts us on a transplant-type watch, whereby when the grafts become available (anytime from now to whenever), we will have to push the pause button on our lives and immediately travel to NY for surgery. We were trying to make plans so this event would have minimal impact on my work and Matthew's schedule. In fact, Miriam's sister was planning to travel with us and if the timing worked out right, we were considering taking Matthew. With everything having to happen on the spur of any moment, all these possibilities are in jeopardy.

After we had spent several days adjusting to this news, we received word from the accountant that our tax bill was considerably higher than I had hoped and that our carefully saved reserves were about to be sent to the IRS. Most of this is carryover crisis from the bankruptcy (another chapter at least partially written by the knee disaster) and the settlement with the SBA to allow us to keep our house. Apparently, all of our "good fortune" is taxable? Wow!

Fortunately, at least for the time being, flooring sales are holding up, and my income as the sales manager for the new flooring company is respectable. Workman's Comp has finally gotten caught up on the back monies we were owed, so although the reserves are soon gone to the IRS, perhaps we can squeak by check to check until we can rebuild them. Attorney Fred has filed for a hearing which is to address some of the back benefits. If and when these potential funds are received, perhaps we will have a bit of a cushion back in the bank. We have always lived carefully and have lived within our means during our entire married life together. Despite never having a very impressive income, we have always managed to save toward retirement and keep our debts at a manageable level. That is until I started the flooring plant, and Miriam fell. In the span of three short months, we lost Miriam's income, and I was forced to miss a lot of work to tend to her care. This combination has been no less than catastrophic for our financial health. Four years ago, I was able to get financing for several hundred thousand dollars' worth of woodworking machinery; today, I'm not sure I could get a set of used tires financed!

Journal

Sunday, March 18, 2001

Miriam had the best afternoon yesterday that she has had in quite some time. We dropped Matthew off for two hours of paintball fun while Miriam and I went after some supplies for the spa room. She was able to use her crutches to motor around two stores, then she rode in a wheelchair for a third. She is getting used to her new brace and it is making a difference for her. She had to get some adjustments made on it this week, get the proper pants and appropriate foot sleeve, and then get a shoe that would fit over the brace, but she is now much more comfortable in it than she was a week ago. Apparently, the tendons are stretching too, (as they are supposed to) because she has far fewer zingers running down her leg now than she did at first.

She desperately wants to go camping this spring. If she can function like yesterday, we may try it. Last spring, we went out one weekend, and she did well. We used the wheelchair a lot and had a cot for her to sleep on, but except for nearly throwing up once in the middle of the night, she had a good weekend, and we had a good time.

Letter to Dr. Robel

Monday March 26, 2001

Well, it is time once again to make a decision concerning attendant care for another month. How much importance do I place on her having round-the-clock assistance?

When I take our son on Friday nights to Boy Scout meetings, I try to have someone stay with her. When we have a once-a-month camping trip with Scouts, I find someone to stay with her.

Am I being overprotective? Is this necessary? If the answer is yes, shouldn't the E/I be bearing this burden instead of our friends and family? To help answer this, I submit a journal entry I made last week:

March 20, 2001

The time is 10 p.m. on Tuesday night. Since no noise is coming from the direction of the bedroom, I am hoping Miriam has finally quieted down. A very rough weather-making frontal system has been moving through the area since last night and may be contributing to her discomfort. Although I must have slept through them, she reported this morning that she had a lot of zingers during the night. These toe-splaying cramps seem to extend almost the entire length of the leg and completely lock the muscles until they decide to let go. She needs help with the bad ones. Less than 30 minutes ago, I was summoned by howls of agony and a frantic tapping on the wall. She was in bed, had on her new brace, and it was as if a demonic force of some kind had control of her leg. Her toes were curled under and splayed apart, and the whole leg was ridged. My goal is to stretch out the toes by bending them up toward the knee. Sometimes I push and pull with all my might before the cramp passes, and she breathes a sigh of relief as she calms down to a quiet whimper.

After supper, I took the family to SAM's CLUB for some provisions. The fact that she went along, if only to ride in the store-provided wheelchair, indicates some progress. When we returned home, I helped Miriam into the spa. I helped her out of the spa and into bed 30 to 40 minutes later. Since getting the new brace, Miriam has had fewer lockups, but the cramps keep coming, and round-the-clock care is required to assist her with the basic chores of living.

Wednesday morning: I can only recall being awakened twice last night, once when my bride was barfing into the porta-potty and later when I had to help her with a spasm. She says she slept very little and wants me to leave a note asking caregiver Peggy to let her sleep.

Wednesday evening

By the time *Survivor* came on at eight, Miriam had been in & out of the spa, and I was working on spasms and lockups. She claims to have discovered a new kind of lock-up she blames on "a loose piece of cartilage floating around in the knee."

Thursday a.m.

She has suffered through three bad nights in a row, and I am beginning to feel the effects of interrupted sleep as well. We have a Scout camp out Saturday night and I am looking forward to it! The opportunity to sleep without being on duty is very appealing, even if I am sleeping on the ground!

At present, as Matthew and I prepare to leave for the day, Miriam is in the spa, but has a "stomach bucket" close at hand just in case the cramps turn into something else.

In short, attendant care and transportation services are still needed and are justified.

~ **Mark Johnson**

Journal

Monday evening, March 26, 2001

Miriam has had a bad afternoon. During her appointment with Dr. Robel today, he encouraged her to begin bearing some weight on the left leg while in the brace. Apparently, she obediently came home, marched around the house, and has suffered for it ever since. She has been restless, fidgety, frustrated, and in more pain than usual since I have been home. It was only a few minutes ago, while we were in the spa, that she told me about the possible cause.

I nearly lost my supper while cleaning up a pile of vomit she deposited on the tray attached to the side of the spa. She is tired of this routine, and the rest of us are as well. I upset her when I suggested that perhaps I should talk with Stacy Casey about getting her admitted into a care home of some kind for a few days, while I get caught up on my sleep and get over this cold. Something must give. Surely this ordeal will soon have a happy ending, right? The sanity and well-being of several people are dependent upon it.

Letter to Dr. Robel

Thursday, April 5, 2001

You will probably want to file this one under "Strange and unusual requests," if you have such a file.

This is really a follow-up to my last communication with you. I wrote to Stacy Casey last week requesting some periodic help at night, so I could get some needed rest. Working all day and caring for Miriam all night has worn me down to the point where I have become an easy target for colds this winter.

I asked Stacy to find a care home of some kind that Miriam could go to for three or four days a month so I could get a break. Of course, Miriam was convinced I was trying to "put her away," until she calmed down enough for me to reason with her and then she understood the nature of my request.

Stacy explained that the place I was looking for did not exist, due to admissions costs and procedures. She then proceeded to offer an alternative suggestion: if I could get you to **write a script for attendant care for one night per week PRN, then she would get it approved.**

Hopefully after this next surgery, Miriam's knee will quit locking up, and she will get relief from the constant barrage of spasms. Until this happens, round-the-clock care will be required to help during these periods, as well as with the nausea and nightmares that often accompany the night.

Journal

Saturday evening, April 21, 2001

What a beautiful day! Contrary to last Saturday when I spent the gorgeous day in bed with the flu, this day was put to good use. The day still ended long before the work, but at least it was productive.

Miriam seems to have become stable. This means the real bad times have improved enough so that life is not quite as harrowing and uncertain as it has been for much of the last nine months. I can talk to her during the day and feel as though I am communicating with my wife, instead of an alien creature with slurred speech and marginal cognitive capacity.

She is beginning to feel like participating in life. Today for example, she began the day (after the first spa session of the day), by going with neighbor Julie to her son's T-ball game. On the way home, she felt good enough to suggest that they stop and browse at a yard sale! Once home, she took a nap but was soon ready to go with her sister Debra to K-Mart for some supplies. This is a sharp contrast to a few weeks ago when sitting upright was how she separated daytime from the night. Perhaps the new brace is partially responsible, but no matter the source, we will gladly accept it and look to the future with new optimism.

I nearly cried today when Miriam told me about a phone call she received sometime during the last two days. Celia Klotz is a registered nurse we have known for several years through church. She has faithfully blessed us (time out to run toward the screams coming from the direction of the spa to unlock the leg of the writhing wife...) on an almost weekly basis with home-cooked food. Now, she has announced that she wants to spend every Sunday night with Miriam to allow Mark to "get a good night's sleep" and she will bring food! Miriam's sister has kindly provided the only breaks I have had in three years. Now Celia will provide some more, how wonderful! Perhaps with the relief their combined effort will provide, in addition to the soon-to-begin one night of attendant care per week, I will eventually recover my diminished health.

Sunday morning, April 22, 2001

Miriam went on Friday to get her brace adjusted. It seems the guy who made it, made it wrong. The short version of the story is that on Friday, she will be recast for a completely new brace; they think it will lessen the strain on the knee and possibly keep it from locking up. There is little doubt in my mind that once the foot was prevented from turning out, she quit getting worse. Why it took so damn long to get a brace like this for her is a question that raises my blood pressure when I stop long enough to think about it.

The weekly checks continue to be very sporadic. For three months now, they have gotten four weeks behind before they send any money. When it arrives, it may or may not be for the amount due and may or may not even be addressed to the correct address, even though we haven't moved in a dozen years. In this age of computer-generated checks and addresses, this level of incompetence on the part of the servicing agency for the E/I is nothing less than astonishing. Our court date is now only a few weeks away; hopefully, some of this will get rectified then. In the meantime, our finances continue to range from ok to precarious, especially since taxes have been paid.

Tuesday night, April 24, 2001

The optimism concerning Miriam's seemingly improved condition I wrote about only a few days ago has reversed. Celia received a baptism by fire Sunday night on her initial stay with Miriam. The night was filled with spasms and, by the time she left Monday morning, she had single-handedly unlocked the knee at least twice after I assisted with the first sometime around 1 AM. I do not know how many cramps or spasms she dealt with while I slept across the hall in the guest bed. Thank goodness for Celia!

The E/I has yet to see fit to send her any weekly checks or reimburse us for the stuff we purchased out-of-pocket for the knee. Attorney Fred, I think, is bogged down in relativism. Because the E/I is treating Miriam better than some other of his clients are treated by their E/Is, he seems to be of the opinion that we should be happy with the way

Miriam's E/I is treating her and just shut up. The unstated implication is that it does not matter what the law says they have to do, they are doing something, so get off their (and his) case and revel in the fact that she is not being completely ignored. No one in his office is glad to hear Miriam's voice when she calls; if I call, we are quickly reminded that I am not the client.

Journal

Thursday night, April 26, 2001

The stark contrast between this week and last continues to grow sharper. The phone conversations I have had this week with Miriam remind me of many in recent months where her speech is slurred and marginally intelligible. I often must ask her to repeat the sentence that she just finished working so hard to wander through. There is no sign of the clear voice and razor-sharp mind that I conversed with as recently as last week.

Miriam met with Dr. Robel today. I talked with him on her cell phone during her visit. I told him about the developing pain in her left hip; about the worsening pain in her shoulders and asked him about a leg-sized heating pad (it is important that I do this, because when Miriam's mind is this fogged in, she forgets half of what she wants to tell him).

Her bedtime routine now includes two heating pads and a "hot pack" to fill in the gaps. She has returned Ambien to the drug medley because the addition of the hip pain has interfered with her ability to sleep. It has been several nights since I have had anything close to a full night's sleep.

I am supposed to be in Palm Springs tonight attending a trade show, but a duty to my wife caused me to beg off and suggest my boss go in my stead. In addition to having to locate someone to stay an additional night with Miriam, there is the remote possibility of getting "the call" from NY and having to return early so we could go for the surgery. The effect this knee has had on my job, my health, our family activities, our income, our extended families, and our neighbors, in addition to ruining Miriam's whole life, are part of "our cost" for which there will never be any form of compensation or relief. Workman's comp law has no provision for these things, and no one really wants to hear about "Our life on the edge of a knee-shaped pit."

Journal

Sunday, April 29, 2001, 10 p.m.

Celia has returned for another night! After the rough night Miriam provided during her inaugural visit, I am astonished that she came back for more. Clearly, some people were born with hearts larger than their heads; or at least the voice of the heart drowns out the logical one in the head. How else do you explain people like Celia or Debra? Debra has been here the last two nights while Matthew and I were on a Scout outing, so I will have three nights in a row where I will not share her "bed of pain."

Journal

Tuesday, May 1, 2001

Some days/weeks, things seem to develop at a snail's pace; other times, it is as if we are zipping along at faster than the speed of life. We are presently in a period of the latter. Sunday night was hard on Celia once again. She was up with Miriam most of the night. At her expense, I was able to get a good night's sleep; only once did she call for help when she was unable to unlock a particularly difficult lockup.

In the last two days, Miriam has gotten a new brace and seen both a pain doctor and physical therapist, Henry. I have felt compelled to write letters to case manager Stacy Casey, orthopedic surgeon Dr. Robel, and attorney Fred. I am contemplating writing to Dr. Wilson too. I can only sit around so long watching Miriam writhe in pain before I begin prodding people into action; doing nothing can only be tolerated for so long.

The Knee Gazette

May 5, 2001

According to the date on the last "*Gazette*," I have not assaulted anyone with one of these diatribes since January! Some saboteur has evidently been sneaking into my world and stealing pages from the calendar; it is hard to believe the clock and calendar would conspire to erode time at such a torrid pace. Of course, it is a perspective thing. For "She Who

Hollers Out in the Night," some days and nights are endless periods of hurting, highlighted by moments of intense awareness when the very worst seconds are mercilessly stretched into hours.

There is no news of pending surgery to report.

Changes continue to affect Miriam's overall condition. The most recent developments involve her shoulders and hip. Dr. Robel has explained that the recent development of pain in her shoulders is due to her wearing out the rotator cuffs from prolonged use of crutches. In addition to everything else, now the poor woman cannot reach for her water, turn over in bed, cast a fishing pole, or a number of other things without her shoulders pitching a fit. The pain in her hip, he says, is due to bursitis developing because of the abnormal use of the joint for such a long period of time! While she is dealing with the new adversity with all the class, grace, and dignity that I have come to expect from her, I on the other hand am looking for someone to yell at and something to kick. The dogs almost never come around anymore.

To her credit, Miriam is not content to simply look at the "cookie of life," she is determined to nibble at its edges, even if she cannot enjoy full sized bites. This defiant determination has allowed her to feel less like an invalid and continues to give us hope for the future. I was an obedient husband and even said "yes dear" as I loaded the van for a one-night trial run at camping; another is planned for Memorial Day weekend. "I won't be any more miserable in the tent than at home, with the possible exception of not having my spa." She declared, as she gave a look that inspired me to obey even more quickly. She has also been fishing a couple of times and has ventured off with her sister to shop on occasion for short periods of time. For the first time in several years, Miriam has replaced the dust-covered silk flower in our home with baskets of real live flowers. This has brought a welcomed taste of spring into our home that is hopefully a sign of better days ahead. In the meantime, my job, as I see it, is to do everything possible to keep the "cookie of life" from crumbling.

~ The Pain and Her Agony

The Knee Gazette

Friday through Sunday, Memorial Day Weekend, 2001

The sun is leaning on the western horizon, a fire is sputtering inside the ring of rocks a few feet away, and we, the Johnsons three, are not at home. This weekend, our abode is campsite #35 at Cloudland Canyon State Park in the northwest corner of Georgia. Miriam is snuggled under a quilt, reading a book while enjoying the relative comfort of the fold-up recliner we bought last night on the spur of the moment.

Although by Friday evening, we had little time to explore our surroundings much, we did meet our neighbor. He seemed pleasant enough when he asked, in a mild state of panic, if we had a coat hanger he could borrow. It seems he needed it to free his baby from a locked car.

Evidently, coat hangers were among the few things that got left at home, so we generously offered to contribute a hot dog fork to his cause. It must have worked because, after a short while, we heard him explain to the relieved mother that "It used to be a hot dog fork." Judging by the racket, the baby was happier prior to his release. The neighbor showed his gratitude on Sunday afternoon by sharing his homemade ice cream with us.

On the way here, we stopped at a nearby Wal-Mart to get some sandwich fixings for supper. Based on my 15-minute visit to this branch of the world's largest retailer, the family trees in these parts may not be full of branches. I had to explain to the 40-something woman working in the deli that eight oz of something, was the same as half a pound! I then took my three items to the express lane and stood directly under a sign attempting to limit patrons to 20 items and waited for the woman in front of me to check out a full cart of stuff. I was kind and did not mention that I had hoped to consume my purchases for lunch, but now it would be much closer to supper.

Saturday morning brother Bruce and his family arrived to spend the rest of the weekend and my parents drove up from Athens to join us for lunch.

After spending two days here, it is my impression that Cloudland Canyon is a beautiful park! Two deep gorges merge before spilling onto a wooded plain, which is also rimmed by distant mountains. On Sunday morning, rother Bruce, his two boys, Matthew, and myself, hiked down to the bottom of the canyon to look at some "water trickles." After a few inches of rain, they could probably once again be classified as waterfalls, but it had obviously been dry, so the falls needed more water to measure up to their classification. The weather this weekend was magnificent for camping, with highs in the 70's and lows in the 50's, with pleasant breezes and low humidity. Although the campground is full, the park is far from crowded. The kids have made some friends and are finding plenty to do, so we adults have enjoyed the simple pleasures of conversation, napping, and sharing time with people we love.

Traveling to and from the northwest corner of the state went much better than I had anticipated. This is by far the longest trip Miriam has had in quite some time, and I was worried about it. Occasionally she gets a spasm that reduces her to tears and causes her to reach for her bucket. The hardest part is dealing with her knee spasms while I am driving.

Miriam did well camping. For several years now, the closest thing to a vacation we have had was when we traveled somewhere for medical treatment. Last summer we made reservations for several weekends in various parks and cancelled all but this one; we either had Scouts or spa room construction, which seemed to devour all our time and good intentions.

I removed the back seat and one of the captain's chairs, which left the seven-passenger van only capable of legally hauling three; somehow, we managed to fill the rest of the space with stuff. Tents, tarps, coolers, cots, clothing, and bedding consume an enormous amount of space, but when the wheelchair, crutches, cane, portable potty, extension cords, a fan (to keep her cool so she did not over medicate), the heating pads, her "drugstore," and half a dozen pillows were added, the van was full! Matthew's bike was strapped to the top.

When Bruce took his shower Sunday night, he ran into another camper who was worried about the possibility of rain. He claimed there was a 70 percent chance last night and 50 today. After such magnificent weather all weekend and a sky full of stars and moon, rain was something we had yet to give much thought or preparation for. Before retiring, however, we made some preparations and within 30 minutes of turning in, lightning began to flash in the distance.

The weekend has gone better than we ever expected, due in no small part to the spectacular weather we enjoyed. Sunday night the dam burst and what seemed like a reservoir full of lightning, thunder and rain poured over our campground. Other than worrying about leaks, this was wonderful to sleep through. The rain slowed by morning and brother Bruce served us breakfast in our tent.

~ Mark, Matthew, and "Enjoys Fresh Scenery"

Journal

June 10, 2001

Miriam continues to display determination to grab hold of what she can of life. Her courage, strength, and willpower are inspiring and remarkable. This week she planted flowers in some pots hanging on a tree that has been empty for several years. Yesterday afternoon we went fishing. We had access to a small aluminum boat that I managed to get a chair into for her and I paddled around the pond. The boat was too narrow to be very stable, and about two feet short of being long enough for three of us to fish from, but as an experiment, I think the outing proved that with the right equipment, she/we can return to a normal level of activity in something we thoroughly enjoy doing as a family. Once she is situated in a boat, she can have access to an infinite number of fishing spots without her having to walk around the edge of the water. Her shoulder was giving her fits as she was casting, but she was learning ways to minimize this strain too. One method was simply to still fish, which she usually prefers anyway. She had a good time and during the time she was reeling in fish, she was able to forget the agony emanating from her lower left extremity.

If I had to classify Miriam's condition right now, I would declare her to be stable. She hurts and still locks up several times a week, and endures spasms several times a day, but I do not see this as any worse than a few weeks or months ago. If anything, she has fewer lockups now than before getting the new brace. Little things, like lifting her left foot high enough to clear thresholds, are a greater challenge today than six months ago, but I do not think she is in any more pain. We use her wheelchair whenever we go somewhere. The wheelchair is the easiest way to take her from the van to anywhere. We go on Tuesday to

Shepherd Spinal in Atlanta to have her evaluated for mobility and transportation needs. There have been many times I wished I could wheel her around the house, but my efforts to build an accessible home fell short. The doors are all large enough for a chair to pass through, but the rooms are not large enough for a chair to really function.

~ A Day in the Life of Miriam Denise

The Knee Gazette

Father's Day, June 17, 2001

Miriam is again sleeping, which indicates that Thursday's surgery to install a new battery for the spinal cord stimulator went well. Considering the sleep lost earlier in the week, this is a welcomed blessing. I will allow her to sleep as long as she chooses.

Monday was our most recent connection with normalcy. Life for our family has been reasonably calm for a couple of months now. Miriam has stabilized to the point where we spent a couple of afternoons fishing and even went camping over Memorial Day weekend. Do not get me wrong, she has still been in much pain, and her activities have been extremely limited, but within those parameters, we have done some things as a family besides sitting around the house and watching each other's hair grow (or fall out, whichever the case may be).

Miriam was evaluated at the Shepherd Spinal Center in Atlanta on Tuesday. The purpose of this visit was to allow their physical therapists to determine what Miriam can and cannot do, given the limitations of her leg, her pain, and the deteriorating condition of her shoulders. Once these limitations are established, they would recommend equipment to help her get around and function better. Since these people are accustomed to dealing with amputees, accident victims, paraplegics, etc., I observed a somewhat skeptical demeanor when a woman Miriam's age arrived under her own power, on her feet, requiring only the use of crutches. This was an opportunity for me to simply be a fly-on-the-wall and watch what they did. I watched initial skepticism turn into genuine compassion as Miriam's condition became evident. Their findings were quite dramatic; they recommended she get a powered wheelchair (her shoulders are in too bad of shape for a manual chair to be of much benefit) and a wheeled walker with a seat to assist her around the house! An architect and an occupational therapist are supposed to come now and evaluate the house for accessibility. How long it will take for any of this to be implemented remains to be seen, but the fact any of this is justified in the eyes of people skilled at making these determinations is indicative of her condition!

During the trip home from Shepherd, Miriam discovered that the spinal cord stimulator was not providing the accustomed level of relief. From her cell phone, she got an appointment to have it checked out on Wednesday. The physician, who installed the thing only 11 months earlier, has moved his practice to a small town about 50 miles north of Athens, so this is where she went in pursuit of relief. While there she learned the code EOL stands for "End of Life" for the battery. It is worthwhile to note that this battery lasts the average patient three to five years and some as long as seven; Miriam managed to burn hers up in only 11 months, because the level of her pain requires her to keep the unit set on such a high setting!

She returned home to wait. Waiting is something we have had an opportunity to practice for several years. If advanced degrees were handed out for waiting, Miriam's would be a PHD; mine would be honorary. If we are not waiting for someone to do something, we are waiting for her to recover from a surgery, or waiting in a doctor's office, or waiting for approval for the next procedure. Among my personal favorites: waiting for the spasm to let go of her leg, so she can return to a normal level of agony. The minimum anticipated wait for a new battery was one week; one week that would feel like a lifetime for the woman in pain!

This time however, we were wonderfully surprised how short the wait was. I had not even had time to work myself into a good rage over the delay when Miriam received a call on Thursday morning informing us of an appointment for surgery that afternoon! Miriam was near tears when she called me with the news. This is entirely due to the intervention of a woman named Rose Bellamy who stopped by on Wednesday evening to check on Miriam. This woman has been a wonderful friend who has brought countless meals, prayed diligently, and visited regularly. She is also employed by the physician who is currently monitoring Miriam's medications. Rose was apparently disturbed by what she saw, because she convinced her employer to do something about getting Miriam some relief. Rose's employer doctor helped Dr. Edwards find time in the Thursday schedule to replace Miriam's dead battery.

On Thursday, Miriam's tour of American hospitals took us to Demorest, Georgia, and Holden County's Outpatient Surgery Department. This was Miriam's ninth surgical procedure, performed in the fifth different hospital, in the third different state, within the last four years! If you think it sounds a little like "all the king's horses and all the king's men," I agree.

A child to whom I am distantly related, once referred to aged people with wrinkles, as being "all wadded up"; this is the perfect adjective to use in describing Miriam's contorted face when she is hurting. Shortly after she was wheeled to recovery, a technician entered the room carrying a computer device built into a briefcase. With it he began to program the new unit residing within Miriam's left buttock. When he turned the unit on, her face was no longer wadded up. At least this time, we were not told she had to lie down for two months while the leads healed in place. This time it was just a fresh wound in her sitter that has to heal.

We are still waiting. We are waiting for a call to come to New York; we are waiting for the new incision to completely heal and for this source of pain to go away. We are not waiting however for a new battery and for that we are most grateful.

~ Happy Father's Day — Impatient and Wait-a-Lot

Journal

Thursday, June 20, 2001

Dr. William's secretary called Miriam yesterday from New York to inform her that the tissue bank has accumulated the parts they were looking for. They are frozen instead of fresh, but I think this will make scheduling simpler for all concerned.

Meanwhile, Miriam is experiencing a new malady. It is as if her left leg is demon-possessed at times. She will develop a spasm that causes her entire leg to shake uncontrollably. Intense pressure must be applied to the back of the knee to relieve it, but then it moves into her foot. I am assuming this is some manifestation of the reflex sympathetic dystrophy (RSD), but do not know for sure. She is looking forward to having the battery replacement incision heal to the point that she can get back into her spa, at least until the next surgery. Twice yesterday she sat on the edge and soaked what she could of her lower leg.

Case manager Stacy Casey has assured us that everything pertaining to the next NY surgery has been approved, so we will not worry over details, we will just go. Where has this woman been for most of the last four years? She is a gift from On High!

Matthew has gone to Awana camp this week. This is the first week of four he is scheduled to be away this summer. He needs the distraction and hopefully a slice of normal childhood. It is quiet around here, but we also realize how much this kid contributes to the household chores and to Miriam's care. Due to his absence, the attendants are working nine-hour days instead of the six they are normally here. Even then, Miriam is alone for a couple hours because they leave at five and I do not get home until seven. It is good they are providing this additional coverage now, but I am not sure how they justify saving money on the back of such a young child?

The Knee Gazette

July 1, 2001

"We should write a note about what is going on and send it out this weekend." This voice was coming from the direction of the wheelchair I was pushing up the sidewalk toward our son's favorite pizza palace. I have been married to this voice long enough that I understood perfectly that "we" meant me. So, in the spirit of obedience, here goes:

During the afternoon of July 11, Miriam is scheduled to once again enter an operating room. We will return to the Hospital for Special Surgery in NYC on Tuesday the 10th in preparation for this procedure. Since all three of the needed allographs are frozen instead of fresh, we have the luxury of having some advance notice of the pending surgery.

This trip will be different from the standpoint that we have decided to take Matthew, and Celia Klotz is going with us and wants to help with Miriam. This makes it possible for Matthew to go along. Matthew and I are planning to do some sightseeing while Celia is tending to Miriam. This will be like a vacation. It will however be seasoned by periods of stark reality, like with every visit to the hospital. All in all, I am sure it will be a memorable trip.

I am hopeful that tying the knee joint back together will eventually allow the incredibly angry nerve to heal and reduce her pain. Realistically, there probably are less than even odds that successful surgery on the joint will solve her pain. This is because the nerves are so traumatized and buried in scar tissue from all the other surgeries, I do not see how this will alleviate this issue, but I won't tell Miriam this, it is, after all, only the opinion of a non-medically trained lay person. Following surgery, they will proceed very cautiously with therapy, to ensure that everything has an opportunity to heal before being subjected to stress. For Miriam, this means eight to ten weeks without the ability to put any weight on the left leg! The plan is to keep her in the full leg brace for six months to a year, even if everything goes right! This will be the last time any attempt is made to reconstruct this knee. I am unable to get anyone to even discuss with me where we go from here in the event of another failure.

We need a miracle. If Tim McVeigh had been sentenced to live only one day with Miriam's pain, the ACLU would have pitched a fit, claiming the punishment to be cruel and unusual. Given a choice, Miriam would gladly swap sentences with him– the thought of going to sleep and waking up at the feet of her Savior sounds pretty good to her! Your prayers and emails continue to bless and encourage us. We have ordered a new battery for the laptop, so we should be able to keep everyone informed about the latest chapter in our "Adventure on the River East."

~ **Mark, Miriam, and Matthew**

Journal

July 4, 2001

Miriam yelled from the bedroom, "Is anyone home?" I mute the TV, slam the footrest down on the recliner and run to the bedroom. By the light spilling into the bedroom from the hall, I can see Miriam laying flat on her back in bed. Her eyes are closed, her right hand and arm are knocking on a door in her dream, and she is yelling "Is anybody home?" I go to her side and try to calm her down by explaining that she is in her bed, in her house, and everything is fine. I glance at my watch on the way back to "my time;" 10 minutes have passed since she went to bed. This should be a good night.

This sort of thing went on for hours. Just before I was ready for bed, I heard a different sort of scream and ran once again to her side. She was on her knees, leaning against the bed, with the portable potty behind her. Somehow, it had tipped while she was trying to get up and get back into bed. I helped her up, got a towel and wiped the splatters off, and tucked her back into bed.

The dream evidently kept changing, but the scenario was awfully familiar. When I enter the room to retire for the night, she often begins screaming in terror as if a stranger has entered her chambers. Once, sometime during the wee hours, I had to help with one of her patented "total leg spasms." During one recent night (they begin to run together after a while), I had to help her with no less than six of these spells! Near morning, she asked me if I had gotten my hair rinsed and would I please wash her back. We had been sound asleep in the bed, not cavorting about in the shower. My next conscious moment was of her rubbing her hand around on my chest. In the absence of any seductive gestures, I was compelled to ask her what she was doing: "I'm making cinnamon rolls, like you asked me to."

Giving up on sleep, I got up, helped her into the spa, started the coffee, and sat down to write this journal entry. It was not long before I heard a noise from the direction of the spa room that sounded like distress, so I fixed her coffee and made my way to spa-side. She was sitting in her hammock with her eyes closed. She jumped and hollered when she awoke from the latest dream; I nearly spilled her coffee when she did. A paragraph later, she was ready for more coffee. Her needs are legion, but I keep reminding myself that she cannot help it or fix it, this is just the way things are. Someone must be there for her 24/7. Her pain, agony and the need for care and assistance takes no time off. Matthew is away at Scout camp, the attendant is not here, so I am "on duty." I get time off when I am at work, on a Scout outing, or when Miriam's sister or another friend stay a night to give me some relief.

Being "on duty" is one thing, but living on the very edge of pending crisis is something else. At any moment of the day or night, she could teeter off the ledge and descend toward a pit requiring help to recover from.

It really does not matter if we are driving down the road at 70 mph or

I am tending to "personal business" in "the library," whatever I am doing must be dropped, or stopped, and her needs tended to instantly. The presence of even a shred of sanity after almost four years of living like this is both arguable and remarkable.

A week from today, she goes under the knife for the tenth time since this ordeal began. For several weeks following each surgery, her needs and the level of intensity increases dramatically; I am not looking forward to what I know lies ahead.

Saturday, July 7, 2001

Miriam's Sunday School class surprised her this afternoon with a send-off party. The new light-weight manual wheelchair, that was prescribed by the evaluators at the Shepherd Center, arrived Thursday. It has already been declared a big improvement by sister Debra and Matthew. The larger and cushier wheels will be delivered soon after we return from NY. These will cushion the bumps that travel toward and focus on the tenderest places on the leg. The electric wheelchair should be delivered by then too.

CHAPTER 12
New York Surgery, Take II

The Knee Gazette

July 10, 2001

Another chapter of our bizarre story has officially begun. The captain just announced that Washington, D.C. is off to our left. Our perch at cruising altitude provides quite the vantage point to watch our tax dollars at work.

I suppose one could label this excursion as: "Adventure travel" or we could expand on the "Dinner and a Movie" thing and call it something like: "Vacation with Surgery." One thing is for sure, whether we go around the block or across country, it is always an adventure!

Miriam and I are enjoying the ride from seats 1-A and 1-C on board AirTran's DC9, which today is transporting Miriam's left knee to LaGuardia in NYC. Upon arrival, we expect to catch a wheel-chair accessible taxi into Manhattan. The rest of Miriam, as well as myself are superfluous, it is the knee they need in NY, we're just along for the ride. The rest of our "entourage," Matthew and a kind-hearted soul named Celia Klotz, are sitting snugly in their seats back on row 17. AirTran's business class provides the legroom Miriam desperately needs, which explains why we are on row #1. The linen napkins, stainless flatware, genuine china dishes and glass goblets that we enjoyed in Delta's first class during our return flight in December, has become paper, plastic, and more plastic on AirTran. We were also spared from committing any embarrassing faux pas with the hot towels, since there aren't any. But I'm not complaining, the seats are less than half the price and serve the purpose just fine! It occurs to me that one advantage of sitting in the front of the plane is that we will be first in line for our seats on the "chariot to heaven" in the event something goes wrong.

Miriam's new manual wheel chair is somewhere below us and will hopefully be waiting when we deplane. The schedule for the day includes pre-op blood work, check-in, and hopefully we will see some sights. Miriam desperately wants to see the Statue of Liberty, something that has eluded us on the two earlier trips. Hopefully we can take a cruise around NY Harbor this afternoon. Perhaps we will see a few more sights tomorrow morning, but 1PM is her appointment with the next chapter of her life.

Celia is with us because she wants to stay with Miriam so Matthew and I can see the sights. I think she is with us simply because she has poor judgment and cannot see what she is getting herself into. Nevertheless, poor judgment or not, I am thankful she is along. Her presence really made the idea of bringing Matthew possible. Bringing him along just to sit in mom's hospital room wouldn't have been much of a trip for him!

With all of the anticipation and preparation behind us, it is good (and scary) to finally be on the way. These endless months of waiting have not been easy for any of us; Miriam especially is ready to get on with it. She has always faced these appointments with nearly unbelievable courage. She looks past the pending misery and grabs hold of the hope for a less painful tomorrow. I feel as though we are once again trading the known for the unknown. One thing is certain, we will descend, at least for a while, into a dark pit called post-op recovery, where agony and despair will reign. Hopefully, we will locate an exit with bright sunny skies full of unicorns, rainbows, and songbirds. That is the goal that has eluded us since her accident. Instead, storm clouds and circling buzzards have prevailed. We have so many friends and relatives praying desperately for a miracle. I am overwhelmed that so many people have taken time from their own trials and lives to assist with ours.

~ The Johnsons Three, Joined by Celia, Winging our Way Toward a Better Future

The Knee Gazette

July 11, 2001, Morning Report

"Could you please move over into that other lane? That one might be smoother." Celia was in the front of the bus/taxi, kneeling beside the very astonished driver. Our previous cab rides have been in Lincoln Town Car type vehicles that delivered relatively smooth rides, but this one was a small transit type bus with a wheelchair lift and very stiff springs. Before the poor man had driven two miles from the airport, Miriam pulled out one of her ever-present "emergency sacks" and looked as though she could use it at any minute. The driver had already noticed the potential problem "brewing" in the back of his bus and had slowed to nearly a crawl on the expressway. Cars were whizzing past and piling up behind the bus. Many were honking friendly greetings and "waving hello" on their way by, yet the poor driver still had to listen to Miriam's "advocate" asking him to get into a different lane; I am pretty sure he felt the tip I gave him did not cover all this aggravation.

We checked into the room and took care of pre-op chores at the hospital before embarking on our first excursion about the city. From the internet Miriam had learned about the Staten Island Ferry. Upon this free vessel designed to transport "working stiffs" from Manhattan to Staten Island, we took our cruise of New York Harbor. The 30-minute trip gave us fantastic views of Lady Liberty, as well as Ellis Island and the Manhattan skyline. Once I had Miriam and Celia situated on the boat, Matthew and I took off in pursuit of an exposed deck from which to better view the sights. Our plan was to get off and get right back on once we reached Staten Island. Once we docked, I located Miriam and we headed for the ramp, assuming Matthew would be waiting for us as we left the ferry. We were told by a Port Authority employee that we didn't need to leave the boat if we were going back. Since Matthew wasn't with us, he missed this useful piece of information and had apparently already left the now empty boat. Fortunately, I soon spotted the silhouette of a short-haired boy with a camera swinging from his left wrist and managed to get his attention. He was calmly walking with the herd of commuters who had just gotten off, heading to who knows where, oblivious to the fact his parents were nowhere around. It would have really put a damper on the trip, if we had managed to lose our 12-year-old boy on Staten Island on our first day here.

For Miriam's "last supper," we chose a place Called Katie Gallagher's. We soon figured out this was an Irish restaurant that came complete with authentic Irish waitresses who spoke with fresh-off-the-boat brogues. While I enjoyed filet of sole stuffed with crab, Miriam and Celia split the largest piece of prime rib I've ever seen. Matthew had a cheeseburger…

Miriam was whipped by the time all of this had been accomplished; after all, the day had begun rather early. Before Tuesday was over, we had managed to travel by car, plane, train (to Concourse C at the airport), and boat. Miriam was hurting by the time she crawled between the sheets. Before she fell asleep, it took the combined efforts of Celia and me to free Miriam from one of the most prolonged leg-shaking spasms Miriam had suffered to date. Normally, after a long, tiring day, she'd get in her spa, but not this day. By morning she was also missing her air bed.

We continue to be concerned about what they are and aren't planning to do this afternoon in the operating room. As it stands right now, there are no plans to do anything with the nerve that has caused so much of her trouble. This may be good, but it may not. We won't know one way or the other for months to come, but it is causing some understandable concern on Miriam's part. Another thing Dr. Wilson mentioned yesterday that surprised us is that he is having second thoughts about replacing the meniscus—a decision I guess he will complete this afternoon on the fly.

Matthew and Celia have gone to find F.A.O Schwartz (large toy store made famous in movie *Home Alone*) and Central Park. Matthew should have a blast at **that** toy store with the $20 he has in his pocket. Miriam and I are savoring some time alone in preparation for the rest of the day; I will try to send an update this evening once we see how things have turned out.

This concludes this report from room 4-O of the Bel Air building, located on the East River in Manhattan.

~ This is Mark Johnson Reporting on Behalf of "The Gang of Georgia Four"

The Knee Gazette

July 11, 2001 Afternoon and Evening Report

Miriam was all gowned up, complete with hat and socks, waiting patiently for her turn in the operating room. I slipped Matthew into the "prep room" for an emotional hug before she was escorted away for her appointment with the knife. Before we were caught and ushered back to the waiting room, I saw Dr. Wilson and took the opportunity to talk with him further concerning the day's procedures. He explained that he had decided to go ahead and replace the meniscus and that he expected the surgery to take five hours. He planned for her case to be his only surgery for the day, so he could give it his undivided attention. He waited until the afternoon, so he would have all the time he needed to complete the procedure to his satisfaction.

I have returned to the hotel room to wait by the phone for news from the operating room, compose a paragraph or two, and take a nap. Matthew and Celia returned from their adventure to the toy store, ate lunch, recharged their "batteries," and have once again gone exploring. Celia is revising her plan for her time in New York. This is the same woman who sat in our living room a few nights ago and told me that she had no interest in seeing any sights. She was coming to NY to stay with Miriam. Since arriving, apparently, some of her stereotypes of the big city have vanished, and she has discovered that she, too, could have fun here. I will take my turn with Matthew on Thursday and Friday prior to their Saturday departure. Celia will have plenty of time for the hospital; for now, entertaining Matthew is a great help. I would not be going anywhere this afternoon anyway, and I prefer to be alone with my thoughts during these uncertain stress-filled hours.

I'm a pacer, so I pace the room. Miriam's empty wheelchair is here to remind me of the drama once again unfolding in our little family. Tears of frustration and anger occasionally break through the stoic demeanor I try so hard to maintain for those around me; being alone allows me to be real. I am angry at a situation I am powerless to do anything about. I am, by nature, a fixer. When something is broken, I fix it, but there is nothing I can do for my broken wife. I invite myself to a one-person pity party and wallow in my despair for a while. Miriam, too, was having a hard time as I helped her out of her clothes and into the gowns (two, one facing front and one facing back); I think her greatest fear is that she will go through yet another surgical procedure and recovery and get no relief from the unrelenting pain. She's human, so she must surely reflect on all the other surgical failures and dashed hopes. She's also tough and determined to do whatever she can to recover something of the life she lost. She amazes me with her strength and unwavering faith. She makes me look pathetic by comparison.

Somewhere near the five-hour mark, I returned to the hospital to see if there was any word on her condition. I learned that she had been assigned to room 546, but she was still in surgery. I returned to an empty surgical waiting room, where even the staff had left for the day. I had lots of room to pace in this vast empty space. Shortly after seven, a nurse entered the room searching for a Mr. Johnson. She had been sent by Dr. Wilson to inform me that all of the parts were in place; he would be another 45 minutes or so closing up but would then be out to talk with me. If my math is correct, she has been in surgery for six hours!

8 p.m.

Dr. Wilson just came out for the post-op chat. His demeanor was almost exuberant. He said the surgery went very well; "her knee is tight, and her foot is straight." He was pleased that he had decided to go ahead with replacing the meniscus. Once he got hers out, he saw what bad shape it was really in. During our initial visit back in September, he and Dr. Ware theorized that a poor meniscus could have caused the last rebuild to fail.

Want some more good news to rejoice over? Apparently, somewhere in the supply chain, someone had messed up because the wrong meniscus was sent from the tissue bank. He thought they might have to locate one overnight and install it tomorrow during another surgery. He sent the request upstairs to the in-house tissue bank and located one that had come from a 19-year-old female that fit perfectly. This spared her from having to return to the operating room for another round tomorrow—P.T.L.! No word on why the 19-year-old was no longer in need of her meniscus.

Dr. Wilson expressed concern about her leg spasms and the possibility that one might cause damage to the repairs. He is going to have the in-house pain management people see her and review her meds while she is here.

The Knee Gazette

July 12, 2001, Surgery #10, plus one day

Apparently, the Hospital for Special Surgery does not carry some of the special medicines Miriam has in her personal pharmacy. At midnight the phone in the hotel room rang. Since the phone was in Celia's part of the suite, she answered it and then knocked on the door to the bedroom where Matthew and I had already gone to sleep. "Telephone, Mark. It's Miriam's nurse."

I staggered to the phone to hear a distressed voice asking for some of Miriam's medicines. After making myself "publicly presentable," I made my way across the pedestrian bridge to the hospital. This route, although longer and less direct than simply crossing the street and going in the main entrance, helps to circumnavigate hospital security, who do not take kindly to wee-hour visitors and would have a hard time believing that anyone within their hallowed halls could possibly need the assistance of a large shabbily dressed, bearded man with sleepers in his eyes.

Miriam was not then and is not now in her assigned room on the fifth floor. Instead, she has been relegated to sort of a halfway status that is somewhere between recovery and "the floor." There is room for four beds in this step-down ward. Three patients were present last night as I entered the room. One woman had both feet in casts and was sound asleep; another patient appeared to be an elderly male of unknown affliction who was also asleep; then there was my bride, her face twisted in agony with tears streaming down her cheeks. I delivered the requested drugs and began trying to calm down the woman with the wet cheeks.

As this is being composed several hours later into the new day, none of the other patients present last night are still here. Some beds, I think, have turned over twice. Even so, I do not expect Miriam to get to the fifth floor before mid-morning. They are moving very slowly with her, possibly because after her December surgery, they had to return her twice to recovery. The first 48 hours post-surgery has always been tough for her.

When the daylight part of the morning arrived, they would only let us into her room once visiting hours officially began at noon, so the three of us went on a walkabout in Manhattan. We ended up taking a cab to the South Street Seaport Museum. Although noon duty at the hospital cut short our visit, we enjoyed wandering through a few exhibits and got to tour a four masted sailing ship. The patient was glad to see familiar faces, but hugging her son was definitely the highlight of her day. I sent Celia to find some lunch, explaining that upon her return, Matthew and I would get something to eat and then relieve her around five. I told her that once they ran me out about eight, we would all go find something interesting to eat. By four, Celia was back in the room asking me to go to Miriam; she was miserable and wanted to see me.

Apparently, I was fortunate enough to miss "the storm" because since I've been here, she has been sleeping peacefully. I found out they gave Miriam a Valium; the nurse said something about her needing one, too?"

"I get one if you get one." I quickly declared. Valium, it would appear, works quite well in conjunction with all of her other narcotics, judging by her lack of consciousness.

Miriam's bed is once again on the waterfront. As I sit here pecking on the laptop, I am enjoying watching the boat traffic plying up and down the East River. The hospital is built over the top of F.D.R. Drive (or Avenue, or Blvd, or something or other), so the windows on the East side of the building have a fantastic view of the river. There are tugs, tugs pushing barges, jet skis, sail boats, motor yachts, etc. There is a lot more pleasure craft traffic on the river now than there was in December.

Last night we dined at the Café Luka. While I enjoyed angel hair pasta covered with sea scallops, Celia had a spinach-pastry something or other, while Matthew dined on fish and chips.

Miriam's condition permitting, I would like for Matthew and me to take a guided tour of the city tomorrow. I'll let you know how that worked out. Until then, I bid you farewell from the Big Apple, on behalf of "The Knee" and the rest of its support team.

~ **Mark**

The Knee Gazette

July 13, 2001, two days post-op

The Silver Spoon served us our dinner last night. Celia savored a dish called Moussaka; I enjoyed the largest plate of broiled fish and scallops I've ever seen, and the "Manhattan Kid" dined on the "Silver Dollar Special," which he chased with Maple syrup. Our fridge is fast filling up with the leftovers Celia keeps having packaged in "doggie bags." Without a microwave, or a dog, leftovers are a problem, but she cannot, or will not, tolerate wasting food. In my mind, taking it back to the room and throwing it out there is the same thing, but not in Celia's...

When I checked in on Miriam prior to retiring for the night, she was sleeping. She is on a nearly unbelievable dose of drugs. She can recall little that has taken place in the last two days. I am in the proverbial doghouse because she has no recollection of my being there when I was supposed to be, or when she asked for me. What good is it to be such a dutiful husband if she is too looped to remember it? My "brownie point account" needs all the credits I can accumulate, but do points really count if the wife is not aware enough to "take notes?" Her speech is so slurred it is hard to figure out what she is asking us to do; rest assured however, that she is almost always asking for something to be moved, filled, hung up, changed, wiped, adjusted, raised, lowered, turned, replaced, cleaned, fetched, shifted, or retrieved. This is in addition to getting the nurse to check on meds or to call someone about something. I keep reminding myself that this is not the real Miriam. Being waited on and served is the opposite of the role she filled the first 37 years of her life. She is just so miserable that she too is looking for ways/things to help her feel better.

I came to her room early this morning. She wanted me to be here When Dr. Wilson made rounds about six; it is now seven-thirty and I hadn't seen him yet. Miriam is groggy. I don't remember her being this heavily medicated this long after surgery. It is probably good, because it allows her (and the rest of us) to rest, but I hate seeing her normally sharp mind so blunted by chemicals. This diminished state of consciousness did produce a rather humorous scene this morning when the girl from the lab came to draw some blood. Miriam was trying to help her by slapping her veins and even offered to stick herself. A short while ago we had an argument about what day it is. When she sobers up enough to dial the phone, she calls me if I'm not already here.

The sun gets up early in these parts this time of year. It was broad daylight by five; the sun was already above the horizon by six; I was by her side by 6:15. She won't remember it though, so the effort will put no points in the bank that I will be able to benefit from at some future date.

I settled onto my perch this morning, with her bed on one side of me and the window on the other. The activity below my window on the East River keeps me from focusing too much on what is happening on the bed. The river was smooth; it resembled a rippled layer of glass rolling gently toward the harbor. I have seen some magnificent yachts slide by. One had two identical tenders lashed to the upper deck that must have each been about 20 ft long and had inboard motors. The vessel looked to be almost new and had a section of glass that began as a wall, turned the corner and ended up as part of the roof/ceiling for one part of the main cabin. The total length of the boat must have been 80 to 90 feet, so we are talking serious money here!

Miriam is so out of it that she thinks this is still the day of her surgery. A short while ago they gave her Valium after a particularly nasty spasm woke up anyone trying to sleep within three floors of her room. The pain "management" guy was by a while ago; they never show up when she's writhing in agony... (It would not bother any of us if the "Pain Cure Guy" would take over and eliminate the need for the pain to be managed...) Before he left, he did mention possibly moving her up onto the floor "in a day or two." There is no word yet on when we will be going home, other than it won't be as soon as Sunday, as we had optimistically hoped. The epidural is scheduled to be removed somewhere around seven in the morning. As bad as things have been the last couple of days, I'm not looking forward to losing the benefit of any medications. No, I was not offered a Valium this time; however, by tomorrow night I expect the nurse and I will share a "Valium toast," as I'm sure she will be needing one too.

My traveling companions will be leaving tomorrow, according to the schedule. I have really enjoyed having some relief, as well as the companionship. Somehow, I will have to remember how to carry on in their absence.

Miriam sobered up enough a while ago to ask to have "the mail" read to her. I will get to read the same ones to her again tomorrow, thanks to the combined effect of the various chemicals. It is nearly time for our evening stroll to find dinner. I will get this sent before bed and fill in today's details tomorrow.

Good night, for now, sign us: "In the Doghouse," "Sleepless Beauty," "The Manhattan Kid" and "Saint Tulia."

Letter Written by Celia, Inserted into a *Knee Gazette*

Hi, this is from one half of the feminine half of this contingent. It's been interesting to spend this time with the Johnson family. I seldom spend much time in the company of the male half of the population, and it has been most interesting. This morning at breakfast I asked Matthew (after saying I had a question he did not have to answer, but if he did answer he had to be honest) if he thinks I talk a lot. (I truly wanted to know!) He declined to answer. His father said that that was a trick question, and for a while the males had the floor. (If they only knew how hard I've tried to NOT talk, how many times I've exercised great self-restraint!)

It's early afternoon and I'm sitting with Miriam while Matthew and Mark have a last (brief) outing together before Matthew and I leave for the airport. Matthew and I just got back from a short tour of Central Park, during which time we went out on a rowboat. Matthew did most of the rowing, assuring me prior to departing that he knew how to row a boat; he later was forced to admit that although he knew how, he had never actually rowed a rowboat. He reluctantly allowed me to row for a while, then demanded the power position to be returned to him, when I had trouble rowing (I COULD have done it! I was just laughing too hard to keep both oars in the water at the same time!)

I've asked Mark for a turn at the keyboard for a more serious reason than sharing tidbits about the pleasure I've had being with them in NY. As I've read Mark's Gazettes, I feel he has not conveyed what I consider to be the desperate situation the

Johnson's face. I suspect there are numerous reasons for this, but I don't want to talk too much.

Miriam's spasms have been excruciating. Twice I've begged her to squeeze my hands instead of digging her fingers into her face in her agony. Sometimes she stuffs some linens into her mouth to muffle her screams. This is serious stuff, dear ones. The toll on Mark, and I'm sure, Matthew, is most likely close to being as great as on Miriam. I've been grateful to hear Mark read the e-mails from people describing how earnestly in prayer they have been. The need for prayer is not behind us.

The road ahead of them is going to be exhausting and challenging to the point of exceeding the resources of time, emotion, strength, spirit, and endurance. Please continue to pray for them. Miriam cherishes visits. She loves e-mail. They need ongoing earnest prayer.

Yours Truly,

Celia (a.k.a. "St. Tulia")

The Knee Gazette

Saturday, July 14, 2001, 5:15 a.m.

This corner of the world is in the midst of transition. It is the time of day when dawn ushers out the night, and judging by the looks of the river, it has just changed directions and once again the water is easing its way toward the bay. It begins the journey quietly, almost like a child trying to get another cookie past the mom; the closer he gets to the door and to freedom, the faster he goes. When the river is in the process of changing direction, it is deceptively calm; at its fastest, it looks angry, able to create swells large enough to roll white caps. Judging by the fits it gives skippers of small boats, it is troubled water they traverse at times. Jet ski jockeys, on the other hand, seem to enjoy the rough water. At times their wakes are only a series of circles because they skip across the tops of the waves almost like a good flat rock when thrown correctly. The tide change is really quite small compared to what we are accustomed to seeing along the southeastern coast. I cannot begin to describe how thankful I am that her bed is beside the window, it sure gives me a lot of interesting things to look at. I have gotten an extra roll of film, just so I can shoot some of the yachts sailing by.

The orange glow will soon become a ball on the eastern horizon. The sky is once again clear, so there is nothing obstructing my view of the celestial ballet unfolding before me. The sun also is gaining momentum, similar to the river, rising again toward its azimuth. Once it slips the bonds of the horizon, it takes off; its beam is the signal for daytime creatures to take over from the nocturnal.

I am a witness to this drama because Miriam's nurse called the room about a quarter to five this morning. Miriam was having bad spasms and was screaming for me. By the time the night was washed off and a fresh set of clothing crawled into, a half hour had elapsed—just enough time for the Valium they gave her to take hold and for her to fall into what appears to be a deep sleep. I will be reprimanded for not waking her and letting her know of my presence, but I will use my better judgment and ask for forgiveness later. She wouldn't remember the exchange anyhow, so what's the point?

After half an hour I return to the room and the bed. Around eight, since the phone has not summoned me back to the hospital, the three of us slip off for a final breakfast together prior to Matthew and Celia's early afternoon departure. After breakfast, I sent Matthew and Celia for another walk around Manhattan while I sat with Miriam.

Matthew and I spent yesterday exploring. We started back at the Sea Port Museum, where we needed to spend more time the day before to see what we (I) wanted to see. While I am looking at the historical displays portraying life at sea during the era of sail, Matthew is admiring a large speedboat with teeth painted on its sides named "The Beast." "The Beast" was a tour boat that gave high-speed tours of the harbor. In the interest of family harmony, I shelved my plans of a narrated harbor cruise offering stops at Ellis Island and the Statue of Liberty and booked passage on "The Beast." At 50 mph we enjoyed near misses with several vessels whose owners somehow forgot to paint large teeth near their bows. The captain, who I imagined to be a direct descendent of a bad court jester or a pirate, was kind enough to stop near Lady Liberty for a historical interlude before resuming the full throttle excursion back to the dock.

To return some hint of educational value to the day, we took off walking toward our next adventure, the observation deck at the World Trade Center. Along the way, we took a short detour so we could walk down Wall Street. It was near noon, so many of the "starched shirts" were walking to lunch or already sitting on a bench or step enjoying the fabulous weather. I was amazed by how narrow the street is. The buildings lining this street are tall and oppressive, so the overall appearance is somewhat overwhelming. This was the first place we really encountered the kind of crowds one thinks of when thinking about NYC. I was also stunned that I walked for several blocks along this center of financial savvy and not once did someone walk out of one of the revolving doors and offer me a high-paying job as an analyst for, uh, drug companies who produce pain medications; or perhaps makers of equipment designed to assist the mobility impaired? I possess information they need, along with lots of firsthand experience. They were probably unaware that I was in town.

The view from the 107th floor of the World Trade Center, some 1,300 ft in the air, was in a word, spectacular! From one window one could see the Atlantic Ocean, the Statue of Liberty, Ellis Island, Governor's Island, the George Washington bridge and all of New York Harbor! The other sides of the building were equally spectacular. It was a wonderful day with my boy. Hopefully he will take home with him some fond memories of the day as well.

For our last lunch together in New York, Matthew wanted some more New York pizza. This was at least his third meal of pizza since arriving, not counting cold leftovers. He wondered out loud why the pizza at home doesn't taste like it does here in New York. The farewell was hard on both of us. We exchanged a tight hug in the hall of the hospital; we were both wiping our eyes as we quickly turned and walked stoically in our respective directions. I think sometimes we try too hard to be brave and strong for one another. Sometimes I wonder if it wouldn't be good for both of us to fall into one another's arms and soak the other's shirt for a while.

I have watched the river change direction no less than three times today and, judging by the shadows, the sun will soon be sucked into the western horizon and give way to another night. Miriam is thankfully sleeping. It has been a long day for both of us.

~ This is Mark, signing off for "Just the Two of Us"

The Knee Gazette

Sunday, July 15, 2001

My wake-up call mercifully waited until seven this morning; perhaps this is an indication of improvement? It is at least a trend that will be further developed. The world looks different when viewed through eyes that have been shut for eight consecutive hours.

New York City is not an early riser on Sunday. At eight, the streets are still nearly deserted, except for a legion of cabs searching for fares. There were no lines at the deli, where my breakfast was prepared (read that cooked) in the time it took me to get out my wallet and pay for it! If fast food is served under the Golden Arches, then what is served at New York delis is instant. They take a space as small as 20 by 20, put four or five employees behind an assortment of counters and display cases, line the walls with refrigerators full of drinks, stack newspapers near the cash register, stick one small round table and four chairs over in the corner to provide for the customers not taking their food somewhere else, and open for business. I took my breakfast to a concrete bench across the street, where I could enjoy my food and watch the world go by.

There is almost constant drama when there are so many people packed so close together. While I am enjoying my hot sandwich, I observe a boy in his young teens standing with his dad and siblings in front of the hospital across the street. It appears he may be learning how to use a brand-new prosthetic arm. In front of me a man is unloading possessions from the trunk of his car; it looks as if he and his wife may be moving into the 40-story building in front of which they are parked. On another bench, two security/police officers discuss where the "Urban Outdoorsmen" bedded down last night. Medical people are often milling about this street corner, probably because there are hospitals in every direction almost as far as the eye can see. Doctors, residents, nurses, and student nurses, all wearing white lab coats or scrubs, gather here to drink their coffee or eat their sandwiches. Dogs of all shapes and sizes are usually visible walking their owners. I think a dog should be part of a parental suitability test people have to pass before they are allowed to become the parent of a human being. If someone is unable to train a dog to walk on a leash, they have no business trying to raise kids. Maybe that's what they're doing with all these dogs. If this is the case, it will be a while before some of these folks get their license to procreate.

Dr. Wilson just left. He is going to have her moved into a regular room today. Her epidural was removed yesterday morning, and the catheter came out this morning. Although she is more sober than 24 hours ago, she is still looped. Somehow though, she often has pulled herself together to discuss her treatment in great lucid detail with people wearing white coats. One resident asked her if she was a physician, when she began talking about the different nerves she has been having trouble with!? The medications have, at the same time, made for some heartrending and hilarious moments.

For four days now I/we have had to deal with both her real and imagined needs. This morning, when she was told it was Sunday, she burst into tears, terribly upset that she had missed another day. At one point yesterday, while I was doing something or other for her and our faces were only a few inches apart, she looked into my eyes and declared, "You're not my husband." Later, she claimed there were two of me.

"Good," I replied. "I hope he's helpful!"

Another time she got "cussin'" mad at me because I was arguing with her about something she wanted to do or thought I should be doing. She "works" a lot while she's sleeping. She is often flat on her back sound asleep and is reaching for things, pushing buttons, or telling someone else to do something. At one point she was helping Matthew with his math and got terribly angry with him over something. I've explained no less than 20 times since yesterday afternoon that Matthew and Celia have gone home. She looks at me, replies with an "Oh" and soon forgets all about it. She often hands me "things" to put away. Watching her eat a popsicle is pretty funny. She can have a half-eaten popsicle only inches away from her mouth and either falls asleep or forgets how to get it to her mouth. When I look over and see her trying to bend her neck to reach her goal, I remind her to move her arm and she returns to eating it normally. What would she do without me?

She has seen a number of cats and rats in the room. She often asks me who is here and swears various people are standing nearby or have just left. Each time this morning that I have handed her a small stuffed dog my mother sent with us, she smiles sweetly and holds it to her chest.

The worst though, has to be some of the dreams. A couple of days ago, when Matthew and I were returning from an excursion about town, I entered the room to hear her sobbing uncontrollably. Apparently, she had just awakened from a disturbing dream about me. Celia declared our timing to be perfect. She has had some bad spasms since surgery, but she has also dreamed that her leg has locked up. She was begging me to "pull down and twist it" to unlock it; no one is going to pull and twist on this knee now! But it was real to her, and I took quite a tongue lashing because I refused to follow her instructions. I will probably endure another when she figures out that I've written about some of the events of the last few days, but there is only so much information that can be left out and still convey something resembling the truth. Besides, some of this stuff is really entertaining. After nearly two decades of marriage, I've become quite accustomed to being in the "doghouse," so another day or two won't make much difference...

A fellow came by the room selling newspapers. I borrowed a nearby cart to carry it on and bought a Sunday New York Times. If you're lucky, it will keep me off the keyboard for a few hours. After that I plan to take a walk along the river. Surely one of these boats could use another crew member, or at least some ballast.

~ **"Woof, Woof" and "Snowed" sending our love from four stories above the River East**

The Knee Gazette

Monday, July 16, 2001

Well, obviously the crew position aboard a yacht did not work out, because I am once again sitting in a chair in a hospital room composing another *Gazette* instead of hanging over the rail of a boat feeding the fish. Miriam has been moved to room 614 and, yes, it has a fine view of the river. Now though, instead of looking across the river, I have a view directly down the river and overlooking FDR Drive.

Miriam seems to have turned the corner. She is better able to handle sobriety than at any time since surgery. She is still enduring more pain than any one person should have to tolerate. There is so little I can do to help with spasms. Prior to surgery, I could apply pressure to certain places around the knee and leg and it seemed to help. But I am not about to start applying pressure to anything near the knee now. They have put her in a new brace that does not squeeze the swollen leg like the last one. They got her up and had her walk to her neighbor's bed. I brought her wheelchair to her room for two reasons: one, so it will no longer be in my room serving as a constant reminder of the ongoing crisis and, two, so it would be here so I can take her for " walks" as soon as they permit it. The best estimate right now for our return home is probably Wednesday.

Last evening, after I had "clocked out," I went to a nearby grocery store to get a bite to eat and returned to the hotel room to enjoy the food. While sprawled out on the sofa in front of the tube, the phone rang. Celia (a.k.a. "Saint Tulia"), was on the phone asking if she could meet us at the airport and help get Miriam home.

During one of her less lucid moments, when Miriam's speech was quite slurred, she called Celia "Tulia." It somehow fit and I added the Saint part, much to "Tulia's" dismay. She has never married, so she has lots of time and energy that is not wasted on some nasty husband fellow. Celia serves folks in need in ways nobody knows. She avoids the limelight and gets ill over almost any accolade. This woman spends a lot of time on weekends cooking food that she delivers to people everywhere. We have enjoyed her culinary generosity for some time. It was perfectly natural in her eyes to volunteer to spend Sunday nights tending to Miriam's needs in order to give me some time off. She has slept (read that: spent the night) on the floor at the foot of Miriam's bed for more than two months now on Sunday nights. When the trip to New York became imminent, in her eyes it was natural for her to use some of her vacation time and come with us. I think "Saint" is an appropriate title for this very private woman who gives so much of herself to other people (she is a nurse by trade). Whenever I came into Miriam's hospital room during Celia's "shift," she was almost always on her feet leaning over Miriam, tending to her legion of needs.

Walking around town with her was quite eye opening for Matthew. He is not accustomed to having his parents stop and talk to anyone pushing a baby carriage or walking a dog. "Congratulations," she gushed to people pushing strollers. "What a pretty dog" was a common greeting to pet owners, no matter how ugly the cur. Few people passed her on the street without a greeting. My son just looked at me in dismay, failing to hide the embarrassment of such a close association

210

with someone so nice. I was pleasantly surprised to return from my late-night visits to the hospital and not find the room full of homeless people that she invited in for the night. She will be upset with me for shedding light on her good deeds, but she has been a Godsend to us and I wanted people to know more about her. Months ago, I told her that one day I hope to simply enjoy the shade from her celestial crown.

~ "Shipmates through life" in search of a calm harbor

Matthew developed a method of summoning cabs that, although unorthodox, was effective. He landed more cabs than all the rest of us put together. When he understood we were ready to hail a cab, he would jump out in front of one and wave his arms. This was, however, much more effective once he learned to tell the difference between a full cab and an empty one!

The Knee Gazette

Tuesday, July 17, 2001

It is an overcast morning both outside and inside room 614. Miriam's pain is keeping her tear ducts flushed and her care-givers busy. When she called the room this morning, Miriam said she hadn't slept much last night. When her leg is not involved in a spasm, she looks good, is able to read some, and can carry on a conversation. When I left last evening, there was concern about her heart rate and low blood pressure. They cross matched a unit of blood just in case a determination was made that she needed it. Soon after I left, they took her for a chest x-ray. As of this morning, her pulse has slowed, her blood pressure has come up some, and they have not given her any blood.

A fender bender just occurred outside my window on an exit to FDR Drive. Two men are not happy with one another; traffic is backing up until they get done gesturing at one another and pull their cars off the road. In Manhattan, stretch limos outnumber pickup trucks, possibly by two to one! In this land, the sedan is king. There are lots of vans and S.U.V.s and, get this, station wagons—go figure...

I feel as though I'm watching the world and life pass by the window. I am getting more and more frustrated. I am ready to get her home. I want to get on with life. I am tired of this never-ending ordeal. Me, mine, and I, do you notice a trend developing? I am getting more and more selfish and resentful. The more insecure and fragile Miriam gets, the more she is uncomfortable when I am not at her side. By necessity, she is dependent upon me; I feel as though I am always on duty. The stress is wearing on both of us. I am ready for her to begin improving; but I know nobody wants her to get better more than she does. She senses my impatience and irritation at her, and it makes her even more insecure, and the vicious cycle only deepens. I cannot imagine enduring the pain this woman has suffered the last three to four years. To suffer hour after hour day after day, for this length of time, with no end in sight, is inhumane. Nor does she know what it is like watching a loved one go through this. She can't stand it if she thinks one of us has a painful hangnail and does everything, she can to fix the problem.

Dr. Wilson is not happy about the level of medication she is on. I am not happy about the intensity of her pain. Miriam goes from hurting really bad, to being too looped to know her own name. I am ready to get her home but would like to avoid the trip! The pain people claim there is nothing more they can do here; their job can be accomplished by her pain doctor at home. Dr. Wilson has rebuilt the knee, so his job is also finished, and he has no tricks up his sleeve to address the pain. Once I get her home, between myself, Matthew, her sister, and the attendants, she will have round-the-clock care and won't have to sit on a bed pan for 30 minutes waiting for someone to get around to getting her off of it. I am trying to get Dr. Wilson to release her so we can come home tomorrow.

We are bailing as fast as we can, but the waves keep washing over our little boat.

~ "The Helmsman" and His Cargo "Precious," Sailing Toward Our Unknown Destiny

The Knee Gazette

Wednesday, July 18, 2001—New York City

Rather than spend another day sitting around the hospital feeling sorry for myself and adding to Miriam's misery, I allowed my quest for adventure to supplant my sense of duty and obligation to the bride. I walked straight out the front door of the Belair building, turned right onto the sidewalk, and began an excursion that lasted more than three hours. Two blocks has been my normal range, simply because most of the restaurants I've written about are that close. Today I set my sights on Central Park.

This was a memorable outing and one that gave me a better feel for the city. As I walked straight up East 71st street, I soon crossed Madison Avenue, then Park Avenue and then Fifth Avenue. I just found out these three legendary streets paralleled one another and were only a block apart. On the other side of Fifth Avenue is Central Park. It rose from the very mortar of the city. Depending on your perspective (whether you're in the park looking out, or out of the park looking in), it is hard to tell whether the park rises from the city, or the city from the park.

I was enthralled by all I saw. Everywhere I turned there seemed to be another fountain, stage, lake, or amphitheater. There were hills, rocky knolls, grassy meadows, historical statues, paved roads, Juniper-lined paths, and dirt trails. There was a great variety of trees and bushes, flowers, and ferns. One pond was reserved exclusively for ducks and remote-controlled model sailboats. Upon another people rowed boats. Central Park is big enough it is possible to lose most of the sounds of the city. If it weren't for an occasional helicopter or siren, one could easily forget they were in the middle of one of the largest cities on the globe.

There was a kaleidoscope of faces to look at. This whole walk was fascinating for a devout people watcher. There were young lovers rowing boats and athletic folks biking or rollerblading along the boulevards. There were young children feeding ducks, old men watching pretty women, and adolescents riding skateboards. There were lots of dogs walking their owners; there were picnics in progress and musicians hoping to have money dropped at their feet. In the center of a small mosaic made of tiles, someone had placed some yellow roses. The vase was simply a two-liter drink bottle with the top cut off, but it was attracting a lot of attention. People were standing beside the flowers to have their photos taken. A group of people from a tour bus walked into the little plaza, took some pictures, and walked back to their bus. It must have been a 30-yard hike! I guess this was their visit to Central Park? A group of Boy Scouts wearing Class A uniforms walked past my perch heading to somewhere out of sight. Lots of nannies and a few mommies were taking their children for walks in the park. Near one fountain a group of people were filming a scene for a movie of some sort.

This was a good outing and provided some needed exercise. I have returned to my perch above the East River and am writing this while enjoying the people, traffic, and boats visible outside Miriam's window. She is having a better day today, and we have made reservations for a midafternoon flight home tomorrow. She has been up some and has walked (with a walker) to the door and back to her bed. Yesterday, I convinced the nursing staff that she needed a bedside commode; after a 30-minute search, one arrived in the room. This relieves her from having to use a bed pan—the designer of which must have never had to use. Since yesterday, every couple of hours, Miriam has mooned FDR Drive and the East River when she uses the bedside potty! So far, it has not caused any accidents that I'm aware of.

Please keep the e-mails rolling in, Miriam has me checking the mailbox several times a day now; emails are the highlight of her day. This should conclude my report from Manhattan. I will attempt to keep you up to date once we return home, but shouldn't put nearly the stress on your mailboxes that I have recently. You all have been very kind. No one has either written and told me to "shut up already" or employed the "block sender" feature on Outlook Express...

Sign us, "The Urban Hiker" and "The Moon Over Manhattan"

CHAPTER 13
Recovering One More Time

The Knee Gazette

Sunday, July 22, 2001

The sights and sounds of the big city have been replaced by a familiar, if not mundane routine at home. Although less stimulating, the familiar trappings are soothing and peaceful. Yesterday afternoon Matthew returned from his latest adventure, so our family is complete again. Since Miriam can recall little about the week in New York, it seemed to her like a long time since she had seen her boy. She was ready for him to come home.

This has been a summer of adventure and diversion for our 12-year-old. Four Saturdays ago, he awoke at a church camp located in Possum Kingdom, South Carolina; two Saturdays ago, he awoke at a Boy Scout Camp located near Rutherfordton, North Carolina; one Saturday ago, he was in Manhattan. Yesterday morning he was in Charlotte, North Carolina with his grandparents. We are still discussing whether he can go to Dalton, Georgia to spend a week with his Uncle Bruce and family.

Matthew has carried a big load since his mom's fall almost four years ago. It is as worn on him as it is on me. I am so glad he has had things going on this summer to direct his attention toward activities and events designed for kids his age. He has spent way too much of his life worrying about and helping with his mom. Although he has shouldered the load admirably, he is ready to get his mom back, or at least as close back, as possible. On another level, there is a connection between the two of them that is unusual and special. Matthew now has a good understanding of what his mom went through as she cared for him during his years of illness, complete with lots of hospital stays and uncertainty.

We have finally got Miriam's "command central" set up yet again. This is the place where she spends her post-surgery recovery period. The room is now set up in a way that would make Martha Stewart proud. Her recliner is backed into a corner and angled slightly toward the windows, TV, and the aquarium. The central fixture in the room, and the one thing that I am certain would bring an approving nod from Ms. Stewart, is the porta-potty sitting right in front of her chair. She will spend most of the next several weeks, day and night, in this chair, so it is important that "her life" be as neatly arranged and in as close proximity as possible.

Overall, I think her condition is slowly improving, at least enough to return a "the glass is half full" perspective to things. It appears to me that the frequency and intensity of the leg spasms have diminished somewhat in the last week or so. Categorical statements or conclusions are hard to make, however, because historically, these patterns run in cycles. About the time we are ready to declare she is doing better, a storm of trouble arrives like a squall line to upend our lives yet again.

Tuesday Morning

Stuff happens in our lives at a pace that eclipses my ability to keep all of you "inquiring minds" informed. Miriam will awake this morning in room 3254 at Altma Hospital. Her knee is apparently infected. When Dr. Robel removed her stitches yesterday morning, he told me he did not like the look of one of the incisions. "If she keeps a fever or this thing starts draining, I will put her in the hospital for treatment." Last evening upon my return from work, she had a small fever and discharge from the area of the incision.

Perhaps I should start a new career as a critic of medical care and facilities; surely, I've enough experience to be qualified for the job...

Mark and Miriam: "Medical Mavens," providing insightful commentary on "Bone Tappers" from coast to coast.

The Knee Gazette

Sunday, July 29, 2001

The red streak that nearly ran over you last night during your periodic pilgrimage to Sam's Club, was there a brunette "driving" the thing who had one leg pointed prominently in the direction of travel and whose hair flew in the direction she had been? That would have been Miriam during her maiden "voyage" in her new electric wheelchair. This was an outing that we had to postpone for nearly a week while she returned to a hospital bed to have an infection in her knee tended to. By Thursday, when Dr. Robel stopped by her room for a visit, he had to endure all her powers of persuasion as she lobbied hard for release. He hung tough and she did not get home until 9:30 Friday night—and then on the condition that she receive I.V. antibiotics twice a day for the next two weeks at home.

The trip to Sam's was my reaction to: "I've been stuck in a hospital room for three weeks now and I'm ready to go somewhere." Why Sam's? Well, it was not because we needed toilet paper; the "lifetime supply" we bought six months ago is still holding up fine. I thought their nice wide aisles would be the perfect place for her to get acquainted with her new mode of transportation. Long ago we got over worrying about what people thought as we have attempted to make the necessary adjustments and still live as normally as possible. During some outings we put on quite a show. When I would push Miriam in a wheelchair while she pushed an orange cart through Home Depot, the only thing missing was a train whistle. When they were available, she often used the scooters many retailers provide for their mobility challenged patrons, but neither their supply nor their function was entirely dependable, so some outings just got scrubbed. During this outing, "the show" started as I got out a six-foot-long ramp and drove her chair out of the side door of the van and parked it beside her door.

She got a prescription for an electric wheelchair after she was evaluated at Shepherd Spinal Center a few weeks back and they determined that her shoulders were not healthy enough to operate a manual chair. She was thrilled with her newfound independence as she motored from one aisle to another, putting things in the cart I was pushing. I had not realized what a blow it had been to her dignity to have to rely on someone to push her around in a wheelchair. It was something I did to facilitate her and did not give it another thought, but she viewed it as one more way she "burdened" us. She has spent a good bit of time in a wheelchair in the last four years. It is so much easier and faster for me to put her in a chair and go, than to watch her clunk around on crutches that were increasingly painful for her to use. I often explained that the chair was a tool to facilitate her life, it did not define her.

Once we figure out the best way to get the powered chair into and out of the van and she becomes more comfortable with its function, it will be an appreciated addition to her life. Even if this latest surgery is a complete success, she will find the wheelchair of benefit for at least the next six months and perhaps on occasion way beyond that, because of the time it will require for her to regain strength in a limb that has atrophied for almost four years. In the meantime, should you see a red electric wheelchair sporting a "student driver" sign on the back, smile, wave, and get out of the way!

~ Mark and the "Red Streak"

Journal

Tuesday, July 31, 2001, 7 a.m.

Tomorrow she will be three weeks post- surgery. Since surgery, I have done all my writing in the *"Knee Gazette."* This recovery has been worse than we expected, and we expected pretty bad. As prior to surgery, most of her current discomfort is nerve related. Apparently, some of the nerves are only now "waking up." She has no feeling in her left foot. You can squeeze her foot, pinch her toes or tickle the bottom and she cannot feel any of it. However, much of her pain is centered on the middle of the foot, way below the surface.

She is "living" in her recliner again. This allows me to sleep through the dreams and when I am needed, she can tap on the wall; I'm just on the other side, sleeping with one ear "tuned" to her "frequency." Celia was here Sunday night, though I do not think she got much sleep, as there was a lot of screaming from spasms that came through the wall. Last night Matthew spent the night in the recliner beside his mom's; it was his turn to help her to her potty and help with her toes. I have some driving to do today and had to get a good night's sleep. Tonight, an attendant will take over. I am weary from the day in day out strain of her care and our situation. I have missed a lot of work in the past month and worry that my job is in serious jeopardy. There was a mix-up at Oconee Health Care yesterday, and the attendant was almost three hours late, causing me to miss more work.

Her overall condition continues to deteriorate. Her shoulders are so bad she cannot even work the lever on the recliner that raises and lowers the leg rest! She sleeps with the Tens unit connected to her shoulder; a heating pad is alternated between her right shoulder and her left leg. She is heavily medicated most of the time and, of course, still has the Spinal Cord Stimulator on its highest setting.

Miriam's pain is as bad as it has ever been. During her time in the Step-down unit at the Hospital for Special Surgery (which is a post-surgical ICU unit with a capacity of four beds), her roommates seldom slept because of her shrieks of pain. Her roommates came and left for normal rooms, while she just stayed put for several days while they waited for her to stabilize before sending her to a room. After their experience with Miriam as a roommate, more than one chose the option of spending the additional $300 per night for a private room! Several of them told me they had begged nurses "to do something for that poor woman" during the night!

After taking a couple of weeks off, her spasms are growing both in frequency and intensity. Every few minutes, I stop writing and bend her toes one way or the other to help relieve the cramp that has gripped some part of her left leg, causing her to holler out in agony and often producing a flow of tears. This may be an indication that the nerves are waking up or are beginning to heal, which would be a good thing, I think. Hopefully, it is not the tip of another iceberg attempting to sink her nearly indomitable spirit.

Last evening after supper was complete and the scorching sun began to lean on the western horizon, I took her outside so she could cruise around the neighborhood on her new powered chair. It did her good to get out. Our lives are wholly centered around her knee and her health. When I am not at work or on a Scout outing, I am sleeping fitfully or engaged in some aspect of her care either directly or indirectly such as making improvements to the house to better facilitate her needs or documenting details of the on-going crisis for posterity. We often wonder if this will ever end.

Journal

1 a.m., Thursday morning, August 2, 2001

I am not sleeping. I sent Matthew to bed. I lay on the other side of the wall and listened to Miriam scream for help three times in the last hour; Matthew sleeps soundly and could not be awakened. The boy has been helping his mom to the bathroom, doing his own laundry and a lot of the cooking since he was eight. He should not also have to sit up with her all night too.

She had an attendant last night, so both Matthew and I slept well. It looks like the sleep "banked" last night will be spent tonight. We have been approved for two nights per month of attendant care but did not use any in June in order to carry them over into July and use them for the expected post-surgical difficulty. Last week she was in the hospital, so we did not need them.

I don't know what we are going to have to do in order to regain a grasp on life. The leg shows no sign of improvement. We are asking the same questions I am sure the E/I would like answers to: what is it going to take to get this woman better and back on her feet?

We are angry but do not know with whom or where to direct the venom. The E/I has been good for the most part about paying for medical treatment and purchasing equipment to help provide for her care; the legion of doctors and medical professionals have done their best, so it is not anyone's fault, but we are still angry. We are fighting a legal battle over her benefits and are trying to get some compensation for the attendant care I have provided during this disaster. I am not surprised they are balking and trying to wiggle free of these expenses!

I often direct anger toward Miriam because she is convenient, not because she is a justifiable target. I am angry and need to vent it somewhere. Last week when she was receiving treatment for the infection at ALTMA HOSPITAL, I could only shake my head as I walked along over floors that shone so brilliantly that I could almost comb my hair while looking down at my reflection. There, those damn floors, that was something toward which I could direct anger! Somehow, I do not think they would care. Besides, being mad at inanimate objects is not as much fun. The shiny floors just seem to mock us. "I won, you lost." In the "playhouse" between my ears, I hear a public address announcement at the hospital: "Security needed on the third floor. Bring a big jacket with long arms. We have a large man stomping on the floor that needs to be escorted to the psych ward."

We find ourselves watching the Travel Channel a lot—dreaming about visiting exotic places where surgery and hospital rooms are not part of the trip. Call this cheap therapy.

What does the future hold? How much longer can we individually and collectively endure this nightmare and retain a shred of sanity?

Journal

Sunday, August 5, 2001

Friday morning, she had an early appointment with Dr. Robel. Later in the day Stacy Casey was coming with a lady from Shepherd Spinal to evaluate the house for accessibility. Dr. Robel sent her to St. Mary's Hospital to get a Doppler vascular study done of her left leg immediately after he saw her. The leg had demonstrated a tendency this week to turn purple on occasion and he wanted to check for blood clots.

Her incision looks good, but Dr. Robel wants to keep her on the IV antibiotics for at least two more weeks and perhaps longer. He admitted Friday that the infection scared him. He was pleased with how tight the knee felt to him. He had no answers concerning the spasms other than to hope they get better over time.

I understand this approach; it's the same one that Dr. Wilson is using. They are both hoping time will provide healing and resolution. This is understandable, especially when they are out of treatment options, but they are not the one writhing in agony every few minutes when one of the "bad storms" settles in for several hours, usually shortly after midnight. Nor do they have to watch it, try to "treat" it, or attempt to function the next day in a mind-numbed, sleep-deprived state. We are desperate. Miriam is ready to talk to Dr. Edwards again about killing the nerve. She has been taking Zanaflex and Dilauded than has been prescribed but is seeking relief from the current reality.

The evaluation of our home went well. Their ideas were similar to mine until they brought up the possible installation of a track system not unlike what is used in packing houses to move sides of beef—a track installed to the ceiling of the home that allows the mobility challenged to ride in a sling (instead of on a meat hook) to get from one room to another, or into a bathroom that is not able to accommodate a wheelchair. The idea of a track system running all around our home is not appealing, especially when I think there are better alternatives for the house that will better serve Miriam and the rest of us (we still live here too).

The dilemma they face is one I understand and appreciate. From the E/I's position, why would they write a check to alter our home when they have just "bought" her a new knee, for the fourth time? It would be much easier and cheaper to get a couple of ramps, a few grab bars, and a track system now and wait and see how she progresses during the next few months. I think the track would not be good for Miriam's mental well- being. She already feels terrible about the strain and burden she has put on her family. The house is already so full of her equipment that we cannot get to the front door. To now alter the appearance and turn it into something resembling a butcher shop, would not, I think, be a good thing.

The Knee Gazette

Sunday, August 5, 2001

Wellll… the electric wheelchair is patiently parked in the front hall waiting for its "pilot" to feel like taking it out for another spin. The news from the knee front is not very rosy at present, I'm sorry to report. The path to the top of our mountain seems to have gotten a lot steeper this week.

The nerves in the afflicted leg continue their recovery from the latest surgery; they are angry, have attitudes, and are making their presence known! The spasms I wrote about a while back as having "grown less frequent and less intense," have reversed the pleasant trend and are keeping us caregivers busy at times. Wednesday night became four o'clock Thursday morning before her leg calmed down enough so I could sleep. Friday night it took until three thirty; Saturday it was three. A state of exhaustion does not come close to describing my condition.

I do not mean to imply that Miriam is having constant spasms, but one every few minutes or even every 20 minutes, hour after hour, is enough to demolish any chances of getting real sleep. Grabbing her foot and bending the toes in whatever direction she nods, will usually cause the spasm to let go. I am very thankful for the three nights this last week when someone else cared for her while I slept. Celia (a.k.a. "St. Tulia") will be here tonight, so perhaps I will get another night of sleep.

Dr. Robel saw Miriam Friday morning and is pleased at how tight the joint is. None of her physicians have ever seen an affliction quite like these spasms, are very puzzled by them, and are clueless about how to address them. Dr. Wilson saw one while he was preparing her for surgery, was quite amazed by the spectacle, but summoned me to deal with it. Her physical therapist witnessed one during one of her treatments several weeks ago and got bug-eyed as he tried to tell Dr. Robel about it. Her knee has not locked up since surgery, and for this, we are very thankful, but the "leg-shaking-cramping spasms" are growing in frequency and intensity. I suspect this is what they call Reflex Sympathetic Dystrophy, or RSD. The more recent title for the sensory nerves trying to take over motor function is Complex Regional Pain Syndrome.

I have been "rifted" (reduction in force) out of the job that I had held since selling my failed flooring business almost two years ago. I was summoned to the boss's office, and after he closed the door and we exchanged superficial chit-chat, the purpose of the meeting was revealed.

"It is certainly not performance related, but purely an economic decision that has become necessary as we search for a way to survive as a company. Here's two week's pay; we wish for nothing but your future success," said the man now sitting in the position I once held.

The only surprise for me was how long they had waited to cut me loose. The "handwriting on the wall" had been pretty clear to me for several months, so I was prepared when it actually happened. Miriam was not prepared and took the news pretty hard; Matthew asked me how soon I would begin searching for another job and then went about his business. I tried to reassure my dear bride that because we live frugally and have saved everything possible, we are not yet broke and are not presently in dire straits.

"I'm sure there will be long line of prospective employers eager to hire someone getting four hours of sleep per night and who is likely, at any time, to have to take off and take his wife to another doctor somewhere. I will begin 'interviewing with them' very soon," I assured her.

Seriously, compared to the life and death struggle we fought for most of the first two thirds of Matthew's life with his health and the crisis we are facing with the "knee from hell," the loss of a job is a rather small ripple on the pond.

~ Mark, Miriam, and Matthew, scaling the vertical faces of "Mt. Life"

Journal

Monday, August 6, 2001

Celia stayed with Miriam last night while I slept for eight solid hours. She kept a log of how many times her assistance was required, as well as the problem she helped with:

- 11:00 foot
- 11:26 take to toilet
- 11:54 foot
- 12:22 foot and leg
- 1:08 foot
- 1:52 knee
- 2:16 knee
- 2:38 foot
- 2:57 foot
- 2:58 foot
- 3:33 knee
- 3:36 knee pain
- 3:38 foot spasm and knee pain cont.
- 3:50 toe spasm

- 3:55 toe spasm

- 4:00 foot and arch

- 4:24 foot and put padding in brace

Celia said that after this, Miriam settled down, and they both slept.

Journal

Wednesday, August 8, 2001

I have been working on cleaning out my office. This process is the final step in the failure of my business. The finality of it all is coming home. All the office decorations, pictures, and art that made my office and conference room "mine" are now irrelevant and are being packed up. I have no idea where it is all going to go, I won't need an office to return to a shop to make furniture. There sure is no need for conference room stuff. As part of the process, I have been sorting through files and faxes. They all tell small parts of the story, like pieces of a puzzle scattered about on a table.

My fall from grace has been gradual, thanks to the men who purchased my company out of bankruptcy and then gave me a job. One day, I had the big office with the private bathroom, the title of president, and owned the majority of the stock in Heritage Flooring. After the bankruptcy, I became an employee of Lake Oconee Flooring and lost my title and position as a shareholder but kept many of the "trappings of power"—the nice office. It was a year later before I relinquished the office and moved into one of much more modest size. Only now am I having to clean it out? So, this has not been a sudden and precipitous fall from the top to the bottom, I've had time to make adjustments along the way.

Even this is about as gentle as it could be; the furniture shop and showroom will stay in its present location, at least for now. There is a finality to cleaning out the office. It does herald the end of my short career in the wood flooring business.

Letter to Case manager Stacy Casey

August 10, 2001

A "new project" for you to direct your considerable talents toward:

Dr. Edwards today wrote a prescription for a long-term epidural. He calls it a "Tunneled Epidural Catheter," for temporary infusion of local anesthetic/narcotics." This is a procedure he can perform in his office once it has been approved. I have the prescription and will fax it upon your instructions.

This is designed to deaden the left leg (it may also get the right one, too) which we hope will allow the needed healing to take place without the trauma that the spasms may be inflicting on the new grafts. Of course, the immediate benefit we are pursuing is relief of this hideous pain.

By the way, during our conversation, I asked him point blank if, "he was thinking RSD might be a factor here." He replied, "That's what I'm thinking, but hoping it is related to the surgery and that once healing is complete, these symptoms will diminish." We share this hope!

One more thing Miriam wanted me to bring to your attention. Her chair, the one I bought for her right after her first surgery and that you were gracious enough to reimburse us for, is wearing out. I have made some structural repairs that are doing fine, but wife reports the padding "ain't where it once were no mo." Since she eats, sleeps and lives in this chair (for a lot of the last four years), I suppose the "paddin'" is pretty important. Should we try to get this one reupholstered, or would you prefer we search for another?

Thanks for all of your help,

Mark

The Knee Gazette

Wednesday, August 15, 2001

No, I've not procured any other employment; I have a job (two really, if you count caring for wife whenever an attendant is not with her), but thanks for asking. For now, I am filling my days with the outdoor furniture business that I started several years before starting the flooring plant. The furniture business was never more than a one- or two-man operation that I continued to run while operating the flooring plant. Now that my flooring business is gone, I am once again working full time making furniture and caring for Miriam.

Speaking of wife, she is sitting beside me in her chair. She has her IV antibiotic flowing in one arm and the epidural narcotics are flowing into the epidural that was implanted into her spine this afternoon. She has a Tens unit sending electrical pulses through her hurting left shoulder. The epidural is loaded with pain killers and muscle relaxants. Evidently, she is a very sensitive woman, because she can still feel pain despite all these efforts to block it!

Saturday Morning

In your subconscious, listen to Willie Nelson's classic "On the Road Again," while you read the lyrics "Uncle Willie" would have composed had he lived in our house:

To the Doc we go, goin' to see another Doc again.

Sometimes we take a plane, been known to use a train.

Seekin' help for the wife, we're off to see the Doc again.

Last Friday, I took her to Demorest so the pain doctor could talk about installing the epidural. Tuesday, I took the van to Atlanta to get a wheelchair tie-down thing installed; Wednesday, I took her back to Demorest (an hour and a half north of here) to get the epidural put in. On Monday, I am to have her back in Demorest for an 8:30 appointment, when we will no doubt discuss what possibly led to her ambulance ride on Friday (details to follow). I actually did productive work on Thursday!

The burden of all this must be showing on my face in spite of my best efforts to project a positive and upbeat demeanor. Matthew keeps asking me if I'm mad about something. Why is it so hard to fool kids? I am sure the uncertainty of Mom's health and our finances probably does furrow the forehead from time to time. My greatest frustration, though, is Miriam's continuing agony. I am certainly tired of the inconvenience of having to empty the porta-potty, to move her from place to place in a wheelchair, having to tend to her every need, as well as the sleep deprived nights, but all this pales compared to watching her suffer. I feel so helpless. I can adjust the pillows; I can keep fresh batteries in her Tens unit, and I can keep her cup of water fresh and full, but there is nothing I can do to relieve her hurting.

~ **Mark and Miriam, Swinging From "Mt. Life" by Fraying Ropes**

Journal

August 16, 2001

Miriam's care is very demanding on those of us committed to delivering it. There are times, even when an attendant is present, that the attendant, Matthew, and I will all be doing something different that is directly related to her care. She does not want it this way, she nearly burst into tears one day last weekend when she told me that she cannot even pick out her own underwear for herself, let alone organize her kitchen and house. In her most lucid moments, she pays bills with the help of this trusty but ailing laptop (one of the hinges has broken, it is out of warranty, and we cannot afford the time and cost to send it for repairs). Much of the time, she simply sits in her chair. She reads if her mind is clear enough and she is not seeing double. Often, she sleeps or talks incoherently while waving her arms around as she 'works" in her sleep.

Her antibiotic must be taken out of the fridge two hours before she gets her dose. This goes into the PICC line that is implanted on the upper part of her right arm. The catheter goes all the way to a vessel beside her heart. This antibiotic is so caustic that to minimize the damage to the vessels, it enters the bloodstream at a place where there is lots of blood flow. The epidural comes out of her back on her right cheek almost directly opposite the generator for the spinal cord stimulator that is implanted in the left cheek. The epidural is permanently attached to a fanny-pack sized black bag that contains the cocktail of medications and the battery powered infusion pump. This goes wherever she goes, until the epidural is removed.

I want to go to Dalton this weekend to see my brother and to get Matthew's eyes checked. He needs new glasses, as his old ones broke just in time for the first day of school. Is she up to the trip? If not, who will I get to stay with her? Our attendant care covers five days and one night per week; the rest of the time, it is up to me. It really galls me that I must appear before the hospital's attorney in two weeks and explain to them why I am entitled to compensation for the time I spend caring for her... by my count, there are 168 hours in every week. The most I have ever had the benefit of an attendant is 78, and this was only for one week since this last surgery. According to my math, that still leaves 90 hours for me/Matthew/friends/relatives to cover in order to provide the care she currently requires, which is still six more than the law allows family members to be compensated for.

In a little while, after the antibiotic is finished dripping in, I will gather her stuff together and move her into the bedroom for the night. This will require no less than three trips! Then it will take several minutes to get her situated in the bed before I collapse beside her.

Journal

Saturday, August 18, 2001

"A new crisis at every turn" will be emblazoned on a flag I'll have made to fly prominently over the front door of our home. An ambulance was called to take Miriam to the ER because she had become over medicated (due to the drugs entering her system from the tunneled epidural,) and could not be aroused by the attendant or later by the RN who came to change the dressing on her PICC line. They called me at the shop and told me what was going on and that an ambulance had been called. By the time I caught up with her, she looked fine and was ready to go home, although she was already hurting from the effects of the reaction to Nar-can, which was administered to counter the effects of the narcotics. This lovely little drug apparently sent spasms through her whole body. This morning she reports aching joints and muscles in places that don't usually hurt. The poor woman cannot get a break! She finally feels no pain, and then she is administered more drugs that cause their own form of spasms...

On Wednesday, before we left Dr. Edwards' office, I asked him specifically about the oral meds and Fentanyl patch regimen and if he wanted anything changed with the addition of the epidural. His reply: "No, not yet -call me on Friday and we will talk about it." In a nutshell, she was overdosed. When I finally got his nurse on the phone (he was standing beside her, because I could hear her talking to him, but he did not bother to pick up the phone himself), their instructions sounded as ridiculous in the other extreme as they did on Wednesday: "Take her off all the meds except Dilauded for the weekend." So, the epidural meds were removed, and she was sent home. I asked Dr. Edwards' nurse about withdrawal: "It could be a rough weekend," she replied. "We want to see her at 8:30 Monday morning (in Demorest), and then we will talk about restarting it."

I did not graduate from medical school, but I was born with some common sense. What they have had us doing with her medications this week defied reason. If I had not taken it upon myself to reduce the oral meds, she could have gotten a lot worse sooner. It is easy for "the deity in Demorest" to talk about a rough weekend; he does not have to see her through it. I will once again employ my common sense and try to give her enough medication to keep her as comfortable as possible and minimize the withdrawal symptoms. Monday I will miss more work taking her to yet another doctor's appointment.

The Knee Gazette

August 24, 2001

"What's that?" Miriam asked.

"I'm not sure, but it hurts my eyes," I replied. Then I asked: "Could it be a sliver of light piercing darkness in our tunnel? Maybe that's why we don't recognize it, we're not used to anything but an echo down here in this dark pit."

Poorly metaphored, but perhaps I can add some illumination...

I ended the last, rather gloomy issue by promising to "deliver some good news when some dropped by for a visit." In the spirit of keeping my word, I am compelled to assault my very patient readers with additional verbiage.

This week began in Demorest, at the office of pain doctor Edwards, bright and early Monday morning. After sending Miriam with a nurse to prepare for his exam under x-ray, Dr. Edwards came into the room where I was waiting and closed the door. After sliding up onto the exam table, he looked at me and began talking:

"I have to look you in the eye and tell you that her overdose on Friday was my fault."

I probably turned around, then looked under the chair and behind the exam table searching for another source for the sound I had just heard. It could not after all have come from the man in the white coat sitting in front of me with his lips moving. I am not accustomed to doctors admitting their mistakes, even in a case this obvious. I behaved myself, as Miriam had been "strongly encouraging" me to do ever since I brought her home from the hospital on Friday. I refrained from jumping out of the chair, grabbing his pencil-sized neck and... no, considering he nearly killed my wife, I behaved rather well, I think.

He discussed the new plan of attack and restarted the pump for the epidural. When we left his office this time, we took with us some instructions that made sense, even to my feebly educated mind. By Monday evening, she declared her leg to be mostly numb. The spasms, although still occurring, were less severe and more infrequent. She retained control of her bladder — another good thing!

Monday night really told the story, she/we slept! She slept like I've not seen her sleep in a long, long time. I will have to spend the weekend repairing the windows because her snoring rattled the windowpanes so hard it shook all of the glazing loose, but let her sleep! Finally, at about 3:30, I decided I had better be sure I could arouse her and see if her bladder needed some relief. She soon returned to her prior state of advanced slumber. Not quite sure how to act or what to do without a middle-of-the-night crisis to tend to, so I joined her.

Tuesday night went well, too. Wednesday night was a little rougher, but compared to where we've been, this, too, felt like calm water. Please understand this does not mean she is living free of pain, she's not. There are still times when she hurts so bad that her cheeks resemble small streams of tears running down them, but things are better. She has been able to come off some of the oral medications and, in the process, has sobered up a good bit. She can carry on a conversation now and recall it an hour or even a day from now—a welcomed change for the husband who has been accused frequently of not telling her anything.

Now Sunday evening, we just returned from a one-night trip to see my brother and family in Dalton, GA. Miriam did well. She travels lying down on the back seat of the van. Surrounded by pillows and with the rear a/c vent pointed on her, she is able to be fairly comfortable. We are easy to spot on the road; ours is the van with the porta-potty plainly visible through the back window and a wheelchair parked just inside the side door. It was good to see our loved ones, and the change of scenery was good for Miriam.

~ Mark and Miriam, resting at last!

Journal

August 29, 2001

This is the eve before I am to be deposed by ALTMA HOSPITAL's attorney concerning my pursuit of compensation for attendant care. I have been reading back over some of my journals and Knee Gazettes to refresh my memory in preparation. It is good we can forget. Otherwise, we would be wallowing in a cesspool of self-pity.

Life at our house is more stable at present than it has been for a long, long time. Mostly, this means we are sleeping. Sleep blessed sleep! Miriam's countenance is beginning to resemble the woman I married. The epidural is working! When they restarted it on the 20th, after Dr. Edwards repositioned it slightly, it began to numb her leg and one "cheek," but thankfully missed her bladder. She is still experiencing spasms from time to time (several a day) but is getting some relief from the constant relentless pain. This has allowed her to cut substantially her intake of oral medications and to have less mental fog than usual.

Dr. Robel is pleased with the way the knee looks and feels. Today marks the 7th week since surgery, only five more to go until Dr. Wilson wants her to put weight on it. From where I sit, I am not optimistic about her walking any time soon. The epidural is covering up and masking the pain, not curing it. At present, although the sole of her foot is numb, if anything so much as brushes against it, she feels enormous pain. Brushing against it is a long way from putting weight on it. I think we may face a situation where her leg is structurally repaired, but the resulting nerve damage may render her wheelchair bound. I hope I'm wrong, but the present trend makes this a possibility.

Journal

Sunday, September 9, 2001

This past week could have been more encouraging. Three out of the last six nights have been eventful, but not terrible, just bad enough to make the night's sleep marginal instead of good. Friday, on the way home from Greensboro, I pulled into the recreation area and took a nap before driving the rest of the way home. Although it is only a 30-minute drive, it is not unusual to need a nap along the way. Fatigue sometimes reaches a point where it cannot be ignored.

Miriam is progressing little at present. This week she saw Dr. Edwards on Thursday afternoon, Dr. Robel on Friday morning, and had physical therapy on Thursday morning. Henry is beginning to turn up the level of activity and put her leg into serious rehabilitation mode. This additional level of activity and stress has contributed to her discomfort. Whatever the cause, it seems that her course of late is charted through choppier seas than she enjoyed for a couple of weeks. The spasm activity is once again increasing, which has helped to elevate her overall level of misery.

While taking Miriam out of the house for an outing, the wheelchair dropped out of our door as it was negotiated down two small steps leading from the kitchen to the garage. This was rough enough that it bruised the area around the spinal cord stimulator box in her left cheek. In retrospect, this "bump" was a disaster. It caused another hospitalization and probably broke the lead in her back for her spinal cord stimulator. At the time, Miriam reported that "the coverage does not seem to be as good as it was."

She was understating the problem. We think this is when the spinal cord stimulator damaged the nerves leading to her bladder and eventually required her to have a supra-pubic catheter. The spinal cord stimulator never really worked after this. It turned out to be another promising ray of hope that was snuffed out by her all-consuming malady.

After all this time, there should be a ramp there anyway; this problem, and no telling how many more in the future, could have been avoided. So far, all the modifications done to this house to accommodate her needs have been done by me, with no help from the E/I. Ramps are simply one of many things I have yet to get around to.

Dr. Robel was pleased with the structural integrity of the joint, but he is deeply concerned about the continuing numbness on the sole of her foot this many weeks post-surgery. Dr. Edwards explained that the epidural can only stay in about three months before the body's white cells shut off the tube responsible for the smile on Miriam's face. "The plan" is to allow this thing to run full throttle for another five weeks while Henry pursues aggressive physical therapy, then slowly reduce the medication over the last month and see how she responds. Once it is determined that she needs the benefits of the epidural to function, he will pursue a permanent implantation of an epidural pump device that is wholly contained within her abdomen and can be refilled when the need arises.

She is now comfortably situated in her chair, not too far from mine. The heating pad lays on her lap, the heater in the chair is on, the massage function of the chair is on, the pillows are placed under and behind her to fill in for the chair's sagging upholstery, and the leg is propped up "just so." She is fine until a heel spasm interrupts the tapping on the keyboard and the rustling of the newspaper. I press on the left heel according to the directions issued and bend the toes in the direction I'm told, and soon the spasm lets go, and our routine is resumed. This is our life, small slices of normalcy seasoned by moments of intense crisis.

Miriam works hard to engage in activities that would help to distract her from the pain. I contribute by feeding birds outside her window and helping with an aquarium that sits near her chair. The time came when she began asking for a lap dog. Keep in mind that we had at least one, and usually two golden retrievers at the house, but she wanted one that could be inside and sit in her lap. She thought playing with the dog's fur and ears would also help distract her from her pain. Missy was a Pekinese Yorkie mix with brown eyes that resembled M&Ms. She had a brown coat and ears that flopped two-thirds of the way toward the tips. The prominent feature on her face was a snaggle tooth and a short nose that looked like it quit growing too soon. So ugly she was cute would be a fair characterization. She weighed about three pounds when she moved in and grew to an astonishing five or six by the time she reached adulthood.

Miriam and Missy soon became inseparable, and the dog truly became Miriam's therapy dog. The dog schooled herself on Miriam's needs and did her best to tend to the ones she could. If Miriam needed help and no one was nearby, Missy went and found someone and barked until they followed her to Miriam. It was good for me that Miriam was never forced to choose between me or the dog because I'm pretty sure I know who would have needed the doghouse. Missy shared Miriam's bed all those years when I didn't, so she was far more useful than was I.

CHAPTER 14
More Crisis and Disappointment

The Knee Gazette

Monday, September 10, 2001

There are some good things about staying in the hospital:

- The doctors come to see the patient.

- Room service

- People come to see us.

- Housekeeping is provided.

- Someone else is primarily responsible for Miriam's care.

- One can take a ride simply by playing with the adjustable bed.

- Rooms sometimes have a view.

- No telemarketing phone calls.

- Someone else empties the bedside commode.

But there are some bad things about staying in the hospital:

- There is probably some undesirable malady that has sent you there.

- The whole family is not together.

- Hospital food…

- Can't bring your own bed.

- Hospital gowns.

- The doctor's bedside manner is not always pleasant.

- The mattress has a plastic cover.

- The nurse may be having a bad day, week, or life.

- People bother you while you are trying to sleep.

Journal

Monday, September 10, 2001, 8:30 a.m.

I spent the night on a cot beside Miriam's hospital bed in room 3254 at Altma Hospital. Yesterday morning, Miriam complained of a headache and fever, which are two things we were told to watch for that could signal a problem with the epidural. By 11, the temperature had crossed the threshold that Dr. Edwards had established as needing to see someone. By early afternoon, she was in a room in the ER. By four, she had been admitted. The concern is the possibility of meningitis.

The epidural is keeping her leg numb and the spasms manageable.

The physicians have paraded through. Dr. Hayes (ACL #2) was on call yesterday and admitted her; someone from anesthesiology came in the room, declared having no knowledge of these types of epidurals, and left. Dr. Cook, a neurosurgeon, was then called in to consult on the case. He arrived around 9 p.m. and spoke of some of the dangers associated with epidurals and spinal cord stimulators. He was abrupt, matter-of-fact, and upset Miriam terribly. Without knowing or understanding the pilgrimage made to arrive at this point, he simply declared that the epidural should be pulled and the SCS removed, and the consequences then suffered. In my view it is irresponsible for him to make such a suggestion without offering any alternative. Miriam asked him if he would provide her with a gun.

His reply was, "I would rather have my wife walking around with an occasional tear in her eye than have her bound to a wheelchair and have to change her diapers."

To which I responded, "Being wheelchair-bound and free of pain would allow her to have a life; she has no life writhing in agony." He just looked at me, apologized for upsetting us, and left.

Dr. Robel came in this morning. He is not sure what to do for her. He talked with Dr. Edwards, who apparently has no privileges at ALTMA HOSPITAL. Dr. Edwards told him to get a CAT scan and, if the epidural is not abscessed, the epidural can stay in. He told Dr. Robel that he had hoped to leave the epidural in another two weeks, instead of the two months he told Miriam on Thursday.

Once again, our lives and Miriam's case is shrouded in uncertainty. I am missing more work in order to be around for the decision-making process. This is part of the cost of being "the common denominator" in her case and for loving someone so deeply.

Journal

Tuesday, September 11, 2001

I am beside myself with frustration and anger. Dr. Robel came a while ago and removed the only relief Miriam has enjoyed in a long, long time. The CT scan revealed some extra fluid around the site of the epidural, so the understandable precaution was taken to remove the catheter. Miriam's back is unhappy, and I am kept busy moving her around to find a position that makes it happy. I have provided her with some relief from the stash of medications I brought from home. None of the doctors here are comfortable with the level of meds she is accustomed to, but I will not allow her to simply writhe in agony if a solution is available. She will soon return to the land of dulled-senses and diminished-mental-capacity. The blessed numbness in her leg will wear off, and we will once again be fighting that pain too, I fear. I do not revel in this role of being a drug pusher but have become one in order to help Miriam survive and, of course, for my own selfishness; I must sleep sometime.

I am missing more work. The attendant will not be here today, so it will be up to me to provide Miriam's detailed care, monitor her drugs, and help Dr. Robel formulate a strategy for the near future. There is news on the television from New York about a plane crashing into the World Trade Center...

The Knee Gazette

Wednesday, September 12, 2001

The epidural responsible for the glimmer of light in our tunnel was removed yesterday morning. An abscess developed around the epidural catheter. A culture of the catheter grew something, but it was too early to tell what nasty organism it was. Miriam's numb leg has been growing less numb by the hour. She has returned to a mind-numbing oral drug regimen that is, once again, keeping her fogged in.

Along with the rest of America, we spent yesterday riveted to the television, staring in disbelief at the events unfolding in New York, Pennsylvania, and Washington. Matthew and I will cherish even more the memories of our visit to the top of the World Trade Center, only eight weeks ago. I cannot believe those magnificent towers are gone. The place was cavernous. During our visit we had to stand in line more than 30 minutes, along with other tourists, waiting for our turn to take one of the non-stop, high-speed elevators to the observation deck. What a view! What a structure! The dominant feature on Manhattan's skyline probably served as the backdrop for thousands of photos taken every day. Although I've watched the film nearly 50 times, I cannot believe they are no more. I am thankful that Miriam's surgery was two months ago and that our protracted ordeal was not made worse by our presence in New York during this most difficult and horrific time.

Dr. Robel told Miriam this morning that if her fever stays down for 24 hours, she can go home on Friday.

Thursday evening

A bacterial strain of meningitis was cultured from the tip of Miriam's epidural catheter. Certainly, the early attention she received helped minimize the effects of this bug. Her fevers have continued to moderate, so she looks much better, except for the fact that her face is mostly wadded up in agony. The nerves in her leg did not forget how to report pain during the month they were numb; her smile exists once again only in my memory. Maybe we can go home tomorrow.

~ Sign Us: Mark and Miriam, One Bum Leg, and Two Heavy Hearts

Journal

Sunday, September 30, 2001

Yesterday, while basking in the pleasure of sitting alone in a boat on a pond with a fishing pole, I was alone with my thoughts for a while.

Angry! Four years ago, I would not have been out here without my mate. She is passionate about fishing, and it has been a shared pleasure since our first date. We got to know one another while sitting on opposite ends of a 10' aluminum rowboat. On this gorgeous fall morning I am fishing while my partner attempts to keep the pain at bay by staying as still as possible.

My focus is drawn back to the pond as the wind carries laughter across the water. Matthew and his grandfather are picking at one another about something and, generally, having a good time. "Boy Wonderful" could not wait to get into the boat and work the oars, but the novelty wore off after the fourth trip against the wind for the full length of the pond. The wind was blowing briskly, so he simply rowed to the windward end of the pond, and we would "sail" to the far end. When he realized Dad was using him as a trolling motor, he decided maybe he had rowed enough and wanted to go fish with Grandpa, which is how I arrived at my time of solitude. It is so good to watch Dad and Matthew together; what fantastic grandparents I gave my son!

Journal

Wednesday, October 3, 2001

Maybe I can finally begin my work week today. Monday, I took Miriam to Dr. Robel's and then waited around the house for a guy to come measure for wheelchair ramps. After he left, I took Miriam recliner shopping. While she looked at chairs, I took a nap in one. Which is an indication of the level of my fatigue. Yesterday, I took her to Demorest to see Dr. Edwards for a midday appointment, from which we arrived home at about 3:30. When decisions need to be made, I make every attempt to be present. When an appointment is regularly scheduled and expected to be routine, I do not mind letting the attendant take her, but given her worsening nerve condition, I did not consider these appointments routine.

Dr. Robel had talked recently with a representative of the E/I named Cindy Harris about Miriam. He told her: "If all of the complications from all of my patients from the last 21 years were put together, they probably add up to what Miriam has experienced."

I have been totally exhausted. Miriam has not been sleeping well. When she sleeps, she dreams and must be comforted and calmed down, even if she is not having a spasm. Celia called and offered to come last night, this allowed me to go to bed and not worry about my bride. I was asleep when Celia arrived and was still sleeping when she left this morning! An attendant is scheduled for tonight, so I could put at least two decent nights of sleep back-to-back.

Journal

Friday, October 5, 2001

We received our first email from Dr. Wilson since the Sept 11 disaster. He is ok, but he lost several patients and has been treating several minor injuries sustained by relief workers.

Sunday, October 7, 2001

Wellll, the nausea demon has resurfaced; this time having managed to morph itself into a strain that offers the afflicted almost no warning of the impending attack. Last evening, while enroute to a nephew's wedding, Miriam spewed all over the dash of the car and on my pants. On the way home from same, she deposited the reception food into a bag that we managed to get in front of her. Matthew and I were helpless to do anything to address the urine she could not help soaking the seat with during each episode.

Yesterday, she wanted to go to the Watkinsville Fall Festival, an event she missed last year and struggled around on crutches the year before that. Once I got "The Red Streak" unloaded from the van and got her buckled into it, she took off and had a grand time. This chair gives her a level of independence that she has missed for some time. It performs well on uneven ground, and with the suspension system and foam filled tires, delivers as good of a ride as is possible.

Journal

Wednesday, October 10, 2001

Miriam is not doing well. This morning she is hammered after having taken enough drugs to allow her to sleep. Last night after I got her out of the spa, I put her stuff beside her bed and came out to watch television while she went to sleep. Several times I ran to the bedroom to help with a spasm. Her foot was paining her so much that she sobbed uncontrollably for some time. When I came to bed, she asked me to chamber a bullet. We talked for a while. She thinks Matthew would be better off without her; I assured her otherwise. She is so weary of the unrelenting pain. She is tired of not being able to cook in her own kitchen, take a bath by herself, or even transport herself from one end of her house to another. This state of total dependence is bad enough but knowing how much additional work she creates for everyone around her is really getting her down.

My latest letter to attorney Fred got some desired results. He called Miriam on Monday and reminded her that this was her case and not mine. Translated, that means he has grown weary of my letters- to which I would reply so sad, too bad, DO SOMETHING! However, he did address every one of the issues brought up in the letter and has gotten us closer to getting her some back benefits. Without us jumping up and down and demanding action, several more months would simply evaporate without any progress on the case.

The Knee Gazette

Friday, October 12, 2001

I'm sure it seems like only yesterday, but according to the date on the last *"Gazette"*, a whole month has elapsed since I assaulted your mailbox with our forlorn tale of woe. Unfortunately, despite the desperate need we all have for good and encouraging news, we can offer little. Miriam's condition appears to be rather stable at present, but we have thoroughly explored the "Valley of the Shadow" during the past four years, are well acquainted with most of the scenery by now, and wouldn't mind a different view, if you know what I mean..?

Good news? How about we have not returned to the hospital in the last month; or she doesn't seem to be getting much worse, that's good news. Although the 12 weeks of not bearing weight have now expired (instructions received upon our discharge following last surgery), I don't expect her to get up and walk anytime soon. The sole of her left foot is still numb, as it has been since the last surgery. Although at first blush this would seem to be rather minor (even a good thing), in her case, although she is unable to feel the floor, any pressure applied to the foot sends her into fits of agony. As with most of her afflictions, I can report on them but cannot fix them.

The first week after the epidural was removed was not awful; she had only a few spasms and was sleeping at night. We were encouraged and thought: "well, we can handle this maybe we won't need another epidural." Let us just say the air left that balloon in a hurry, dropping us once again to the bottom of this boxed canyon filled with darkness, despair, and almost no hope.

People around us continue to shower us with love and thoughtfulness. Folks from church are still delivering meals twice a week; friends drop in to visit; people take time to send us humorous emails, sometimes adding personal words of encouragement. I could not count the number of the folks who faithfully pray for strength, grace, wisdom, and healing for us on a regular basis. Even though we can be depressing company, people still come to see us. So far, at least, none of our extended family has changed their name in order to escape us "millstones," and none of the neighbors have put their houses on the market to move to someplace with less shrieking and crying. No, our community of friends and family have really wrapped their collective arms around us and are helping to keep us from drowning in our own despair.

'Tis the season for anniversaries, some good and some not-so-good. The 10th marked the fourth anniversary of Miriam's fall. The 11th was the one-month anniversary of the terrorist attack, and the 15th will be our 18th wedding anniversary.

~ Mark and Miriam, Explorers in Search of the "Promised Land"

Journal:

Monday, October 22, 2001

It is noon on a gorgeous fall day. I've a thousand things to do, but am seemingly paralyzed by my own thoughts, so I am writing instead of performing useful work; is not that the very definition of an excuse?

I took Miriam this morning for an appointment with Dr. Robel. He is concerned that the foot is trying to rotate outward again and admonished us, using very strong words, to do whatever we could to prevent this from happening. He read the report from the nerve study performed last Thursday, examined her leg, felt the temperature difference between her feet, used a Doppler machine to check blood flow in the foot, and shook his head a lot.

"This case is so far over my head I don't know what to do," he said after many long pauses for deep thought. He is concerned about the risks involved with the epidural pump. He wants to talk with Dr. Wilson. He thinks Dr. Wilson will want to see her.

The cynical voice inside my head begins speaking: "I am certain the E/I would approve another trip to New York for a check-up without hesitation."

There was a prolonged discussion about RSD. The one symptom usually associated with RSD that Miriam has not suffered from is swelling of the affected limb. This is keeping him from making an official diagnosis, hoping it be nerve damage only and not RSD. "Dr. Edwards needs to make this call," he says. I'm not sure an official diagnosis would change anything with her treatment, but it might give us one more arrow in the quiver that may one day be useful on the legal front.

Stacy's assistant asked the doctor about attendant care, how much and for how long, to which he promptly wrote a prescription for the next six months! He wants her to see a neurosurgeon.

During the visit there was discussion about amputation and sympathectomy and the inherent risks associated with the implantation of a permanent pump.

My heart is heavy, Miriam hurts like hell. She is plastered on drugs and the relief we have been anticipating from the epidural implant may be too risky to pursue. What is next for her/us? How much longer can she endure this level of agony while the doctors in her life search for a solution to this pain? Hope, along with options for treatment are fading, as one option after another is eliminated. I know not where to turn or what to do for her, nothing provides the relief we are so desperately seeking.

The Knee Gazette

Sunday, October 28, 2001

"Aren't you cold?"

"No," I replied to the thoughtful neighbor, who had noticed my blue legs and chattering teeth.

"You are aware that it is almost November, there is frost on the ground, and you are dressed for July?" He continued in a tone of voice that clearly questioned my sanity.

It was Saturday morning, and I was busy working on the spa room. The short sleeves, shorts, and flip-flops were my attempt at denying that another winter was upon us, and I was still working on one spa room. Yes, I will deny that this is the 16th month I have been working on this 12 x 32 addition to the back of the house. Yesterday afternoon I wheeled Miriam to the room so she could nod approvingly at the latest piece of molding I had nailed in place.

"This is really coming along; how much longer before you'll be done?" she queried in the most supportive tone of sarcastic voice she could muster.

"March," I deadpanned. The demure look of support was chased off by a you've-got-to-be-kidding expression. I did not try to explain further; after this many years of marriage, I didn't figure any was needed. True, it appears that only a few pieces of molding and some paint are all that are needed before the project will be complete, but given the pace of my progress, I was being realistic.

A difficult week has mercifully come to a close. On Monday, during an appointment with Dr. Robel, much of the hope we have been holding onto in anticipation of having an epidural pump implanted was cruelly dashed. "This could be risky," the well-meaning Doctor declared, not realizing he was snuffing out Miriam's will to live. By Friday, he informed us that his mind was not entirely made up and that this was not the end of the discussion, but the days between these off-the-cuff comments were not easy ones.

The despair was only made worse by a hormone-altering medication she started taking on Tuesday that had been prescribed by her gynecologist and further aggravated by the nerve-related problems that only seemed to intensify. One of the risks associated with having multiple doctors trying to address different problems. By Thursday morning, when I discovered the potential problem with the medicine and got it removed from her regimen, she was extremely depressed. Her eyes became too dull to reflect light; her face lacked expression, and her conversation centered on how much better Matthew and I would be without her. She was seriously talking about suicide. I was too worried to work on Wednesday and returned home soon after arriving at the shop in Greensboro.

Fortunately, the combination of getting her off the medication, and the assurance that her doctors would continue searching for some kind of relief, helped restore some of the fighting spirit I am accustomed to seeing when gazing into Miriam's coal-colored eyes.

I realized this week how important it is that we continue to dream. We talk about places we want to visit and things we want to see. It is important that we all have goals to stretch and reach for; in our case, it is perhaps even essential. Thankfully, it costs nothing to dream, yet the process can be very uplifting, therapeutic, and perspective enhancing.

~ We are Mark, Miriam, and Matthew, Would-be Voyagers "Booking Passage" on the Vessel "Kneed Therapy"

Journal

Monday, October 29, 2001

I used up all the levity I could muster on the latest issue of *the Knee Gazette* I composed and sent out yesterday. The following paragraph is what I wrote about last week:

I made it sound as good as I could, but the fact is my wife was suicidal and for the first time I was faced with the prospect of thinking about life without her. It was a dark and depressing day. I plan to grow old with her and experience many more adventures along the way. This damn knee is simply one protracted, devastating detour that we had not planned for. Who'd have thought that a slip and fall on a waxed floor could eventually be terminal? If she dies from one form of complication or another, or by her own hand, (or mine for that matter) then that is exactly what it would be!

When I came home early on Wednesday, I called the case manager and Dr. Robel's office, leaving messages for both. Stacy called first and listened to my plea for psychiatric help for Miriam. This is something that had been mentioned on more than one occasion in the last couple of years by Dr. Robel, Stacy Casey and Fred, but until Wednesday I did not think it necessary. Stacy made an appointment with a woman in Conyers with whom she has had personal experience with other clients. We will meet her at 1 p.m. tomorrow. These arrangements were in place when Dr. Robel's nurse returned my call at about 6 p.m. Dr. Robel was very concerned and asked her to find out from me if he needed to hospitalize her; I told them that at this time, I did not think this would be necessary.

I have time to write this morning because no attendant has arrived to spell me. Miriam has not been sleeping well lately despite the incredible dose of medications. Last night she left our bed and went to her chair so she would not keep me from sleeping. I am doing everything I know to do for her. Last week I got some dowels so she could make some desensitization sticks with which to treat the RSD. The physical therapist recommended that something be done to keep the covers off her feet during the night, so I took a stick of conduit and shaped it in a way to accomplish this task. I am slowly making progress on the spa room and, since things are slow at the shop, have been spending some time working on it during the week.

Journal

November 2, 2001

Tomorrow is Matthew's 13th birthday. This is a painful holiday for Miriam because it marks another year in the life of our son that she feels has been impacted by her knee and the resulting limitations. She would love to bake him a birthday cake but had to settle for going to

Kroger and helping him pick out one that someone else will make.

I took her to see Dr. Edwards this afternoon. Stacy Casey had a representative present that asked questions of Dr. Edwards concerning the possible implanting of a pump to deliver medication to the intrathecal space in her spine. As it stands right now, she is scheduled to receive a trial next Thursday. The pump could follow as soon as a week, if the procedure is approved by the folks who write the checks. We left the office with a new shred of hope which helped bolster our spirits.

One of Stacy's questions pertained to a diagnosis of RSD. Dr. Edwards made it clear that he was prepared to make an official diagnosis of RSD in Miriam's case and would include it in his notes from this visit.

After arriving home, we sat down to a wonderful meal brought to us by Renie Richards. Miriam ate well, better than I have seen her eat in a long time. She was sitting in her wheelchair at the dining room table and went to push (roll) herself back, the knee bobbled, and she hurled her supper into the garbage can; what a disappointment. Of far greater concern than the lost meal, is the bobble in her knee. It appears the knee is getting looser by the week, a fact that Dr. Robel has documented during the last two visits.

Journal

Thursday, November 8, 2001

Tuesday morning, I woke up in Pigeon Forge, Tn, where I had a 9:30 appointment to peddle furniture to the largest timeshare condo outfit in the country. Last Thursday I was in Knoxville making an initial contact with the parent company.

I am doing everything I can to run my furniture business and take care of Miriam too, but many days it doesn't feel like I'm doing much of a job on either front. Like last week, two days of this week will be consumed by visits with one doctor or another with the common goal of relieving Miriam's pain.

Journal

Sunday, November 11, 2001

Journal entries have been sparse of late, not because of a lack of material, but because most of my "writing time" has been spent corresponding with the attorney, multiple doctors, or Stacy Casey. I invest this time to keep Miriam's case on their front burners, so she can hopefully receive some relief sooner, rather than later. Some of them appreciate it more than others, but at least Miriam's name crosses their desks and hopefully their thoughts a lot more often than if we suffered in silence. I make time to periodically update the journal so important details and events are not lost with the passage of time and other distractions.

Celia came again last night. When Miriam told me she was coming, I told her, "We really do enjoy a special friendship with Celia. After all, there are not many women who could call us, invite themselves for the night, and be warmly welcomed by you because your husband needs some sleep." Because Celia's work schedule has changed, she needs to be able to function at her job by 8 a.m. on Mondays, so she finds Saturday nights an easier time to miss sleep. This is fine with us, because we have more time to visit now than we normally have when she arrived at bedtime on Sundays. Although I heard Miriam hollering three or four times through the wall, I slept on, assuming Celia was at her side. I did not even awaken to relieve the bladder that so often requires attention since crossing the 40-year threshold.

The Knee Gazette

Sunday, November 11, 2001

By six o'clock Thursday morning, we had been on the road and already covered the hour and a half distance between home and Demorest, Georgia. Demorest is a speck of a town that probably is omitted from many maps. U.S. Hwy 441 once used main street to carry through traffic to points north and south between Clayton and Cornelia. I suspect very little of the traffic tarried in Demorest. The primary industry appears to be education since it is the home of Piedmont College. A smattering of shops and stores are strung out along 441, for about a mile on either side of the college. Somehow it seems odd that

I bring wife to this small town nestled in the foothills of the Appalachian Mountains for medical treatment, but this is where the pain doctor settled when he left Athens more than a year ago.

We were pulling into the parking lot of Habersham County Medical Center. We are here so Miriam can receive a trial dose of pain medication administered into the intrathecal space around her spinal cord. This is the first step toward implanting another battery-operated device into her body (this one would occupy the cheek that does not presently contain an electronic device) designed to relieve her pain.

What? You have never heard of the intrathecal space? Well, I can relate; only five short years ago, I did not even know what an ACL was, let alone that severing one could be a life-changing event (in less than 5% of cases).

The results of this experiment were disappointing. Although the spasms took two hours off, she still felt pain she would rather live without. We had to spend the day in the hospital so they could watch her and deliver assistance for any adverse reaction, which thankfully did not occur. Dr. Edwards agreed to give her a sciatic nerve block before we began the trip home. Although this would only numb her leg for a few hours, it should give her at least a short vacation from the relentless spasms that often dominate her days.

After months of speaking of the possibility from time to time, her doctors have officially diagnosed at least part of her nerve-related malady as RSD, or Reflex Sympathetic Dystrophy. This is a hideous condition where the sympathetic nerves attempt to take over motor function. It can take hold after the motor nerves suffer some severe trauma (such as from a fall or multiple surgeries). It is not unusual for its victims to take their own lives in order to escape its terrible grasp.

As Dr. Edwards waited for her foot to twitch, while using an electrical probe on her upper thigh to check for responses (which would be an indication he was closing in on the right spot), he patiently answered a steady stream of questions. This barrage was intended to keep him thinking and address some of our concerns at the same time. The interrogation may have paid off, in that he mentioned two heretofore undiscussed courses of treatment that may offer some promise. The first is a procedure he called a "sympathetic block." Essentially a series of nerve blocks (shots) administered to the sympathetic nerves at the spinal cord that may, if performed properly, provide pain relief that would last several months. The second was to reposition the leads of her spinal cord stimulator, to get better results from the box already residing on one cheek. Miriam is scheduled for the first sympathetic block the Monday before Thanksgiving. As usual, the response to this will dictate what happens next, but since the results of this test were so underwhelming, we will try both the sympathetic block and repositioning the spinal cord stimulator leads before pursuing further the intrathecal pump option.

What? You want to know how the spa room is progressing? Well, it's still on schedule to be completed by March, some March, pick a March. We have taken somewhat of a detour in order to devote some time and attention to the refuse that seems to be consuming our living quarters faster than we are able to organize it, toss it out, or give it away. I am presently one office, a storage room, and a garage away from returning to the trim in the spa room. Remember, we must have enough space in our home to shelter an impressive inventory of orthopedic devices and mobility enhancing apparatuses. It would be fine with me if we could benefit from a miracle and then have a sale, but in the meantime, Miriam needs a path shoveled through the house that is wide enough for her wheelchair.

Thanksgiving this year has been planned for Myrtle Beach, S.C. This has provided Miriam and me about the only non-medical-related travel we have had for the last five holiday seasons. Although I always worry about potential problems and having her so far away from her "medical team," every trip has been an adventure and a great time, as well as being very therapeutic. This year, with its proximity to the ocean, I will have another opportunity to work on securing that crew position on a boat of some kind, so I can sail off into the sunset. "…sorry honey, I'm going to sea."

~ **Holding Tightly to the Knot We've Prayed Into the End of Our Rope**

The Knee Gazette

Thanksgiving week 2001

"I assure you officer; we have not knocked over a medical supply store; all of this is for the use and comfort of one special lady. Yes sir, that is a potty in the back of the van. What? You've never seen a potty in a minivan? We are careful to pull the curtains when it is in use. No sir, I am not a wheelchair dealer. It's a little like golf, you use a different wheelchair for different locations. The skipper of these fine implements is buried under the pillows and blankets in the back seat. Well, no, it wasn't easy, but as you can see, I did manage to get two wheelchairs, three people, their luggage and a potty in one little van, pretty amazing, huh? Have a good holiday."

Our little entourage arrived in Myrtle Beach, South Carolina Tuesday evening for a time of family togetherness. Thanksgiving week has become a much-anticipated change of scenery and pace for the extended family, but especially for Miriam, Matthew and me. This year's holiday abode is in Cherry Grove Beach, a little burg located only a stone's throw from North Carolina. This beach-side tourist destination is only a few minutes' drive north of enough shopping and entertainment possibilities to drain any pocket.

A three-block walk has us strolling on the beach admiring the expanse of the Atlantic Ocean. Step out the back door and onto the second story deck and we are overlooking a man-made channel that eventually connects with the Intracoastal Waterway. The two-story house is on stilts, which puts the second floor three stories in the air. There is a deck on the back and a porch on the front. A private boat ramp spills out from under the house and into the water. Fishing from the ground-floor deck is possible when the tide is not all the way out, although the fishing has been much better than the catching.

We brought the Johnson family yacht, a leaky, oar powered, 10-foot-long aluminum vessel that has been in the family for nearly three decades. This will allow the kids to explore the basics of navigation and seamanship. By the time we pack up to leave on Sunday morning, most of the next generation will have acquired some skill at rowing a boat. When the tide is out, the kids have bicycles, board games, and every shape of ball ever invented with which to create an argument.

These are rich times for our family. Three generations gathered for a few days of reminiscing and memory making. One very fresh, very scary memory involves Miriam, the wheelchair, and the two flights of stairs separating the main floor of the house from the ground. Houses in this area are all built on stilts, so the first floor is two stories in the air. Reservations for this six-bedroom six-bath house were made nearly a year ago. Similar to the last several years, we were certain that, by now, Miriam would be walking and would not need a handicap accessible destination... Each trip up and down the stairs is another opportunity to try a "new and improved" solution to transporting her from one level to the other. So far, we've tried the "three-point tote," where three adult males take a different part of the wheelchair and physically carry it up or down the stairs. This is probably the best, safest, and least traumatic for all concerned. We have also tried the "one legged hop;" the "butt slide," and a brainstorm of mine that nearly ended in disaster.

My bright idea was to get behind and down a step or two from the wheelchair, which I thought I could back, one step at a time, down the stairs by myself, using my bountiful mass to keep her from careening out of control. The flights of stairs are separated by a landing, conveniently located at the halfway point. Fortunately, brother Bruce was skeptical of the scheme and was ready to intervene if needed. Step one, and half of the second, went according to plan, but then I lost control, and the rest of the steps came all at once, which nearly bowled me over in the process. My retreating foot found a railing on the landing, which I instinctively pushed against, attempting to arrest her descent as the large back wheels bounced from one step to the next in a rapidly increasing procession. The carpenter who assembled the railing must have been running short of nails but put the railing in place anyway, counting on luck and gravity to keep it there. It was not built to withstand what we were using it for that day!

My foothold gave way as the nail-free bottom rail swung free and my right leg began reaching toward the ground, still some eight feet away. In that moment, I realized there was a good chance I would fall, and the wheelchair, along with my terrified wife, would shortly follow. Thankfully, brother Bruce grabbed the chair and stopped the certain disaster. The local emergency room was cheated out of at least two new patients thanks to his effort. I survived with only a bruised shin and Miriam received only a few more frayed nerves, but this could have been so much worse!

Miriam has done remarkably well and is enjoying the company of loved ones, along with the different scenery. Spasms and pain still accent her days and nights, although they have not been nearly as frequent, or intense as they have been at other times.

At my father's suggestion, the entire family gathered around Miriam's wheelchair last evening for a very emotional time of prayer. This was really a localized manifestation of something that takes place daily by untold numbers of prayer warriors scattered far and wide. I cannot explain why these petitions have gone unanswered. Perhaps we are all supposed to learn something about perseverance and patience? I do know that quitting is not an option. We desperately need and covet your continued intercession on our behalf. One day her leg will be made whole again; we prefer it to be on this side of eternity, if possible.

~ We are: Mark, Miriam and Matthew, along with our precious loved ones, counting together our many blessings with thanksgiving.

Letter to Stacy Casey

November 28, 2001

Thank you for taking up the issue of transportation. I have never had a full-sized van, so I am starting from scratch with my homework and am trying to find out what the options are. When approval comes, we will at least be educated enough to talk intelligently on the subject.

We love our current van and, were it not for Miriam's needs, would not be planning to replace it until the junk man hauls it away; we usually don't trade vehicles until they won't go anymore. Last week for Thanksgiving we went to Myrtle Beach for the week. By the time I got the power chair, the manual chair, the potty seat, the ramp, the luggage, and three people on board, we were packed! But even at 10 yrs. of age and with 150,000 miles, this old van is comfortable, dependable (it has been well cared for) and efficient (25 mpg on this trip!). So, you can see, it is with some mixed emotions that we begin this process. However, I am convinced it will be better for Miriam, and I know Old Blue, like the rest of us, is not getting any younger.

As always, your suggestions and input are welcomed and encouraged.

Journal

Wednesday, November 28, 2001

Were I to characterize her condition of late in one word, I would choose the word stable. I don't see her in any more or less pain than two weeks ago. The quantity and intensity of the spasms is also about the same. Most of the time, she is remarkably clear-headed and able to carry on a conversation. It is important that we don't mess with her medication schedule, but within those parameters she is functioning and is less vegetative than she has been at times.

She has decided to get another sympathetic block because it apparently was able to increase the circulation enough in her foot to lessen the spasms. She wants to postpone the repositioning of her leads until after the holidays, so her bed rest won't get in the way of the activities she enjoys so much.

Ramps, van, and renovations to the house, are all things Miriam needs for safety and to better facilitate her life. Without any additional surgeries on the horizon, it looks like her need for these tools will continue for the foreseeable future. Her safety, as well as the safety of her caregivers, are our top priority. She deserves to have as great a quality of life as possible. Since I obviously am unable to fix her, tending to these needs has become my primary focus. Only a few moments ago, while care-giver Peggy was helping her get out of the shower, her foot slipped, and the knee locked so that it would not move. Peggy was unable to get it unstuck; fortunately, I was still here (writing this entry and waiting on the guys coming to build a ramp) and was able to run toward the shrieks of pain. I lifted Miriam up, which allowed Peggy to pull the leg out of the shower and Miriam was able, eventually, to calm down. It is amazing there have not been a lot more serious incidents during this ordeal.

Journal

December 8, 2001

For several days I have been nursing another knot in my stomach, as I try to figure out where we are headed as a family. Our financial reserves are dwindling; the furniture business is floundering; Miriam is not getting any better and the lawyer continues to do nothing on the legal front. The question of where we will end up gnaws at me almost constantly. Yesterday, as I drove by a group of homeless folks standing on a street corner, I couldn't help but wonder if that would be me in a few years. One thing I know for sure, the current trend must be stopped, or our future will become increasingly precarious with each passing week. Any one of several things could turn our economic picture around, but at present, they all elude us.

On Thursday Miriam met with a neurologist in Conyers. This was requested by Dr. Robel and arranged by Stacy Casey. He seemed to wonder why she was there. What was he supposed to do for her after seeing some of the most respected physicians in medicine? He offered little hope; gave her a new medication to try and sent her on her way. Peggy drove Miriam home and I went a different direction with a truck and trailer loaded with furniture toward Tennessee. The entire trip I listened to my thoughts, never touching the box of cassette tapes I took for company. I prayed some, yelled at God some, had a pity party for a while, and then was put in my place as I watched a bus unload several "special needs" children into the arms of waiting parents at a gas station. I was quickly reminded of all I have to be thankful for.

Miriam seems to be on a downward trend again. Her pain is more intense, her sleep more fitful. She looks through her tears of pain and asks me to do something. I check her meds to see if anything is due, grab hold of any spot experiencing a spasm, and try not to cry with her. I feel so helpless. She has been sleeping in her new chair more and more because she sleeps better than in the bed. I do not have the opportunity to hold her and provide the comfort of a hug or a caress when she sleeps in her chair.

We have a beautiful fall day to enjoy, and Matthew has been marching around the house for several hours already wondering what we will decide to do with it, so I better close for now.

Letter to Dr. Wilson

December 9, 2001

The trial for the intrathecal pump did not produce the desired results, so, for the present, we do not see any point in proceeding with the pump that I wrote about a month ago. Dr. Edwards (pain doctor) is trying a series of sympathetic blocks and will probably attempt to reposition the leads for the spinal cord stimulator sometime after the first of the year.

The good news on the orthopedic front is that the joint integrity is stable. The news from the pain front is less encouraging. Spasms and pain prevent her from receiving any benefit from the joint you built for her.

Dr. Robel is getting worried about loss of bone mass because of the time that has passed since she was weight bearing. A recent bone density exam confirmed a loss of bone mass in the hip and lower back.

We need help. Somewhere there must be someone who could help with this nerve that is devouring her life. If not, we need to again have a dialogue about amputating this leg above the knee. How long would it take for the phantom pain to diminish? At some point the brain would surely reprogram itself and realize the stimulation no longer exists...? Are there other options your pain guys can offer? Does she need to return to NY for a follow up evaluation by yourself and Dr. Ware and, while there, see the pain and or nerve guys? What about your associate in Atlanta; is it time for him to evaluate her?

Journal

Monday, December 10, 2001

Stacy and Anne, two of Miriam's former co-workers, have come this morning to help her wrap Christmas gifts. These times are very special for Miriam, and I appreciate them taking time for her. The attendant had a sick child this morning and didn't come, so I am staying home from work to stand in. I managed to get most of the morning chores finished, so Miriam was ready when her friends arrived.

I have enjoyed watching Miriam wrap and talk, while listening to Christmas music. On occasion the banter and crinkling of wrapping paper suddenly come to an end while Miriam deals with a tear-producing spasm. They will be fine without me, so I will soon leave and go about my business. Watkinsville home health has just called to inform me that someone will be here before one to take over for the afternoon.

Letter to Dr. Wilson

December 11, 2001

I received your email just in time for two important appointments, to which I carried a copy. The first was lunch with the case manager in charge of Miriam's case (Stacy Casey). The second was with a psychologist who has been seeing Miriam for a couple of months now.

> 1. Chemical neurolysis would be a better, more palatable option to amputation in my mind, should it come to that. However, 2. Psychiatrist consult. There may be some voluntary / volitional component to Miriam's spasm condition. I certainly would not move on point one until this has been investigated. I will touch base with Dr. Robel.

Re: item number one —chemically killing the nerve is a

conversation I've had with her pain doctor (Dr. Edwards) on more than one occasion. He contends that this is a good plan only in terminal cases when the patient is expected to expire prior to the nerve regenerating. Once it regenerates, he says lots of problems can result.

Item two is what I specifically wanted to get the case manager and the psychologist's reaction to. They independently shared the same opinion: neither think there is a volitional component to her spasms. I concur. Believe me, I have been searching for a pattern of some kind that would shed some light on the stimulus for these episodes. They are completely random and arbitrary with regard to time of day, location of spasm (usually limited these days to the left foot), climatic conditions, activity, or position. These things can happen during the deepest part of her sleep, while soaking in her spa, sitting in her chair with her feet up, riding in the car with her feet down, it does not matter whether we are talking, or she is "expressing frustration" with the boy or me. These things can come quickly and leave just as fast once we intervene. They can arrive in a storm that will involve several minutes or even hours of nearly constant activity, or they can take most of the day off. The only pattern is that they have no pattern.

Letter to Dr. Robel

December 12, 2001

Good Wednesday morning!

Miriam and I had lunch yesterday with the caseworker managing Miriam's case for the hospital (Stacy Casey). **One thing she asked us to get from you is a prescription for a "dependent passenger evaluation to identify vehicle accessibility and/or modification needs for long term."** *If you will have someone call us when this is ready, we will arrange to pick it up. Miriam is not scheduled to see you until the 21ˢᵗ of the month. I would like to get it into Stacy's hands before this, to keep things moving as rapidly as possible.*

CHAPTER 15
Through Miriam's Eyes

Let's take a trip back in time and "try on" Miriam's "shoes" for a short "stroll" while viewing life as best as one can through her eyes.

In today's mail was a letter forwarded by your lawyer that was written by the adjustor for the company administrating the hospital's self-insured workman's comp program. The contents stir fresh feelings of rage and anger, which are accompanied by a new river of tears. It is May of 2000, some two and half years since the accident that radically changed your life; in your mind begins to replay the "tape" that is your story...

You are a medical laboratory technician employed by a hospital to perform the tests ordered routinely by most everyone's doctor. For 19 years you respond automatically to the various alarms sounded by the different lab machines when they need attention. Alarms go off when a test or cycle is completed, when intervention is required for one reason or another, or when something is wrong. Your ears are tuned to the hum of the machines; their various pitches and tones "speak" to you and in this way and you know exactly where each machine is in its respective cycle. This is going on in your subconscious, leaving the conscious thought processes to focus on tasks at hand, and to plan a logical sequence for what will be accomplished next.

Although this routine that might seem mundane and monotonous to others, to you it is a life and death drama! Big and potentially life-changing decisions are made based on the information you report to the doctors. It is the life and death importance of the work that keeps your focus intense and causes you to find great fulfillment in doing this job well.

The weekend night schedule you work allows more time to be with your son and to help with your spouse's fledgling business. Working this crazy schedule provides many challenges and responsibilities that are normally shared by a much larger crew on every other shift, but now you enjoy more independence, variety, and responsibility by working several departments at once, and the pace makes the time go very quickly. Although you hate giving up weekends with your family, the contribution to the financial well-being of the household makes it a good choice for this stage of the family's life.

A familiar noise interrupts your thoughts. You stop what you're doing and make your way toward the alarm. Since it is on the other side of the lab, you walk at a fast pace through several departments and cross several walkways. As you near the machine, you round the last corner and time suddenly crawls. You are spinning; there are two faces with bug-eyed expressions watching you. There is a noise, not unlike that of glass being ground into asphalt by a shoe. You hit the floor and eventually quit moving. Your left leg is bent behind you and the foot is pointing the wrong direction. Searing pain hits you with the force of a tidal wave. You hear screaming but can't tell if the noise is coming from you or someone else; you are overwhelmed by excruciating pain in your back, hip, and knee.

You are lying in the Emergency Room feeling again the burning pain in your leg and your mind begins replaying "the tape." You are told that you fell, your knee "is badly sprained" and your spouse has been called. When co-workers come to check on you, they begin filling in missing details.

"They were waxing the floor. You fell on some wax that was fresh laid and still wet."

"I didn't see any signs. There was no tape on the floor," you quickly reply.

"You're right. We went back and looked at where you fell; they had not put up any warnings or barriers there."

After x-rays, they report that nothing is broken. There is a possibility of torn ligaments or a sprain.

You close your eyes and remember the faces with the big eyes. You drift to sleep because of the pain medication you have been prescribed to quiet your agony. When you awaken, you check to be sure the appropriate reports have been filled out and signed. Soon your spouse arrives. You are wheeled out to the van, given a pair of crutches, and sent home with instructions to see the orthopedic doctor on Monday.

The spouse makes you as comfortable as possible and begins tending to your needs. The crutches provide some mobility until the swelling subsides enough to try bearing weight. It feels like no sprain you have ever experienced before...

A few days later, you are examined by an orthopedic surgeon for the first time. He evaluates the knee, takes some x-rays, and declares that the ACL is severed and will have to be replaced. You begin going to physical therapy, trying to strengthen knee muscles in preparation for the surgery scheduled a month later. It all hurts! Trying to function, going to therapy, everything you do is now accomplished through a fog of pain and over the counter painkillers. Your spouse is getting frustrated because normal is gone and has been replaced by limitations caused by the injury. You sit while the rest of the family attempts to "plug" the holes left by your incapacity. This is not what you wanted, the novelty of being waited on wears off quickly, and you, too, become frustrated.

The month waiting for surgery seems like a colossal waste of time; the sooner they cut, the sooner you will be on the road to recovery and can recover your life. The pain and frustration cause you to look forward to "knife day." The spouse shares your sentiment, and it is with a hopeful kiss that you are sent off to the operating room for the procedure that will surely at least bring the road to recovery within view.

The next few days you would have rather skipped. The pain you feel now made the pre-surgical pain seem minor. The knee feels like it is the size of Rhode Island; the nerves are angry and make the brain aware of their fury. You are nauseous. Every time you move, you try to vomit, but there is nothing left to "hurl." Your spouse is standing there trying to help, but mostly looking helpless. When the noise and nausea become too much for him, he summons a nurse—again.

At times you experience almost an out-of-body sensation, where you think you are "hovering" above the bed watching the activities going on in the room; other times, the sensations breaking through the medication-induced fog are all too real. How can anything hurt this much, you wonder during your more lucid moments?

Finally, after three days, you get to go home. Your spouse, having seldom left your side during the entire stay, looks terrible. You both cannot wait to get home, until the reality of the situation dawns on both of you.

"What now?" In the hospital, there was an entire staff of folks to tend to your needs; suddenly you realize that now it is up to your already worn-out-looking spouse and young son...? How are they going to manage? The spouse has already been away from the business way more than he should, and son must go to school. The impact of all this is sinking in. When the van crosses a bridge, the bump in the road jars the fresh-cut knee and a bolt of pain displaces all other activity of the brain like a mortar hitting a fox hole interrupts whatever activity had been taking place before the arrival of the shell. The explosion of pain makes you nauseous and you begin to heave; fortunately, spouse has planned ahead and has a bucket nearby to catch the contents of your stomach.

Again, and again, this is repeated until four knee reconstructions have taken place. One day at a time is the only way to deal with this kind of pain and disappointment. Will it ever end?

The Knee Gazette

New Year's 2002

At the dawn of another new year, life for us has settled into what I would describe, at this moment in time, as stable. This does not mean she is pain free and walking, because she is not, on either account.

Six months have elapsed since her last surgery, which took place only four miles from "Ground Zero" in Manhattan. We had hoped that, by now, she would be able to bear weight on her afflicted left leg and would have gotten some relief from the unrelenting pain that dominates her days and nights, but this has not gone as planned. Although her knee joint is probably more stable today than at any point in the past four years, the nerves in the leg act at times as if they are possessed by demons, intent on driving any remnant of sanity from her.

I am part husband, part dad, fulltime caregiver, and part fireman. I am on call more than 100 hours per week, ready to respond to the "fires" when something happens with which she needs help. I am extremely grateful for the 50 hours per week she is being cared for by a professional attendant hired by workman's comp. In addition to this, friends and extended family continue to give of their time, so I can go with Matthew to Boy Scouts, or just have an occasional "night off" to sleep soundly. The constant state of high alert has worn on me as much, if not more, than the work required to provide her care. She wants so much to do things for us, but in her condition, even the simplest tasks can lead to more crises. Bumping her leg on something, a cool draft that hits her leg, or just a random spasm, can send her into orbit and one of us scurrying to her aid.

I think she has adjusted to life in a wheelchair to the extent possible. The limitations she finds most debilitating, however, are her state of dependence and her diminished mental condition caused by the medications. She often gets frustrated with not being able to hop in the van and go like she once could; because of her medications, she has not had driving privileges for more than a year now. Since our van is not specially equipped for wheelchairs, getting out and going places presents challenges and frustrations. But we are glad we have a van and not just a sedan of some kind. Trying to get around a house not designed for wheelchair accessibility creates challenges as well. Workman's Comp has provided a ramp for the front door and is getting one for the kitchen door—it only took them slightly more than two years to install two ramps! We are hopeful that one day they will also address the rest of the house, as well as the transportation needs.

We continue to have many things to be thankful for, not the least of which is the army of "angels" that continues, even after all these months to bring meals twice a week. Our church family has "stood-in-the-gap," so to speak, ministering to us in this way. They are joined by a legion of family, friends and acquaintances who offer up a steady river of prayers on our behalf. People often call or stop by to visit with Miriam. This Christmas, two former co-workers spent an afternoon here helping her wrap presents. Others drop by, or take her to lunch, or out shopping. These efforts have kept us from any feelings of isolation. We try to get out and go when we can and where we are able. Physical therapy and doctor's appointments provide all the activity she can handle most days. Workman's Comp has continued to provide

Miriam with the best medical care available, and although we have been frustrated at times, we realize that we could be much worse off.

It would be fair and accurate to characterize this crisis as the focal point of our family's life for several years now. The steady barrage of surgeries, the preparation required prior to and the recovery afterward, have understandably precluded and usurped most normal activities. We are trying to do the best we can to keep Matthew's home life as near "normal" as we are able, as well as to engage in productive work whenever possible.

What does the future look like? In a word: uncertain. At the present time anyway, there is not the cloud of major surgery looming on the horizon.

Journal

Sunday, January 6, 2002

The holidays are over and tomorrow the normal routine will resume in earnest. It has been a good season, full of family time and relaxation. On New Year's Eve Miriam got the sympathetic block that was never received on 12/26. Although a new year has begun, it does not feel like a fresh start—too many things seem awfully familiar.

Miriam informed me Thursday that she is losing feeling in her right leg. Is this a result of the block on Monday? Is the RSD moving into the other leg? The passage of time may answer the question of what is going on, but it is one more thing for Miriam to worry over and to pull her down. How did I respond to the news? By covering my ears and singing la la la la la la la.

The Knee Gazette

April 1, 2002

"Bedside potty?"

"Check."

"Wheelchairs?" It takes two, one manual and one powered.

"Check."

"Drugs?"

"Check."

"Ramp?"

"Check."

"Luggage, food and water?"

"In the van."

"Dad, where's the bike gonna go?" asked Matthew as he looked into the full van with the squatting tires and sagging springs.

Once again, our tired blue van is loaded way beyond the legal limit, with more orthopedic equipment than some third world hospitals even own, along with enough narcotics for several felony convictions, provided we were lacking the all-important prescriptions. The bike was strapped to the roof.

"Honey, I assure you, they would not have put the rack up there if they did not intend for it to be used." This was my response to the expression from the spouse, which was obviously questioning my judgment.

I ignored "the look" one more time and continued with the preparations. This time we are not headed out of town for surgery, we are taking a vacation. As we pull away from the house, the opening scenes from "The Beverly Hillbillies" keep flashing through my mind. I swapped some furniture with a bigwig of a Pigeon Forge resort in exchange for a week's vacation. This had a lot to do with determining our destination.

Miriam lies on the bench seat in the back of the van, Matthew sits in the front seat beside me. Before we are out of the county both have on their headphones and are listening to music. Miriam is also reading a book; Matthew is playing with his Game Boy. I may as well be traveling by myself; I would have the same amount of company and conversation. The silence is only broken by pronouncements of hunger or the need to "go."

Once we encounter rough and crooked roads in the Smoky Mountains National Park, the moaning and screaming starts; at times, it becomes so intense the radio volume can't drown it out!

"We must go home a different way," is one sentence I was able to make out amidst all the sobbing. Bumpy roads, speed breaks, potholes, gravel roads, expansion joints, bridges and railroad crossings all conspire to add misery to Miriam's agony—at least that is her claim. It does not help that my faithful "assistant" is willing to attest to my ability to hit every bump in the road. Note to self: talk to son about the need for us guys to stick together and form a unified front.

These are nice digs! This unit appears brand new, still lacking stains in the coffee pot and on the stove eyes, which I am certain we will rectify within a few short hours. We are staying in a two-bedroom, two-bath unit complete with three televisions, a washer, dryer, stereo, and VCR. The best part so far appears to be that Miriam can ride in her powered wheelchair from the parking lot to anywhere inside the condo she cares to travel. These are appreciated amenities our regular abode does not offer.

"What size are these doors?" asks Miriam as she drives from the living area into the bedroom, where she transfers to the bed for the first nap of the young day.

"Thirty-six inches," I answered, but I think she was already asleep.

I plan for this to be a working vacation for me. After all, I have the cell phone, the laptop, and an internet connection, so I feel a little like "Paladin" from the 60's western "Have Gun Will Travel," only this is the new millennium version: "Have Laptop Can Work." I plan to make some sales calls up here this week. It seems to me like there are an awful lot of porches in need of some comfortable furniture.

Sometime in the first half of '02, Dr. Dean became her pain doctor.

Letter to Dr. Dean

June 11, 2002

Something happened this weekend that was very upsetting to Miriam and may provide a clue about what lies ahead. In the middle of the night Friday, she began howling in agony. Although this is not unusual, it was her left arm and not a leg that she presented for assistance. Her fingers were pressed tightly into her palm and the rest of the limb was rigid as a board. It took a while, but I finally found a combination of twists, tugs, and pulls that caused it to release its grip. On Sunday she experienced a "zinger" that began at the shoulder and went down the arm to the tips of her fingers.

She has been under assault lately by waves of intense spasms. The only limb that has not been involved within the last three days (or ever) is the right arm! The right leg, from the hip to the foot, has begun routinely contributing to her agony, although with less regularity than her left. Waves of nausea often accompany these spasms and cause us to scramble for the "emergency bucket," although there is rarely a deposit these days, thanks in part to the benefit she receives from the electronic relief band she wears on her wrist. She spends several hours a day in her spa, which helps keep her extremities warm and provides as much massage as she can tolerate. The spa also allows her to perform many of the exercises at home that she has learned by going to aquatic therapy.

The spinal cord stimulator (SCS) is useful only part of the time and is still very positional.

What lies ahead for her? What are your plans for the S.C.S.? What other treatments are you considering?

Mark Johnson

Letter to Dr. Dean

August 14, 2002

Miriam has promised me for two days that she would write; since it has not gotten done, I will attempt to write for her.

She is not doing well. She has not slept much in three nights and has just endured two tough days. Since you saw her, she has experienced more intense and prolonged episodes of burning sensations in her left leg, highlighted by random and arbitrary episodes of spasms. Although in recent days, burning sensations seem to be the dominant complaint. This afternoon I returned from work to news from her caregiver, that her blood pressure was 151/112 and she had a pulse of 112! She was sleeping fitfully in her recliner and her face had a familiar expression of pain. Prior to her surgery in July of 2001, her blood pressure had always been below normal. Something happened in that OR that has affected BP and pulse. The problem was first noticed in the recovery room and has been with her ever since!

She hopes you will review her medications and discover a regimen that provides relief. She has some 50ug Duragesic patches (A.K.A. Fentanyl), can she add this to the two 100 ug patches she is already wearing? She says the current Duragesic and Dilaudid are just not covering the pain. Note to readers: Fentanyl is 100 x as strong as Morphine; Dilaudid is 8 x the strength of Morphine. She was on some powerful stuff!

She has been heeding your suggestion that she work on activities of daily living (ADL), by exercising as much as she can in our spa, in addition to the visits to the hospital's pool, where she has physical therapy, I do not know that there is any connection to the recent increase in activity and her pain. This appears to me to be more of a gradual trend that has been developing for nearly two months.

Mark Johnson

~ Husband and care provider for 2nd and 3rd shifts

Narration:

Once we settled in from the second surgery in NY and got the infections and hospitalizations behind us, our efforts and attention turned more to living life as best we could with the challenges of her condition instead of looking for a miraculous surgical intervention. We accepted the fact that was not going to happen. My attention turned more to caring for her than fixing her. If she was not going to get better, then it was my job to facilitate her condition to the best of my ability. By this time, my job was gone, my flooring business was gone, and although I was still making furniture, with all the time her care and case required, this business was not doing too well either. Much to the chagrin of her doctors, the lawyer, and case manager, Miriam was my all-consuming job. My mental energy was no longer burdened with managing an employer, a host of employees, and a slew of suppliers and customers, it was free to focus on what she needed and who needed to do something to provide that for her. Unlike every professional involved with her care and case, I had only one client. I was not burdened by knowledge of how things "should be done" or "how things are handled in other cases," I was the proverbial bull in a China shop. There was not a "lane" for me to stay in and I was not afraid to step on toes if it helped my poor wife.

Knee Gazettes and even journal entries got very scarce as the years elapsed. The only time many people heard from us was through annual Christmas letters. We were busy surviving just like every other family in America. We all have burdens and challenges to deal with, so I did not feel compelled to continue adding to the burdens of others by sharing ours. Except for the pain doctor, my letters to the medical community diminished considerably too, there just wasn't much else they could do for her; the same cannot be said for letters to the lawyer and case manager. My focus primarily turned to the legal case because this is where we could get things needed to facilitate her needs and care…

CHAPTER 16
The Legal Drama

The next two chapters could be a book all by itself. If legal wrangling is not your thing, you should skip this part of the book. If you choose to descend into this hole with us, remember much of it was written in the heat of the moment while we were already embroiled in a medical and financial crisis. The medical battle included staying in communication with a team of doctors, as well as the case manager; both of which often had legal aspects that often-required legal input or intervention. In other words, it was similar to a 3-ring circus where activity takes place simultaneously in multiple arenas. In this circus, I was part ringmaster, part performer, and part clown. My job was simple: hold the family together, manage one or more businesses, and for a time, a real job with a real boss, while providing and managing Miriam's care. Additionally, I worked to keep the legal case off back burners in multiple offices. This was a stress-filled time that I do not wish to repeat. In retrospect, composing this book from a far more placid place many years later, I wonder how we survived.

Some of the wording in this chapter is rather harsh, but to sugarcoat or leave it out would, I think, lessen the story and certainly temper the intensity of the crisis we were in. Our legal battles went on for nearly two decades and at times were as all-consuming and as mentally fatiguing as the surgeries. The day it ended a huge burden left our collective shoulders.

Important note: most of the book to this point has been telling the story in a linear fashion- today follows yesterday and precedes tomorrow; because I wanted to confine most of the legal stuff to one chapter, this chapter will bounce around some and for that I apologize in advance for the confusion it is sure to cause.

Letter to Mr. Eddie Harris, personal bankruptcy attorney

November 8, 1999

The following is an outline summarizing our financial situation. This is intended to provide you with information you may need prior to our upcoming meeting.

Heritage Flooring, Inc. was incorporated in July of '97 and filed chapter 11 in April of '99. Tim Boone handled the corporate bankruptcy case, which is nearing completion. The assets were sold, and the business is continuing under a new name; I have been retained to serve in a sales capacity but have no equity in the new entity.

I expect to have to file a Chapter 7 bankruptcy, and my wife may have to file Chapter 13 in order to convince the Small Business Administration (SBA) to come to an agreement on the equity in our home.

I look forward to talking with you very soon. This process is so very painful. We are anxious to get this mess behind us, so we can soon begin rebuilding our financial lives.

Mark Johnson

Narration

So, how exactly does a work-related injury generate legal drama? A reasonable question, and if we lived in a perfect world where everybody did as they were supposed to do, we would need no lawyers, judges, mediators, or courts. If Miriam's accident had taken place in a public place because of someone's clear cut negligence, the case would have included things like punitive damages and loss of consortium, which would have increased the monetary value of the case exponentially. In Miriam's case, the accident happened at her place of employment and was instantly subject to the laws put in place by the Georgia state legislature for workman's compensation. These statutes clearly define how injured workers must be cared for and they protect employers and insurance companies (E/I) by limiting their liability. Negligence, pain and suffering, or loss of consortium are off the table. It does provide for medical care and **some** loss of income for the injured worker, as well as things needed to facilitate activities of daily living (ADLs) of the injured worker.

More than two years after her accident, with no improvement in sight, and the statute of limitations for her case fast approaching, we reluctantly hired a lawyer. Why didn't we hire one sooner? Accidents happen. She was going to have surgery, recover, and we would go on living life. Unfortunately, that was not the way it worked out for us. Mr. Harris, the attorney who handled our personal bankruptcy, referred us to Fred Hill, who specialized in workman's compensation cases. Attorney Fred was the poor fellow who agreed to champion Miriam's interests in the legal arena. It is not clear how many times he regretted this decision over the years, but to his credit he persevered until its conclusion. In the coming pages you may often wonder why he did not kick us to the curb. Maybe he should have, but in our defense, remember what was happening in the other "rings of our circus" while I'm pitching fits in the coming pages...

Letter to attorney Fred Hill

January 8, 2000

Our research indicates the E/I must provide certain things, if her long-term therapy requires them:

"A seriously injured worker may be entitled to a panoply of services ranging from in home attendant care to specially equipped automobiles to specially adapted housing to spas and swimming pools. An excellent analysis of the employer's potential liability for these and other items may be found in Richard C. Kissiah's treatise, Georgia Workers' Compensation Law published by Michie."

-

It is time to play hardball with the E/I (employer/insurer). Miriam is not getting better, and she has been denied access to the temporary relief that a spa would provide. On the financial front, we have heard nothing concerning the request for Temporary Partial Disability past, present, or future. She should be due total disability for the recovery period following each of her six surgeries. Also, again according to our research, I could be compensated for the care I have delivered during each of these periods! I was providing care for "their" patient that they were not. Some compensation is due for at least some of the sleepless nights over the last 30+ months:

"A frequently overlooked item and the subject of potential tremendous exposure on the part of the insurer is in home non-medical attendant care. An injured worker who cannot take care of his own basic personal needs and cannot be left alone may require the 24-hour presence of a caretaker. Most frequently, this is the individual's spouse. This may require the spouse to either cease working or to refrain from obtaining the employment that he or she now must seek in order to compensate for the loss of income from the injured worker. The fee schedule discussed below contemplates that a family member can provide these services, finding that the usual, customary and reasonable charge would be $7.00 per hour with a maximum of 12 hours per day. The hours can be extended if the Board deems it to be reasonably necessary. Chatham County Dept. of Family & Children Services v. Wilson, 221 Ga. App. 366, 471 S.E. 2nd 316 (1996)."

Fred, please take whatever action is necessary to get things moving **quickly***. Each passing day seems like a week and each night drags like a month for someone in constant pain and for people in our desperate situation!*

Mark Johnson

Letter to attorney Fred Hill

June 19, 2000

After talking with Miriam following your conversation with her, I understand the following to be true:

The E/I has said no to the spa.

The E/I's "no" to evaluation/surgery in New York still stands.

We will find out soon about the spinal cord stimulator, but at this time do not know what they will do.

They want to settle.

You are filing papers concerning the temporary partial disability (TPD) which should get us a hearing soon.

Will this hearing include anything besides the TPD? Can the E/I keep saying no to things, or do we have any recourse? Although their posture makes sense from a business perspective, it is contrary to information we have located on the internet. You are aware that we agree with the opinion you expressed in January, about never settling this case.

The balance of power will improve once we get in front of a judge.

Journal

5 a.m., Saturday, July 1, 2000

Fred told Miriam on the phone the other day that we would have a difficult time proving that the hours I submitted for compensation were wholly for Miriam's benefit and not something that the whole family benefitted from, such as preparing meals. There have been hundreds of nights like this in the last three years. Through my journals and the testimony of those familiar with our situation, I think this hurdle can be jumped. I do not think there should be a problem justifying my request for compensation.

Although I took her to only one doctor appointment this week, I have taken her to a spa three different times! Getting her in and out of the van, in and out of the spa, and waiting for her usually takes nearly an hour and half for each visit. Since neither Matthew nor I have ever joined her in the spa, except for during family vacations, this can hardly be described as a "normal family activity." The doctor appointment was to see Dr. Edwards for a nerve block. I took time from work, took her to the appointment, and afterwards had to transport her in a wheelchair to the car. Her leg was so dead, she had no control of it whatsoever; it followed her, much like a piece of firewood that was tied to her waist. Once home, I had to help her into her chair, where she stayed the rest of the day. I arrived three hours late for work.

Back when I took her to the plant, it was as much for my convenience as for her help. She could sit and answer the phone while I could attend to her other needs. I knew where she was and how she was doing. On many occasions she laid down on a sofa that was placed there for her use. Does this sound normal to you?

We now have a hot tub. Some tender-hearted people in our church had a cheap, five-year-old unit that they had replaced with a new model. This one is **on loan** until we get a "real" one, but it should be better than what we had; and far more convenient than the friend's we were using. Several hundred dollars have been spent on parts to get it functioning.

The hours I submitted for her care on the invoice are justified and conservative. Her care has been nearly all-consuming. Although I am not complaining, if compensation is available for some of this time, it would certainly be helpful and appreciated.

Letter to attorney Fred Hill

Sunday, July 16, 2000

I have forwarded to you the letter I sent to Dr. Robel this morning. I will also send you a copy of the instructions we received upon checkout Friday from Winder/Barrow following the spinal cord stimulator implantation. Please notice the 30 days she is supposed to spend lying down. It would have made little difference, but we were not aware of this prior to the procedure.

What is your strategy at this point? Time is "of the essence" and with RSD apparently gaining momentum, time is not on Miriam's side. She probably will not be able to travel for several weeks, but it would be good to get on Dr. Ware's schedule ASAP. Have you filed the papers you said you were going to file requesting a hearing? Does ALTMA HOSPITAL have anyone else they would like for her to see for another opinion? They cannot simply say, "No," and do nothing, right?

Yes, the top priority is getting her to NYC. However, I fail to understand why this pursuit must be exclusive of other items on the master agenda; the macro and micro are not exclusive of one another.

The loaner spa is functioning for now, but it is obvious why it had been replaced. This unit will cost us a fortune to operate in electricity and chemicals and will likely require almost constant repair and new parts to keep it running. I am hopeful we will have something else before cold weather arrives, but for now it is greatly appreciated.

My greatest complaint, at this point, is the poor job you have done communicating with us. Please try to put yourself in my place. If this were your wife and you had to watch her writhe in pain day in and day out, month after month, while other people held control of her destiny, what would you be doing in order to get her some relief? Sitting idly by, doing nothing, and hoping the physicians and attorneys involved at least glance at her file occasionally is not an option for us anymore. During the first several months of this year we relaxed, confident that you were implementing the plan you outlined during our January meeting and that the doctors were busy developing another plan of attack. As it turns out, nothing happened on any front, except the calendar and clock kept singing a noisy duet. The clock is like a beating drum; the calendar chimes in with a crescendo every four weeks when it loses another page.

We are naive and inexperienced in legal matters. You are our "point man" for the legal stuff, just as Dr. Robel is on the medical front. During your last phone conversation with Miriam, you mentioned that we may want to seek other council. If you are weary of us and this case let me know, and we will make other plans. In January you and Mr. Harris convinced us that you were the man to help her. We have not been seeking other counsel but can if you so desire.   We have honored your request not to pester you by phone; too bad you did not say anything about faxes, huh? At the same time, you have been informed of everything I/we are doing to keep her care (and case) moving forward.

Her case and her pain need and deserve your prompt attention. Everything you have asked us to do, get, or provide was done in a very timely manner. This included in depth research on a spa and requests for information from different doctors. I think we share mutual goals for the outcome of Miriam's case. Please help us put these on some kind of timetable or correct our misconceptions and expectations. If you desire to be shed of us, inform us of this also.

Letter to attorney Fred Hill

May 1, 2001

As you are probably aware, Miriam's condition is not improving and, in fact, is growing more challenging by the day. The latest involves collateral damage to her shoulders and left hip, just more pain and agony for one who has suffered more than her share.

This, of course, requires even more care and assistance from those of us obligated to provide it. She requires around-the-clock care. Someone must always be here to provide basic assistance and to unlock her leg when it locks. This care is exacting a heavy price from my son and me that should be compensated for.

My question for you: we have a hearing coming up which is scheduled to address the E/I's inability to write checks in a timely manner and mail them to the correct address. Would this be a good opportunity to bring up family compensation for attendant care and the issue of having her case designated as catastrophic?

I have no sympathy for the E/I, because I must live with the consequences of their shiny floors every day. There have been enough delays in her treatment over the last three and half years to make my blood boil. I am ready and willing to fight for what is due her (and us). Mr. "Nice Guy" has left the building.

Letter to attorney Fred Hill

May 2, 3, and 4, 2001

Re: Our phone conversation of 5/2

Thank you for your prompt call after receiving my last letter. I have spent a lot of time thinking about our conversation.

We should anticipate a continuance instead of a hearing on Wednesday. Any idea how long this will delay the hearing?

I have given considerable thought to this attendant care compensation and have the following additional points for you to ponder on:

1. *Robel does not know what Miriam's days and nights are like. This is also true concerning her physical therapist, who spends more time with her than all the other "professional care providers" combined. Peggy,* **the attendant who spends six hours per day five days per week with Miriam, has seen it all**: *vomiting, spasms, lockups, medication induced delirium, and the nagging, on-going, unrelenting pain.*

2. **Nights are the worst for Miriam,** *and only a handful of people have had the "opportunity" to see what we deal with night after night. How would Dr. Robel have enough information to write a script for 'round-the-clock' care? He only spends 15 minutes with her once a month (on a good month).*

3. **Could her condition and needs not be established through the testimony of those who have spent time with her**? *This would include the day-time attendant, myself, her sister, a friend who has spent two Sunday nights with her "so Mark could sleep," a multitude of friends and extended family, and then of course, there is my journal.*

4. **All the post-surgery recovery periods prior to this past November, have been borne entirely by my son and me** *with the help of some friends, and extended family. I would think it would be*

possible to build a case for attendant care for these post-surgical periods.

5. *As her condition has continued to deteriorate, especially over the last year, her care requirements have grown.* *Three years ago, when she was not recovering from a procedure, she was able to drive, work some, and at least, maneuver about independently. All this has now changed. Her driving privileges were probably revoked a year later than they should have been, but she has not driven now since June of 2000, when Dr. Robel took away her ability to drive legally.* **Now that her shoulders have become involved, the poor woman cannot even turn over in bed without assistance and maneuvering about with crutches is becoming increasingly painful!**

6. *The attendant arrives shortly after we leave in the morning and leaves about 40 minutes before Matthew gets home from school in the afternoon. During these periods Miriam is confined to the couch, having hopefully taken care of all personal needs before being left alone. Clearly the rest of the load is left for us to bear.* ***Her nighttime care has allowed an average of only two or three good nights of sleep per week since last summer!*** *This has taken a tremendous toll on my health in addition to affecting my performance at work and what I am able to accomplish around home. I have been sick more this winter than the last four or five combined!*

As I understand the statute, family members can be compensated for attendant care at the rate of $7 per hour for a maximum of 12 hours per day. **If Miriam were single, she would be in a nursing home of some kind right now**! I understand you have never considered her case to be nearly this serious, but I can convince you that it is as bad as I am claiming.

I would like your assistance in getting us compensated for as much of this time as possible.

Journal

Sunday, May 27, 2001

On Thursday Miriam gave a deposition to the Attorney representing the E/I. Prior to the meeting, we met with attorney Fred for about 30 minutes. I have asked him in more than one letter to develop a strategy for getting me some compensation for providing her care. On Thursday, his attitude toward the idea appeared to have shifted and he informed the hospital's attorney that he wanted the issue put on the table for discussion. Right now, anyway, it looks as if she may get the back benefits that are due her, as well as possibly some back attendant care, as well to get set up for benefits going forward. Timely checks would be a welcome start, but attendant care compensation for me would be a big shot in the finances and would relieve a lot of pressure. Time will tell how it will all shake out, but both lawyers agreed that the E/I does not want to defend this case before a judge; gee, I wonder why?

Journal

Sunday, June 10, 2001

The drought that has plagued our region for nearly four years is taking a breather. We have been blessed with over four inches of rain in the last 10 days and the earth is looking lush again.

The same sort of thing seems to be happening with Miriam's legal case. After much pushing, berating and bad-mouthing attorney Fred, he seems to be paying greater attention to Miriam's case. This attention may provide some desperately needed nourishment to our finances. He has gotten serious about recovering back and underpaid benefits for Miriam that date back more than three years. In addition to this, he appears to have listened to my assertions that I am due compensation for attendant care. Workman's comp will not compensate me for "the loss of consortium" by law; but should, I think, pay me for the care delivered for which they do not have to pay an outsider. It has taken quite some time to convince Fred that this is due, just, and defendable, but judging by some of the correspondence he has sent out this week, it appears he has decided this too is worth fighting for. If and when all of this comes through, we will be able to shore up our financial world and feel as though we are not living quite so close to the edge. For now at least, it feels as though Fred is on our side, which has been something we have questioned from time to time.

Letter to attorney Fred Hill

June 27, 2001

Good Wednesday morning!

Mr. Martin's (hospital's lawyer) letter is certainly no surprise to either of us or to you, I am sure. Please inform him that I am willing and eager to be deposed.

The simplest way to explain what has happened to our family would be to picture our little nuclear unit as a Conestoga wagon rumbling through life. Our son, house and businesses, responsibilities and obligations are piled neatly upon the wagon. On October 9, 1997, Miriam and I are harnessed in tandem, on the same end of the wagon, leaning into the load and pulling it ever so slowly down our chosen path. On October 10, 1997, Miriam was not only unable to remain in the harness but became tied to the back and had to be dragged along behind the wagon.

Just keeping the wagon from falling off a cliff has been my goal most of the time. When Stacy Casey came on board, we finally began receiving some attendant care following the December surgery in NY. Prior to this, who do they think was providing her care?

Celia Klotz is a friend and an RN by trade. Her heart is larger than her head, which explains her offer to spend Sunday nights with Miriam to give me some time off. Although she has spent only eight or ten nights with Miriam, she can attest to what they were like and provide an objective (and professional) opinion regarding what the other nights are like for Miriam's primary caregiver.

I realize I have once again violated your request for brevity, but I wanted you to understand how passionate and justified I am about what we are asking for. A lot is at stake, but I do not think the requests are unreasonable. In the event they refuse to compensate me, ask them which nursing home they want her deposited at; I want to get on with my life.

I could fill a courtroom with witnesses who have attended church with us, worked at her side prior to her injury, worked with her since her injury, helped to transport her to and from appointments, attended aquatic therapy with her, visited us at home, etc... There are people from many differing walks of life who have known her for up to 20 years, and they could attest to her daily agonizing struggle to function and to recover, as well as the impact this has had on our family. In other words, I think an air-tight case can be built around her credibility and integrity. Neither of us have ever received or pursued any kind of settlement or compensation from any litigation, insurance company, or government entity, including unemployment or any other government relief programs. This is simply not how we were raised or how we planned to live our lives.

Our family's future welfare may depend on pursuing and procuring whatever satisfaction the law allows.

Soapbox Digression:

Following a work-related accident, the injured worker is usually overwhelmed by questions and uncertainty and can be easy prey for unscrupulous operators. An employer of any size probably has an entire staff of people to protect their interests and minimize the financial damage to the business from accidents. Some employers readily provide needed assistance and care for the injured employee; others prefer to play hardball. How can they play dirty? They deny claims; they put pressure on doctors and lawyers to write opinions, and direct dialogue in directions that minimize costs and get people back to work, sometimes before they are ready or able to do so. This is generally a strategy that places the interests of the employer above those of the injured individual. Remember, it is the E/I who writes ALL the checks to everybody, and money does a lot of talking!

Fraud exists on both sides of the equation. Employees fake injuries all the time so they can sit on the couch and collect checks, so I understand the employer/insurer must be diligent and carefully assess the validity of each case. Fortunately for us, Miriam's case was pretty cut and dried. There was no doubt about where the injury occurred or what the injuries were, and it was all well documented. We suspect these facts however did not keep the E/I from hiring investigators to lurk around our residence to see if they could film Miriam walking to the mailbox or dancing with her husband. We noticed several black SUVs parked at the edge of our property through the years. The E/I never really believed Miriam could really be as bad as she was; heck I lived with her, and I had a hard time comprehending her condition, so I understand their skepticism.

Once we returned from New York in the summer of '01, her care plan changed from finding a surgical fix, to one of how best to manage the pain and facilitate her life. Unfortunately, this is where the legal case began to heat up.

By the fall of '01 and winter of '02 our little family was not in a good place. On the morale front we were very discouraged. The story of Humpty Dumpty kept coming to mind, because all the king's horses and all the king's men were also not able to put him back together after his great fall either. To the credit of the E/I, they really did spend what should have been necessary to get her restored to health and it was not their fault the effort failed, but neither was it ours. Any hope we had of getting Miriam on her feet and freed from pain was, by this time, mostly gone; there was nowhere else to turn for a medical cure. Financially things were very bleak. We filed personal and corporate bankruptcy in 2000. Following her last surgery in NYC in '01, following six extra days of recovery prior to travel, I was laid off from the sales job at the plant I had once owned.

The fixer in me kept communicating with the medical staff trying to keep her pain managed, but mostly I turned my focus to the legal case that was in a perpetual state of going nowhere.

Although there were several doctors I could badger, there was only one lawyer, poor Fred! According to my records, Stacy Casey was the recipient of "only" 33 of my letters while Fred got over 125! This is probably why on more than one occasion, he reminded me that I was not his client, Miriam was. His secretary gave Miriam several tongue lashings about my involvement in the case. The problem for him was that we did a lot of research into the Workman's Compensation statutes in Georgia and were able to read for ourselves what should be getting done for Miriam but was not. If the hospital had been doing what this lay person understood was their obligation under the law, our financial situation would not have been nearly as dire. To fix this problem, my focus, attention, and mental energy were turned toward trying to get the E/I to do what I understood they were supposed to do. My only leverage was legal recourse, and my conduit to the legal system went through poor Fred.

Although not his client, I was Miriam's voice, and he was going to have to deal with me. Another thing about my adjunct position was that I did not feel compelled to make nice in order to keep peace or make friends. I could not be fired, and I was not bound by any "rules of engagement;" I was the squeaky door, constantly reminding the entire system that Miriam's case needed attention. After looking back over how many letters I sent him, Fred was probably overwhelmed by my demands and impatience, but I was a desperate husband trying to solve a myriad of problems that by necessity required him to do things.

My philosophy was that if Georgia's statutes made provision for injured workers to receive certain things, then we needed to go after those things. Fred, and to some extent Stacy Casey, were more of the opinion that if not many people get accessible vans, spas, attendant care, compensation for family members or accessible housing, then those were buttons we should be careful about pushing. They thought we should be satisfied that medical bills were being paid and the E/I was graciously allowing us to keep the medical team we liked. We should be happy they were paying for some attendant care and providing a check that covered a portion of her lost wages and just not worry about how badly she needed things that would help facilitate her limitations that were, by the way, caused by the E/I.

If your boat was capsized by the wake from a passing cruise ship and you are fighting to keep your head above water, would you be satisfied if the ship that caused the problem and was fully capable of restoring you to safety, simply tossed you a life vest and waved as it continued its journey? I was not either. Miriam's work-related injury had swamped our little family-shaped vessel, and we were desperate for rescue. In my mind, the E/I needed to step up and do right by us.

Part of the problem, as you will discover in the coming pages, is that it is hardly a "fair fight." The E/I can load their side of the table with all the legal power, doctors, evaluators and experience they are willing to pay for; where the injured worker has one lawyer who gets a state mandated percent of a weekly benefits check, which also technically comes from the E/I. They remind injured workers and their lawyers of this periodically by suspending the weekly checks.

While defense attorneys get to charge for every phone call and every item of correspondence either read or composed while dealing with the case, the plaintiff's representative receives nothing. (This is also true, for issues such as attendant care, items of durable medical equipment, fighting for medical treatment etc.) This makes for a very unbalanced playing field! Obviously, the patient (injured worker) cannot give up 25% of their house, medicine, attendant care, or wheelchair allowance to compensate their attorney, but this also takes away the attorney's incentive to mount a good fight on behalf of their client. Not, by the way, an allegation being made in Miriam's case. While the E/I has lots of incentive to deny, delay, and aggravate; the other has no incentive to perform. **How does this system serve the best interests of the injured worker?**

It is a colossal waste of time and resources for the E/I to spend money year after year after year fighting a well-documented case, when those resources could be providing needed care for the injured worker. The strategy of "starving" the plaintiff (and their lawyer) into settling an issue or an entire case is immoral and should not be legal! This is also why many workman's compensation lawyers work to settle cases as quickly as possible, because they can bank a check and move on to the next case. To his credit, this was not the way Fred operated.

My radical proposal to solve this inequity is as follows: it should apply for all cases deemed catastrophic. **Every time the E/I cuts a check for their lawyer, they also must write a second and equal check for the plaintiff attorney**. The playing field would be leveled, and the injured workers would get what is needed much more quickly, because all parties suddenly have an economic incentive to resolve and address issues rather than wage war! I speculate that actual attorney fees paid by the E/I would go down, because cases and issues would be resolved much more quickly.

I apologize for the digression...

Miriam's need for the legal system focused on weekly benefits, accessible transportation, accessible housing, and attendant care. Things like spas and wheelchairs fall into the category of adaptive equipment. Left to their own devices, the E/I would prefer to deny some or all the above. All together now: "Poor Fred."

Journal

Sunday, September 9, 2001

The deposition went fine, all I had to do was tell the truth; the truth is far worse than any fiction I could compose. Since then, I have spent countless hours reducing more than 130 pages of this journal to the 20 or so Fred wanted so we could enter it as courts evidence. It has been a time-consuming job that has kept me from doing any additional writing. Reading back over the past four years has reminded me of many things I had mercifully forgotten. It also convinced me that we need to ask for more attendant compensation!

Letter to attorney Fred Hill

September 27, 2001

The almost imperceptible pace of progress on Miriam's case compels me to, once again, serve as "the squeaking hinge" for our family.

In January of 2000, as Miriam was signing the agreement to have you represent her in this case against ALTMA HOSPITAL, you made the following statement: **"We will probably be in court within six weeks and will get a check coming very soon."**

We are frustrated! Last week we received the notice from the judge's office that because discovery had not been completed (in four months!), "the file was removed from the docket and returned to the file room." **The weekly checks are once again four weeks in arrears; there has been no word on her back benefits; late fees have not been paid on the checks she has received; trip expenses are** *desperately needed and are past due; any mention of seeking reimbursement for the spa has not been acknowledged, and we do not even have a court date to further discuss attendant care.*

Stacy Casey remains convinced that a catastrophic designation on this case would be very helpful to your side of the case, as well as to hers.

According to Dr. William's protocol, Miriam is to be full weight bearing within one week, but so far, because of the nerve problems, has not made the progress she was supposed to have made six weeks ago! **In my opinion, if she ever walks again, it will be sometime in the distant future (six months to two years),** *certainly no time soon.*

I understand this is a complicated case that will not be resolved for years to come. However, in the interim, **we have got to have some resolution and relief on these current issues.**

Letter to attorney Fred Hill

January 25, 2002

Dear Mr. Hill,

We received a copy of the Catastrophic application today, thank you for taking care of this. Having Miriam's case designated Catastrophic should help Stacy Casey get around some of the E/I's foot dragging. It also eliminates the statute of limitations and caps on benefits.

One thing about Dr. Robel's reply warrants a correction. I think you are aware of this, but we wanted to clarify it just in case. In a letter dated January 8, 2002, Dr. Robel writes: "She is basically a household ambulator." This is not true. Stacy Casey, Celia Kotz, or any of her care providers can attest to this fact.

Miriam does not walk at home or anywhere else.

She uses a wheelchair all the time. No one, including her immediate family have seen her walk, even with the aid of crutches, for at least six months. Our memories are not clear on exactly when she became 100% wheelchair dependent, but I am certain she has not been able to use crutches since the July surgery, and probably for several months prior, but the July date is one of which we are certain.

Thanks for your help,

Mark and Miriam

Letter to attorney Fred Hill

May 3, 2002

Dear Mr. Hill,

Several things are on my mind, that I am compelled to share with yours.

I am glad of the recent agreement over a portion of the back benefits; this is good and long overdue.

Miriam needs to do better. The latest trial for the intrathecal pump (her second), ended more than a week ago; the recovery from the complications related to this trial, a profound leakage of spinal fluid, is only now in its final stages. Spinal fluid leaked from the site of insertion for the intrathecal trial. When it was removed, the stupid woodworker Miriam hangs around with asked the almighty doctor if the hole at the base of her spine needed to be plugged?

"No, it will be fine," said the doctor to the woodworker.

After we arrived home, we measured a teaspoon of spinal fluid every 11 minutes flowing from her back. She was in horrible pain, but she had to wait for the next day and return to Atlanta so the good doctor could put her to sleep and do a blood patch to stem the flow. The local ER doctors wouldn't touch her and said we had to return to the doctor that caused the problem. We were pretty upset by the time the problem got fixed; it's as if no one cares how much agony this woman is in, even when their incompetence caused the problem!

Frustration is understandably building. She/we have done everything asked by a legion of professionals and she seems to only be getting worse. Around every turn, we encounter more disappointment and get farther away from any meaningful cure, or even reprieve, from the nearly constant pain.

Thanks for your help,

Mark

August 2002

The much-anticipated hearing was cancelled. We were furious that Fred allowed this date to get away. Basically, attorney Martin agreed to settle some of the issues and convinced attorney Fred that there was no reason to go to court. No one, unfortunately, thought to ask patient Miriam what she wanted. What a disappointment! They agreed to buy a van, pay for part of a spa and to pay me for six months of attendant care. The other issues are to be discussed before a mediator. The attorneys will retreat to their respective lairs/offices, and several months will likely pass before anything else happens.

In the work comp system, the primary doctor is called the Authorized Treating Physician, or ATP. In Miriam's case this was Dr. Robel. He was the first to see her after the accident because he was the orthopedic doctor on Altma Hospital's W/C doctor panel. Someone needed to oversee her case and lend continuity to the medical treatment. Doctor Robel was important to us because he knew her whole story, including surgeries, medications, treatments, etc., AND the argument could be made that he was the choice of the E/I since they decided who was on the W/C doctor panel.

When opposing counsel thought Dr. Robel was writing scripts they deemed too favorable to Miriam, they would send her to an Independent Medical Exam (IME). This exam is performed by a doctor of their choosing and there are no limits to the number of IMEs they can demand she attend. They used this tactic often. They would try to locate someone with a medical degree who would declare she was able to return to work and did not need as much, if any attendant care or medications. Miriam went to IMEs in Athens, Lawrenceville, and several in Atlanta. Additionally, she had an in-patient evaluation at Shepherd Spinal Clinic in Atlanta and another intense day-long evaluation in Jacksonville, Florida, where she was poked, prodded, and examined thoroughly.

There was a lot of legal maneuvering concerning her medical caregivers. There were many attempts to wrest her away from Dr. Robel, and later, pain specialist Dr. Elliott. Fred spent a lot of time and energy fighting attempts by attorneys Martin and later Mr. McKay at the State Board of Workman's Compensation. The subject of Dr. Robel being the ATP was discussed at numerous rehab conferences and mediation sessions. They were convinced these doctors were too "patient friendly," so they wanted a change. To accomplish this, they went "Dr. shopping."

The evaluation at Shepherd Center was by far the most intense. It was in-patient, so Miriam was put on a floor with patients trying to recover from profoundly serious accidents or conditions that often involve spine trauma. Compared to these patients Miriam's condition looked good. After all, even though she was confined to a wheelchair at this point, she had the use of most of her limbs and she could transfer into and out of her wheelchair.

Over the course of two days, she was evaluated by a host of medical professionals, each with their own field of expertise. At the conclusion, everyone gathered in a conference room along with the lawyers from both sides, a representative from Altma Hospital, the pained patient, and her not-so-patient husband. It was a room full of white coats and business suits, one woman in a wheelchair, and me. Each specialty delivered their report then answered questions.

This was another frustrating day for Mr. Martin, et al, because they failed to accomplish their goal of accumulating opinions favorable to their side. I was not allowed to spend the night with Miriam during her time at Shepherd, so when she had one of her leg shaking spasms in the middle of the night, she was left to writhe in agony for 30 minutes while the nursing staff attended to other patients. Thankfully, it was mentioned in the report, so we had proof she had spasms whether I was present or not. I was also prevented from joining her for the evaluations. This fit the narrative that I was part of the problem, so needed to be kept away from the evaluators while they were evaluating.

The question-and-answer portion of this little get together is where I scored big for team Miriam. I asked a simple question that each evaluator answered in turn: "How many hours per day should Miriam be left alone?"

"None" was the unanimous response, much to the chagrin of Mr. Martin, et al. I have no idea how much money the E/I spent for this evaluation, but I know it failed to accomplish what they had hoped. Their plan, as I understood it, was to secure enough opinions contrary to Miriam's treatment and existing opinions of her condition that the expected lifetime cost of her care could be reduced to a much smaller number, and then they could force us to settle the case for an amount the E/I thought reasonable. At the conclusion of this meeting, Mr. Martin took Fred aside and told him they wanted to settle the case and that he would hear from them with an offer "soon."

"Soon" never arrived, so when Fred followed up on the conversation with Mr. Martin at a conference a few months later, Fred was told, "It's going to be too expensive to settle." Translated, that was lawyer speak for "We are going to wait and see if she dies." Although not officially trained in this arcane language, by this point in the case I was understanding more than mere mortals untrained in the law are supposed to.

Attorney Martin's replacement, Ralph McKay, 13 years later, decided she should go to Jacksonville for another evaluation. This time it was to see if she could be admitted into a program where she would be taken off her most expensive pain medication and put onto something much cheaper. Of course, the reasons given were always about how much better off Miriam would be if this would work. Again, my newly developed language skills helped me to understand that this was really an attempt to reduce the cost so they could take another stab at settling the case for a more palatable sum. It evidently is highly unusual for cases to linger this long in the system without being resolved through settlement.

We drove to Jacksonville, where she was evaluated by several more specialists. During one evaluation, they measured the temperature difference between her feet at 11 degrees Celsius! When the report was sent to the lawyers, it stated that "She was not a candidate for their program." Wow, yet another whiff and miss. Team E/I sulked back to their dugout.

Journal

Sunday, November 24, 2002

"How is Miriam doing?" "they" ask, projecting a demeanor of genuine, but-please-make-it-brief concern. Something happened last night that may offer as good an answer as I could come up with.

We were watching a movie entitled "The Third Twin" on Lifetime. What made this movie different from almost any other movie we have ever watched together is that we had both read the book, written by Ken Follett, within the previous two months. The storyline involved a medical mystery that included laboratories and DNA, etc.—the kind of stuff that really turns Miriam's crank. I had stumbled across an audio version that I listened to while driving to and from work, knew it was a story written just for Miriam, and checked out the hard cover version for her. She read it, enjoyed it, we talked about it, and then apparently it was gone.

Last night, while we watched the movie, she had no recollection of having read the book or of any coming twists as the plot unfolded. This, from a woman who I once considered as having a photographic memory! She burst into tears when she was brought face to face with irrefutable evidence of the condition of her once razor-sharp, perfect memory. She is aware from time to time, but, apparently, suffers her loss privately. Last night it was out in the open and it could not be ignored. As we prepared for bed, I reminded her that we still were not sure if the condition was a temporary thing brought on by the medications she is taking, or if it is permanent. Of course, if she does not come off the drugs, we may never know.

This is Thanksgiving week and this year our family will travel to a state park outside of Nashville, TN to celebrate the holiday in traditional togetherness. We had thought that surely by this holiday we would make the trip in a new van equipped for her needs, but in truth, the "new van" remains a fixture in our fantasies, as it has not yet even been ordered! What makes this all the more remarkable is that the evaluation which declared her need for a van took place more than a year ago; the first quotes were procured last February or March; back in the summer the E/I agreed to buy a van, and a court order for an accessible van has been in place since September. It is now late November, and we have no van and no order for a van.

Journal

January 24, 2003

Three weeks into the new year, there is at the same time more hope and more frustration than we have had in some time. Hope, because an accessible van will soon be ordered and progress will soon begin on the house. Questions concerning our decision-making constantly swirl inside my head. Should I push harder for results, or am I making things worse? Lately it seems like I have made Stacy mad and Fred pretty much stays upset with us. Doing nothing just prolongs things, and my badgering makes folks mad. I guess I am supposed to watch my wife writhe in agony and endure one sleepless night after another and keep quiet about it. It should not bother me to watch my productive life get washed away like footprints on the beach by the surf of crisis, along with our financial security and future dreams. I should quietly ignore all this and do nothing. This is the part I could improve at — doing nothing. Perhaps we should fold our hand of cards and start talking settlement? There are no handbooks for victims on the best way to handle these kinds of crises. Laws are different in every state, so strategies and procedures might have 50 different approaches. Miriam's case is in "rare air." Only a fraction of one percent of work-related injuries are close to this complicated or expensive.

On or about January 30, 2003, I had had enough of the nonsense and excuses about why an accessible van had not been ordered, even though a consent order had been in place since the prior summer. I went over everyone's head and sent a letter directly to Deborah Krotenberg, who was in charge of the State Board of W/C. In it, I explained that E/I attorney Martin seldom returned calls to case manager Casey or to Miriam's attorney Fred, and consequently no progress had been made on getting Miriam a van. Evidently Mr. Martin was able to find time to take Ms. Krotenberg's call, and very shortly after that he found the time needed to order a van!

I was duly chastised by Fred for my end run around him with my letter to the State Board without his knowledge. Much to his chagrin, it would not be my last. Shortly afterward Mr. Martin was replaced by Mr. McKay, which was probably just a coincidence. Mr. Martin's method of operation was to stonewall any progress by simply not taking or returning phone calls from Fred or Stacy. His strategy was to wear us down by being incommunicado, which was sophomoric and unprofessional. They would both leave messages day after day, then never hear back from him, not just for a day or two, but for weeks! He kept costs down by not picking up the phone and authorizing expenditures. He complained loudly to Fred about me but knowing this did not cause any loss of sleep on my part. His replacement was tough, not very sympathetic or compassionate, but at least he would communicate with Stacy and Fred. His conduct never inspired any letters of complaint to the State Board. Unlike his predecessor, Mr. McKay was just doing his job.

Letter from Miriam to attorney Fred Hill

July 23, 2003

After reading the deposition from Dr. Dean, there appear to be a few items that require some clarification:

The thing about Mark not being "trained" in attendant care is baloney! He's had six years of on-the-job training. Every single CNA or other (remember Celia is an RN) that has walked through my door to take a turn at caring for me, has had to be trained by me or Mark on how to release my spasms. Remember that prior to the last surgery the tibia was actually rotated to the left so much it would mechanically lock behind the femur and had to be rotated and pulled down to bring it back in alignment. The physical therapist, Dr. Robel, and the doctors at the Hospital for Special Surgery all noted and observed this. The doctors and nurses at the Hospital for Special Surgery looked to Mark when I had the lockups or spasms while in their presence! The nurses after each of the two surgeries in New York called Mark from his room across the street from the hospital in the middle of the night to come to my room and assist them with complications because they realized Mark had far more experience in treating me, and they did not know what to do!

Since he is the ONLY common denominator through this entire ordeal, he has a perspective no one else possesses. He has also seen and felt the repercussions of mistakes, delays, and inaction on the part of the medical decision-makers involved in this case. I am not surprised he is becoming a "thorn in the side" of the opposing counsel. Watching his spouse suffer for six years while people "play chess" with our lives has had a big effect on him!

I know it is out of character for me to write letters, **but I'm tired of people assuming that they know what I feel but don't take the time to really find out,** *or if they do ask, they seem to tune me out about the time I say, "Well, every day is different, but..." Dr. Dean's deposition really set me off.*

Thanks for allowing me to set the record straight.

Miriam Johnson

Letter to Stacy Casey

September 28, 2003

I am sorry you got dragged into court on Wednesday. Just remember, we are not the ones who requested your presence, although it was good to see you.

Fred recently told us that you have expressed concern that you have lost our confidence and should be replaced by another case manager. This follows on the heels of the comment you made following the Shepherd meeting: "I don't think I can take another two years of this case," or something to that effect.

Fred has given me permission to reply directly, so here goes:

Miriam needs you; I need you; Fred needs you; and Mr. Martin, et al, would probably make the same claim, which is a testament to the neutral ground upon which you tread so carefully. Your reputation and conscientiousness lend credibility to Miriam's cause that would be seriously damaged if you left.

Please rest assured that you are wanted and needed on this case.

Fred has promised to file a motion to change the pain doctor from Dr. Dean to Dr. Elliott immediately.

Thanks for all you do,

"Mr." (because that is the only way she ever addressed me) Johnson

Saturday, November 1, 2003

Delays and postponements sum up the year. The house plans, which were supposed to be completed by the end of April, were completed in August, but they still need to be delivered to us or be put out for bids. The evaluation at Shepherd was delayed a week; the court hearing, which first appeared on a court docket for May, was delayed until July, then finally took place in September. The briefs, which were supposed to be submitted "within 10 days," have now been twice delayed and are now scheduled for this coming Wednesday. The only thing that does not delay or postpone is Miriam's agony. It took several months, a script, and two false starts, but Miriam finally got a footrest for her wheelchair, a footrest!

CHAPTER 17
The Fight for Compensation

What are the exact number of hours of care I've provided?

For the first three years, along with help from family and friends, I provided all the care Miriam received outside of hospitals. Thankfully, except for a few days immediately following major surgeries, round-the-clock care was not necessary, and for much of this time, she was also able to drive herself to appointments.

On the day of her accident, I was 39 years of age, had an almost nine-year-old son, a 37-year-old wife, and was the president and majority shareholder of Heritage Flooring, Inc./Heritage Casual Furniture, located in Greensboro, Georgia. This was in addition to owning and managing several rental properties located in Athens, Georgia. Miriam and I were on the same end of the "family wagon," pulling together and trying to build a life and a future for our little family.

Heritage Flooring employed 20 people in the manufacture of hardwood flooring. It was a brand new three-month-old enterprise on October 10, 1997, when I received the early morning call concerning Miriam's accident. Would the enterprise have failed even without her accident? It is impossible to say for sure, but given the economic downturn of the mid-2000s, it is entirely possible. The people who bought the company out of bankruptcy failed during that downturn, and they were much better financed than was I. But of this, there is no doubt—immediately dropping the demands of running the plant and taking care of Miriam hastened the end by many years. At a time when I needed to spend 80 hours a week at the plant in Greensboro, I was instead at her bedside in Athens, Watkinsville, Birmingham, or New York.

It is important to remember that I did not create this injury or the resulting complications. I am not the villain here! The injury to her leg was terrible but the collateral damage to our family was considerable. We suffered the loss of her income, the loss of retirement contributions, the loss of a normal mother for our son, the loss of a healthy wife for me, etc., and the entire thing has been nothing short of an overwhelming disaster (physical, emotional, and financial). I have contributed over and above for my part and am due compensation for the time stolen from my productive working years. I do not recall signing up to be a "candy striper" volunteer for the benefit of the Employer/Insurer (E/I), and I did not intend to give away the most productive years of my working life benefitting a large institution!

Attendant Care

An attempt will be made to explain this, so it makes sense: When Miriam is no longer able to care for herself, the caregiver becomes an "attendant."

This may be the most controversial demand we made to the E/I; I married her, so am I not obligated to provide whatever care she needs? I have and am, but since her employer set this slow-motion chain reaction disaster in motion, shouldn't providing for her care be their responsibility? Why did we need a lawyer? The E/I sat quietly for two years while I provided for her care through all those surgeries, all those appointments, and all those recoveries, and they never once offered us any help. I wore out and used up our friends and family, lost my business, and then my job, to provide for her care. Dr. Robel even wrote a script for "in-home care," but because it was not written using the correct nomenclature (he didn't know what to call it either), the script went unfilled. When Stacy Casey joined the "team," she knew what to call it, so Dr. Robel wrote another script using the correct nomenclature, and we began receiving a few hours of help per week. The E/I was quite content with the fact that Matthew and I were still providing more than 100 hours of care per week. We saved them a ton of money. The funny thing is, the issue of whether or not we were properly trained to care for her was of no concern to them and never came up until we asked to be compensated for a portion of those hours.

As her situation continued to deteriorate and more care was needed, they fought hard against any increases in hours. As a businessman and employer myself, I understand their position. On the victim side of the equation, it seemed callous and immoral. By the time attorney Fred joined team Miriam, our level of desperation was reaching new highs almost daily. Since this case was new to him, it took a while for him to get up to speed with the severity of her case. Unfortunately, we had already been immersed in the mess for more than two years, so our reserves of patience had already been spent. We needed help and relief NOW! But as we were to eventually learn, the legal system does not have a **NOW** button.

This was a long and protracted fight due, in no small part, to the fact that attendant care would have a huge impact on any potential future settlement.

Letter to attorney Fred Hill

February 20, 2002

I am very angry they have taken this amount of time to present this insulting offer to me for the attendant care I provided. In view of what this case has cost them already, this money, which would directly benefit our family, is peanuts. If the full amount of the spa, back temporary partial disability and attendant care are added together, it amounts to only about seven percent of her total medical expenses to date! Although some compromise might be in order, the offer on the table is less than half of what was requested.

As you know, weekly benefits and attendant care are as close as we can get to collecting reimbursement for our losses. Perhaps you can afford to walk away from a large portion of the fees due you, but we have no other "cases" we can look to for any forfeited funds. Our answer to their offer is "No." We need every penny the state statutes entitle us to receive.

Thanks for your help,

~ Mark and Miriam

Letter to attorney Fred Hill

February 26, 2002

You will be shocked to learn that I have a few follow-up thoughts to our phone conversation...

Concerning attendant care:

At present, we are getting 40 hours of daytime weekday care and one night per week of care from an outside provider. In addition to this, Stacy has been great to cover weekends when I am away for business or on Scout trips—big help, no complaints here, doing a great job!

On average, this probably leaves around 110 hours per week (out of 168) where I am providing 100% of her care. I should point out that 110 hours per week fails to consider the two or three days per month I take off work to take her to important appointments or to have procedures performed when the outside attendant is not on duty. The actual average is closer to 115 or 120, of which I am asking to be compensated for 56. This is reasonable!

Establishing the need for round-the-clock care is likely the toughest battle. The list of people who have spent multiple nights in our home providing her care continues to grow. These people, in addition to the journal entries should be helpful in this endeavor.

Original thought for the day: The path of least resistance is not necessarily the one best traveled.

Thanks for your help,

Mark and Miriam

Narration:

Although I feel I am due some compensation for the care I've been providing Miriam, I've never expected to get paid for near all of it. I do think that somewhere there is a "line" that separates the "moral obligation" I have as her spouse and the "moral obligation" the hospital has as the party that caused the injury. Where this line is, is probably an issue the judge will have to decide.

We had a hearing before a mediator. This session was mostly about attendant-care compensation for me in the past and future. I presented my case for compensation for the thousands of hours of care I had provided from the time of her accident until the point they agreed to begin providing outside care. They made an offer that I considered so close to zero, I rejected it. Attorneys Martin and Fred were dismayed that I was digging in my heals on this. The mediator said we should see a judge. Fred explained we might lose and get nothing. I told him to file for a hearing. Was I gambling? Maybe, but it looked to me like the potential upside was far greater than the pittance they offered me.

When we finally went to court, the items being discussed were the two parts to my claim for compensation. For reasons that baffled both the judge and us, Fred inexplicably took the first period (the time from the accident until 2001 when some attendant care was provided) off the table for the hearing and instead chose to focus entirely on the second. This shorter period involved only a fraction of the hours in the first. He assured us after the hearing it would soon be revisited, but it never was. I was pretty angry over this strategy that was never really explained. "Take the pawn and just put him in the corner," was what I heard in my head.

The hearing went well. Miriam, Celia, and I testified on our behalf; Stacy Casey and the claims adjustor for the other side, but they offered no evidence to refute our claims about Miriam's pain or her need for constant care. We hoped for a ruling by Christmas.

In the meantime, we continued to wait, Miriam continued to hurt, I continued to care for her and work as much as I could on whatever sleep I was able to collect each night.

Journal

Thursday, November 13, 2003

Judge Murray's decision arrived yesterday. He received the briefs only last Wednesday, issued the ruling Monday, and the "letter fairy" placed it in our mailbox yesterday. I am shocked that we have this ruling so promptly, but his findings are even more stunning. He awarded me 54 hours per week! This is far more than we had ever dared hope for. I feel vindicated. It is a tremendous shot of encouragement to have the judge declare that my contribution to Miriam's care has tangible value, especially after so many months of listening to Mr. Martin and Dr. Dean imply that I could be part of her problem. Obviously the "tangible value" will be helpful in shoring up the decimated family finances, but the boost to my flagging self-esteem is nearly as important, even though it is less tangible.

As a man, there is an intrinsic desire to care for and provide for our family. For much of recent history, I have felt consumed by circumstances and boxed in by one crisis and then another and have been unable to exercise any control over the course of our family "vessel." The idea of "charting a course," setting goals, and maneuvering toward those goals has been completely out of my hands. I have been the captain of a dismasted ship with a broken rudder, completely unable to impose my will upon the wind or the sea. Instead, we are blown by the winds of crisis and carried by the currents of disaster, while living in fear of uncharted shoals that at any moment could shatter what remains of our tattered vessel.

Judge Murray has, in effect, thrown us a lifeline and ordered that we be towed toward a safe port where repairs can be made in preparation for the rest of the journey. He has declared that the career of caregiver that I have fallen into by default, does have monetary value!

This is only one battle in a long war. After so many disappointments, this is a gratifying victory. No matter the turn of events lying in wait on the next page of the calendar, on this day, we have procured a victory!

The cork was pulled on a bottle of red wine that we purchased last summer from the Habersham Winery. The bottle has been lying in our refrigerator awaiting an occasion worth celebrating. This bottle was salve for our souls as well as pleasing to our palates. Celia arrived for her regularly scheduled Wednesday night keeping-of-the-wife-so-the-husband-can-sleep shift, and she shared our joy and a taste of our wine.

Tuesday, November 17, 2003

Whhhheeeee... the roller coaster ride continues. Attorney Fred called yesterday and informed me that he had talked with attorney Martin and was told they plan to appeal Judge Murray's ruling. In the meantime, they plan to provide us with an additional nine hours per day of attendant care through Oconee Home Health. Mr. Martin is determined that our victory will remain a moral one. He is thoroughly committed to keeping every dollar possible away from our household, even if it costs them double to do so! How determined is he? He will have to pay Oconee Home Health three times what the state would require them to pay me, so that's pretty determined! His obvious strategy is to squeeze us as much as possible financially, so we will become desperate enough to settle the case for a number they consider reasonable. No matter the reasoning behind the strategy, the additional help will make my life easier. I am also emboldened! Having the judge declare I was standing on the right side of the argument was a big deal to me.

Friday, December 26, 2003

Another year is drawing rapidly to a close, with little progress available to report. At the beginning of the year, my goals included getting Miriam to a new pain doctor, finally getting the much-anticipated van, and seeing the house renovated. One out of three is the best I could do; if I were a baseball player, I could demand a new contract with a seven-figure raise, but I'm not and I can't. The van is the sole accomplishment, and this came only after I wrote to Ms. Krotenburg at the State Board of Worker's Comp and asked for her help.

The hospital's appeal, attempting to gut Judge Murray's ruling following our September hearing, has been filed by the opposing counsel. Contrary to Martin's verbal promises, no additional attendant care has been forthcoming, as I expected. Meanwhile, they continue to oppose the idea of changing Miriam's pain care from Dr. Dean to Dr. Elliott. An official request was finally filed by Fred on Tuesday, "only" 15 months after she was first examined, and we decided it was in her best interest to have him treat her—15 months!

Wait, it gets better! Fred called the shop about 10 days ago to tell me he had received a call from Wright Rehab Services, the catastrophic rehab provider with which Stacy Casey works and is a part owner. He said, "Stacy was burned out and overworked and was excusing herself from Miriam's case and wanted to hand the file to someone else within her firm," or something to that effect. I listened as carefully as I could, while pondering the best way to break the news to Miriam. This was going to be another in a long list of bitter disappointments she would have to swallow somehow. Interesting that he wants me, "the not his client" to break the bad news to Miriam, don't you think? Fred mentioned a couple of names that Stacy recommended, but my mind was busy trying to come up with a positive way to spin the news and lessen the blow to my wife, so the names escaped me.

"Honey, you know Stacy has gotten weary of your case, is terribly busy, and really doesn't want to deal with the housing issue. Perhaps her replacement will have more time to dedicate to your case..." She did not hear half of what I had so carefully rehearsed, due to the convulsive sobbing that drowned out my hollow-ringing words. What I said was true, Stacy is busy, too busy. Case in point: she has been in possession of the plans for our house renovation since August and has only in the last week gotten them distributed to the "legal eagles." Every little step seems to consume three pages of the calendar. There's no need to hurry, life goes on forever, don't you know? No, I don't know.

Since Stacy has Cuban roots and speaks Spanish, she is uniquely qualified to address the needs of injured Hispanics. They are often neglected, railroaded, and taken advantage of, because of their immigration status, lack of education, lack of language skills, etc... Stacy is good and I am sure she provides a desperately needed service to many individuals. Although we are not illiterate, we have an attorney and we possess some ability to stand up for ourselves, Miriam's case is neither small or simple, and we also need her help. While I sympathize with others who need Stacy's help, it is not my job to worry about the rest of the world but to focus entirely on Miriam and her needs, someone must! The hospital has given us a simple choice: fight and litigate for every single dollar needed for her care or forget it and go away. Stacy brings credibility to Miriam's "table" that is neutral and respected in the lofty reaches at the state board level. Stacy had been part of our lives for more than three years. The prospect of losing her is a disappointing setback and the sobs coming from Miriam's chair indicate her understanding of this fact, too.

Two days before Christmas, Fred called the shop again and this time admitted to having good news. He explained that Stacy Casey had called and wanted to remain a part of Miriam's case after all. It was with great joy that I delivered this news to my wife later that afternoon.

Per a ruling delivered by Judge Murray on 11/10/2003 and **upheld** by the appellate court on 6/1/2004, I was compensated for the period from 8/1/2002 to11/4/2003, which was the extent of the time period that was included in that hearing. This ruling only covered 15 out of the 60 months that I have provided her care (thank you, Fred), **but we prevailed in TWO courts**!

July 23, 2004

The appeal for the attendant care issue was finally decided in our favor. Mr. Martin reconsidered the idea of appealing further and agreed to write a check. "Would it be okay if we write a check for part of it while we do a thorough accounting to determine how much additional is owed? We will provide a summary with the balance due by the 15th of July." Of course, Mr. Hill agreed, (as would have I). As of yesterday, neither the check or the summary had arrived at Mr. Hill's office. The well-established pattern of delay, deny and ignore, is firmly in place.

Another legal victory was passed down from Judge Murray about 20 days ago: "Yes, she can see Dr. Elliott." An appeal on this issue does not look likely as their 20-day window of opportunity (to file an appeal) slides quietly closed. October will mark the two-year anniversary of Miriam's initial consultation with Dr. Elliott, as well as our two year-long battle to get pain care transferred from Dr. Dean to Dr. Elliott. Two years to change physicians—this is one efficient, patient-oriented system we are mired in!

CHAPTER 18
Her House

A rehab conference is scheduled to take place August 12, 2004, in Atlanta. The topics for discussion between the lawyers, Stacy Casey, a representative from the State Board of Workman's Comp, and us include housing and possibly wrangling over a spa. Mr. Martin has already spelled out several reasons for delaying the conference, on the grounds that we are not prepared to discuss "all of the options." Thankfully, Mr. Hill has refused this suggestion, but I will be surprised if the hearing takes place on the 12th. If it does, I anticipate that we will return with little or no progress to celebrate, then have to badger our lawyer for three months while he "immediately" files the forms for a court hearing on the same subjects. Delay and ignore is not always limited to opposing counsel... October will mark the seventh anniversary of Miriam's injury; she has been wheelchair bound for almost three and a half years- I think it is past time she has a place to live that will safely accommodate her needs!

Speaking of counsel, Fred spent about three hours at the house Wednesday afternoon discussing preparations and strategy for the August 12th meeting. Attempting to fully understand our options, we have spent time looking through and researching available housing in Oconee County (since they have made it clear that our home is too costly to renovate). Mr. Martin's most recent idea to save them money is to find a house we can purchase with the proceeds from the sale of our present home that would cost less for them to renovate. A "lateral move," he calls it. My response when Fred mentioned this was to highlight several relevant points:

"... We have gone bankrupt (some of the collateral damage resulting from her injury) and cannot get another mortgage. Starting over with another house and adding the time required to find a suitable house, complete the purchase, and sell ours, will not work. If they want to renovate something we own, let them go to work on this house. We like the plans they've had drawn, like the neighborhood and already have a mortgage! It has taken these folks eight months to secure three bids on renovating this house, I cannot imagine how many years would pass before this ingenious delay tactic could be exhausted."

In some respects, there is a vacuum where hard information is concerned. Dr. Robel has admitted on many occasions that Miriam's case is unique in his experience; Stacy Casey has often stated that Miriam's case stands alone in her career's "most interesting and challenging case column," Fred admitted Wednesday what we have long suspected—Miriam's is the largest case he has ever handled. These three professionals probably have a combined total of more than 80 years of practice in their respective fields dealing with injured workers, yet Miriam's is the most difficult and challenging case they have ever handled! Certainly, it's a dubious distinction we would have preferred to avoid, but of far more tangible concern is that no one really knows where we go from here or how to get there. Direction from the State Board is either too vague to be of much help or no one knows how to direct us. The net result is similar to a sailing vessel stuck in the doldrums. Month after month we wait for a breath of wind to fill our sails with anticipation and restore our hope for the future, but the wind refuses to blow.

There is a consensus among all parties (Martin, Hill, Casey, and Johnsons) that the housing issue should be "stipped out" or separated from the rest of the case with the simple cutting of a check to resolve this issue. This would make everyone's job and life much simpler, as well as expedite the goal of getting Miriam into accessible housing. Although the concept makes sense, no one has made an offer for the other side to accept or reject either.

November 15, 2004

It is very early Monday morning. My mind, busy sorting, herding and corralling thoughts at the speed of light, has managed to push sleep toward another night. I crawl out of bed, start the coffee and sit down at the computer, while savoring the silence of a sleeping household

Hopefully my random ideas can be organized into something resembling rational thought.

A busy three days now, going on four, began with a six o'clock departure from home on Friday morning. We drove through rain, fog, and darkness, toward a mid-morning appointment in downtown Atlanta. Getting Miriam up and out the door at that hour is not easy, as the normal rest, medication and meal routine is interrupted. A later departure would have ensured a tangle with even more rush-hour-bad-weather traffic—a schedule-wrecking combination around Atlanta these days. The meeting was to be a "rehab conference"—sort of a mediated discussion to attempt to resolve a three-year-long impasse over the issue of accessible housing.

At the appointed hour, we were herded into a conference room, where we took chairs around a long table. In attendance were two participants from the state board of workman's comp, one to conduct the proceedings and one to observe. On Miriam's side of the table, sat Miriam's case manager, me and Miriam's attorney, Fred. Representing the E/I were their lawyer, two claims' adjustors from an insurance company and one current employee from the hospital where Miriam once worked. We were never informed of the name of the insurance company involved.

During the next three hours, emotions, and anger, mostly mine, that was bottled up and then fermented during years of frustration, periodically bubbled to the surface and spewed across the table. This process has given me a new understanding of the depth of Miriam's attachment to her home and neighborhood.

I waved toward a tube containing blueprints, which were the result of several thousand of the E/I's dollars spent during three years of delays and untold hours spent evaluating our house for appropriate renovations to accommodate Miriam's unique needs. Once the initial evaluation was complete, the project was handed over to an interior designer who specializes in creating accessible spaces. She had done an extraordinary job of rearranging the walls and eliminating hallways. She turned our house into a place with minimal obstructions with larger doors. She had designed a beautiful kitchen that put things in easy reach, so Miriam would be able to cook when she felt up to doing so.

"We like this floor plan," I declared.

"It does not make sense to spend more than twice the market value of your home to renovate it." The hospital's lawyer answered, referring to the three quotes to renovate our home using the plans to which I was still pointing.

Their insistence that we look for another house that would be less costly to renovate, caused Miriam's floodgates to open. Tears have flowed ever since, every time the subject is discussed. Our roots are pretty deep here, in this house we built with our own hands, among these neighbors we've known for so long. Sticks and bricks can be assembled anywhere into a shape that resembles a house, but history, memories and relationships turn it into a home.

These people knew Miriam before her accident, before her razor-sharp mind became dulled by pain and medication. Their children were often entertained by the "TGIF" parties she threw on Fridays after they got home from school. They knew her before she needed round-the-clock care and the ever-present wheelchair. Miriam can look around this house and recall nearly every day of progress as it rose from the foundation. She looks out her window and can see the Elm tree we planted. It now shades the house six months of the year. She looks around the rooms and sees the stenciling she added in several rooms. The day we moved in, we had a party and celebrated our son's first birthday. In this nest, she once held him through countless days and nights of uncertainty. It is also here, where he has now grown into a fine and blessedly healthy young man. This is the home where she and her husband shared the fires of mutual passion, before they were quenched by pain, drugs and nerve damage. Memories are tucked into every corner and scratched onto the woodwork. This house, along with the memories that linger here, mean more to her than I understood until now. But it is now apparent our neighborhood will become another casualty of this crisis. We will adjust as necessary and try to make new memories somewhere else, but not without some initial additional pain and frustration.

Since returning home Friday afternoon, Miriam has been busy, working to accomplish the charge we were given before leaving the Atlanta conference room. She has spent hours scouring the internet and the newspaper in search of housing that would save her former employer money, by being less costly to buy and renovate—after they steal the equity from our existing home and apply it as salve to their bleeding checkbook. On Sunday afternoon we spent several hours and over 60 miles driving around the county following leads gleaned from her research. We spent an hour last evening talking with a realtor friend, who stopped by with some additional houses to consider. I looked in one house under construction that might work—if purchased before the sheet rock is installed. I took her into one home that advertised an open house, but nothing about it would be acceptable to anyone sitting at the conference table on Friday. Additional possibilities will be examined in the coming days, as time allows.

The money we have saved in an account called "our home" through frugal living, is not the business of her former employer or an agency of the state! Nor should this be a factor in determining how the mandate is met to provide Miriam with a safe and accessible place to live. If they can annex the equity in our home, a good portion of it the result of our own calluses and perspiration, accumulated from two houses and 21 years of marriage, why can't they also grab other assets? What makes home equity unique? Why not go after retirement funds too?

The emotional agony caused by forcing her to abandon a home she loves and move into another house surrounded by strangers, is not necessary, is avoidable and downright immoral! Requiring us to help finance this miscarriage of justice is beyond comprehension.

Monday, February 14, 2005

By now we have resigned ourselves to moving to a different house—somewhere.

Stacy informed us that in South Carolina, Miriam would have been kicked out of the system long ago with no housing or attendant care to fight over.

I perceive she is growing weary over her place in the middle between Mr. Martin and us. Both sides are dug in deep and neither appears willing to compromise. I asked her this question: "If we forfeit our equity, leave our neighborhood and I give up my shop, we could get a deal done without going to court. Is that the way you see it?"

She replied by nodding her head. Fred said he thought we would win in court, but they would appeal us to death.

Fred began scratching some numbers on a piece of paper then started talking: "Altma Hospital has agreed to finance your equity at a very reasonable rate. This might allow you to stay in your house..."

I looked at him dumbstruck, then glanced at his paper. I took a deep breath, trying to calm myself before speaking: "Fred, we have never had a mortgage that large, and I don't intend to have one now!" I think he understood how stupid I thought the idea to be. The idea that we would have to pay them for equity that was ours, so they would renovate the house to accommodate a work-related injury they caused, stunned me. My blood has boiled every time I have thought about it. It is not enough that Miriam's life is over, that Matthew and I have lost his mother and my wife, or that our financial security is gone, we are also supposed to assume a huge debt because our house is nearly paid for?

The meeting ended 90 minutes after it began, with little having been accomplished. Perhaps a dry run for the rehab conference scheduled for later this month?

February 22, 2005

Tomorrow, we have our follow-up rehab conference. Fred called this morning. He received a call from Martin at 8:30 this morning. He asked Fred why we were going to the conference, if neither party had changed its position– this is a conversation that could have taken place two months ago, but Mr. Martin waited until the day before a scheduled meeting to pick up the phone. Before Fred could call us, Martin called him again. This time, he had actually looked at the information he had received from Stacy Casey and noticed we had been looking at a house. Now he wanted to tie it up and cancel the conference. I contend we have a bunch of stuff to talk about and work out.

Fred made arrangements to look at the house this afternoon and asked me to meet him there. After we had completed the walk through, I suggest a proposal for him to consider and pass on.

February 24, 2005

We returned yesterday from our day in downtown Atlanta around four, totally exhausted. Caregiver Cathy went with us and cared for Miriam during the trip. I was glad she was there since Miriam had several spasms on the way home.

Everyone came to the meeting with the intention of getting a deal done. There was haggling and posturing back and forth. They attempted to bundle several issues together and save piles of money, but we preferred to keep the discussion limited to housing.

I finally made a cash proposal that would save them money, did not involve surrendering equity in our current house, would resolve housing and put us in control of resolving the issue. They did not say no but claimed no authority to make the agreement without first consulting their counterparts in California.

The possibility of resolving the issue of housing and putting some control of our future back into our hands has rekindled some optimism.

It was raining this morning and Miriam needed to return to Atlanta for an appointment with Dr. Elliott. I decided against letting Cathy take her to the appointment by herself, so I took another day off from work and returned to the big city. It was good I was there, because Dr. Elliott wanted to discuss Stacy's request to comment on Miriam's need for attendant care. We answered his questions concerning the coverage we now have and what services they perform for her. At the conclusion of our appointment, he agreed that the coverage in place made sense and he would back up Dr. Robel! This is a big load off my mind and possibly the second victory in two days. We are overdue for some good news... these events are encouraging.

I called Fred to relate the encouraging news from Dr. Elliott's visit; he said he had not heard anything from Mr. Martin. He went on to tell me he thought my last counteroffer was extremely fair and reasonable. "If James Martin comes back with some of his jujitsu, we need to take the matter to court."

I replied: "If they reject my counter, we need to accept their last offer and go on down the road. This is the only way we'll get a house done before our son leaves home."

"Okay," he sighed.

Friday, February 25, 2005

I need some couch time with my therapist. Although there is certainly some value gained from banging on the keys of the laptop, the ability to have the rumblings in my head appear before my eyes is cheap therapy and probably helpful in the decision-making processes!

Do we have a deal or not have a deal on accessible housing? We should have, either for my last offer or theirs, but Mr. Martin hasn't called Fred to tell us anything for certain. Better to have us dangling through the weekend, I suppose. One thing for sure: if you have money, you have options; with no money, you are at the mercy of someone else who makes decisions for you. But this is one of those things in life that must be done correctly the first time, because no one will step forward and offer "do-overs" like we enjoyed as kids on the playground.

The claims adjustor made the comment Wednesday that "they were having a hard time explaining to the excess carrier in California why they needed to buy Miriam a house, since in California they don't buy people houses."

I have been thinking about this. When I asked, "Where do wheelchair-bound workers live in California?" they just shrugged. Perhaps Georgia's workman's comp system is among the best in the country. Considering how woefully inadequate Georgia's system appears to someone from the inside, this thought is scary! I guess in some states it is ok to toss people on the scrapheap of humanity and forget about them.

Tuesday, March 1, 2005

Fred called twice yesterday. In the early afternoon he called to tell me that Mr. Martin had left a message on his machine Friday afternoon. The message said simply: "They had agreed to my offer but wanted a completion date stipulated in the agreement."

"That sounds reasonable," I told Fred.

"I expected worse. I thought he might try to pin you down to a specific house or location, which would not have been acceptable," he said.

"It could take us 90 days to figure out exactly what we're going to do and then it would be good to have a year to complete it. I don't think it will take that long, but I hate to get backed in to too tight of a schedule. See if you can get 15-18 months. I think it is interesting that all the sudden they want instant house."

"You know, to Fred Hill you are the devil incarnate, don't you?"

"He's just upset that I'm not as stupid as I look."

"I'll call him and see what he's thinking."

The second call came about six.

"I couldn't get a hold of Joe, but he sent me a fax. He wants to allow 12 months from the date Judge Murray signs off on the deal and this is to include the lap pool– it's not a lap pool, those things are 40 foot long!" Fred said.

"He seems to be getting reasonable all of a sudden. I guess I boxed myself in when I opened my mouth at the rehab conference and told the room, "It wouldn't take Mark four years to solve Miriam's housing needs."

Fred went on to give me credit for the compromise that got us a few more dollars and a deal. He admitted he was ready to "beat a dead horse." I told him it was important for all parties concerned to get a deal done and go on down the road.

Miriam spent the day on the phone with the realtor and doing on-line research. The results of her arm-chair efforts make an impressive pile of paper. When I got home, I delivered to her lap a stack of current real estate books. The search is officially on. Lots to think about, but it is good to be able to make plans instead simply talking about "what if!" Wait, is that a rudder I feel in my hand? Is the sail really filling with wind? Are we really charting a course toward the future?

Sunday, March 6, 2005

House hunting is in high gear. We spent several hours yesterday afternoon with a Realtor. We looked at houses in Oconee and Clarke counties, including a 5,200 square-foot behemoth priced cheap, but wouldn't have been practical for our needs. Three of the houses we looked at had swimming pools! A pool is something about which I know nothing. If we could make it useful for Miriam, it might have some value to us, but it would have to be enclosed and heated. If something like this proves practical and not budget-blowing, we might consider it, but we have certainly not gone hunting for a house with a pool. We have, however, been hunting hard for a home that fronts on a body of water that would allow Miriam a place to fish. A tall order, but dreaming is cheap therapy! We are scheduled to look at one lakefront house tomorrow. This is a private lake of maybe 50 acres 10 miles east of Athens. I have a friend who has lived on the lake for 13 years and I have coveted, shame on me, his picturesque location since I first saw it. Could we find something we could afford on this same lake? We may find out tomorrow. Of course, finding a house and trying to tie it up without knowing when our funds will be available may be tough…

Our minds have expanded in the last 24 hours. Spending this money on the current house would make little sense financially, so we have got to go somewhere else. It occurred to me only yesterday that it may be time to dream again! I've built two houses for the family since we got married. Should we go for three? I'd rather not but sweat equity really can stretch a budget.

Thursday, March 10, 2005

"Good morning, Fred, this is Mark Johnson, have you heard from your counterpart yet?"

"No, I haven't. I called on Monday and was told he was in meetings in the office all day, whatever that means."

"I think it means he didn't want to talk with you."

"I plan to call him today. If I still can't speak with him, I plan to call Valerie Hill and ask for her help."

"I was going to offer to call her, in case you had some reservations for professional reasons." I don't ever have to see, talk, or work with any of these folks once Miriam's case is resolved, so I don't care who I anger at this point.

"Naw, I'll call her. I'll tell her you've found a house but can't do anything until you have some money."

"I'm not as concerned about getting my hands on the money as I am to know what's in his agreement. Until we know, we don't know how to plan. We either have an agreement or we don't. It has been two weeks since the verbal agreement was reached in principle; plenty of time to write a paragraph that says: xxxx amount of money resolves forever the issue of accessible housing and the spa. The house will be completed within one year from the date of the judge's approval."

"You're right. I know. I'll call him right now."

"Thank you."

"Goodbye."

Monday, March 14, 2005

Fred called this morning: "I talked with Martin on Thursday morning. He answered his own phone!"

"Good. What did he have to say for himself?"

"I told him one year was ok, to write it up. He said he might could have it done by the middle of this week. I have also talked to Stacy Casey, and she agreed with Martin that a year was enough time to get Miriam into adequate housing."

"What will they do if the house isn't done in 12 months, come take away her money?"

"That's the point. The money will be sitting in a bank account waiting to be spent on a house or its completion. Taking away money won't solve anything. It's kind of silly if you ask me."

"Thank you. I appreciate your calling."

May 6, 2005

Two months and one week post verbal "agreement" and we still don't have one in writing. Fred calls a couple times a week to assure us he is calling Martin almost daily but cannot manage to talk to the man. He is pondering the idea of filing for a hearing; we may not have much choice. Perhaps a hearing notice will put Mr. Martin in a mood to get something done.

We looked at another house late yesterday, this one is on the backwater of a reservoir 20 miles south of our current home. It borders a national forest, is in a small neighborhood, has a level lot, a shop and several hundred feet of waterfront. The water is shallow but can be reached by a pontoon boat. The one-level house would require an addition and modifications, but the kitchen and great room are already perfect for her needs. If we want to live on a body of water, this is probably our best opportunity. It is hard to get too excited however, because we do not have any money and if we go to court, it could be another year before we are in a position to negotiate with the ability to do something. My preliminary sketching and cost calculations look like this house could work and checks many boxes on our list of dreams.

May 10, 2005

Before leaving the house this morning, I composed and faxed another letter to Valarie Hill at the State Board of Workman's Comp. She called as my hand was on the doorknob and I was finally headed out the door.

"…Agreements are worked out when both sides are willing to compromise…"

"…That's not easy to do when one side is incommunicado…"

For 20 minutes her syrupy sweet voice essentially said the same thing four different ways and so did I. The funny thing is that she apparently put in a call to Martin before calling us, because she knew he was in mediation. When we explained the remaining issues of contention, she repeated the compromise line three more times, reminded us of our options which we "should discuss with our attorney" and suggested another face to face which she would gladly facilitate.

When the call ended, care-giver Cathy was grinning broadly. "Looks like you stirred the pot this morning!"

Once I finally arrived at the shop, I picked up the phone and called the seller's realtor daughter and requested a plat and a copy of the covenants. Miriam and Matthew are beginning to get excited about this house. If the agreement could be finalized and a check cut, we could become legitimate negotiators; until then, all I can do is stall for time with the sellers.

The agreement was signed and approved by Judge Murray in time to get the place we decided we wanted.

We closed on the property in August of '05 and moved in the following March. I beat their one-year deadline by several months. I was able to add a wing that provided Miriam a spa room, accessible bathroom, and a large bedroom with "ride in" closet. We also added a garage with a ramp into the house. I hired skilled help and managed the project myself while working on it as well, along with Matthew and another boy we hired, so we had a lot of sweat equity in it by the time it was finished.

The legal battlefield was littered with years of frustration, but in the end, we prevailed on every major item we pursued: van, attendant care, some compensation for Mark, keeping Dr. Robel, getting transferred to Dr. Elliott and housing. Fred and the Johnsons did not, however, spend a lot of time celebrating victories. Usually, we were so bruised and battered by the time a victory came, that we barely had enough energy left to exchange pleasantries and drag ourselves back to our "corner" and begin preparing for the next round.

The one thing the other side mentioned several times over the years but never really made a concerted effort to accomplish was settling the case. I am surprised they allowed it to fester so long, but we refused to blink, so if a deal was going to get done, they were going to have make the ball roll, so to speak, and this did not happen for many years.

My concern from the very beginning was Miriam's welfare and that of my family. As long as she had everything she needed to live as full and comfortable life as possible, I was content with letting them pay the bills until the day she died, because that is what they were obligated to do. This way Mark did not have to worry about whether an agreed-upon sum of money would expire before she did. Would it be nice to be in control of our own destiny? Yes, maybe. As the years went by the E/I became convinced she was going to live forever, but increasingly did not want their checkbook to remain open for that long. Pressure was slowly building from, and I am guessing here, because I have no solid information, the re-insurer to settle the case. Their efforts to reduce the costs of her care lasted several more years and were mostly a waste of time. She was relatively stable, but still required round-the-clock care and a plethora of medications. The only surgery discussed after NYC was possibly installing another spinal cord stimulator, but Miriam was not interested. The cost of her care was the cost of her care, and once this was understood and accepted, rumblings about settling the case began anew.

What happened from '07 to 2012? A lot of the same, but the legal battle cooled unexpectedly. My guess is that the opposing counsel was monitoring her health looking for a trend that would convince them to wait her out rather than try to settle the case, but this is just speculation on my part. We did not complain about not having to worry about legal stuff; there were plenty of other things needing our attention.

Although relatively medically stable, Miriam had monthly appointments in Atlanta with pain doctor Elliott, which maintained her medication regimen. She also had regular appointments with other doctors who were treating her for some of the myriad of side effects caused by the intense dose of narcotics she was taking. She spent many hours a day in her spa, where she exercised and read a lot of books and listened to Christian music between naps. When not in the spa she sat in her recliner, where she read or napped. Most of these activities were to take her mind off the ever-present pain. How she dealt with this pain all these years was something I never could quite get my head around. I think she was just determined not to be beaten.

When not caring for Miriam, I worked on building my fledgling dredging business and being a dad. The dredging business was started after we moved into the northernmost house on the lake, which was made affordable because it was surrounded by shallow water. I saw an opportunity after learning that one dredger served two good-sized reservoirs, bought some equipment, and went into business. I was a one man show in those early days while I learned the business the hard way. Having my own business was the only option, because it gave me the freedom to care for Miriam when it was necessary. Fifteen years later the fledgling operation has grown into the largest in the area, so I must have done something right.

Although we thankfully had caregivers most of the time, "my share" still covered more than 40 hours per week and stretched to 24 per day when we ventured out of town. The nine-year-old we had the day of her accident grew up and left the nest. Evidently the time we spent worrying about having damaged his formative years was wasted, because he turned out rather well. His greatest fear all those years, and perhaps even now, is that something will happen to me and leave him to care for Mom. Ahh, the burden of being an only child.

Mostly, we lived one day at a time as best we could.

January 20, 2012

Last summer we went to Indiana for a family wedding. It was the first time in several years we had traveled more than a couple hundred miles from home. Mother and dad traveled with us and as we returned home, we began talking about taking a trip west we have discussed often through the years.

A trip like this was a daunting challenge to get my head around. I would have to care for Miriam 24hrs/day, drive and keep an eye on my aged parents. My siblings and close friends thought I was nuts for considering it. Depending on the outcome, I would be a god or a goat—it could easily break either way. The inspiration to even try it was knowing how fragile everyone's health was and knowing there may not be another opportunity.

Miriam has seen her son become an Eagle Scout, graduate from high school then college, then the police academy, the DNR academy, become a game warden and get married. Now her sights are set on one day holding a grandchild. She and I are more determined than ever to not be completely defined by her accident and limitations.

In October 2013, I loaded my parents and wife into our little van and went on a 30-day road trip around the country. My dad had Parkinson's, mother a heart condition, and Miriam's afflictions are well documented. Dad was dead within two years, so we either went then or never.

Upon learning of our adventure, the opposing counsel had a dying duck fit. The result was that Miriam, and I were deposed to get us under oath, so we'd have to disclose all the hiking and dancing they were sure we did while we were out of town, which of course we did not, because we could not. We did sit in the van, look, point, take pictures and ooh and aah a lot.

July 13, 2014

We are four months from completing the 17th year of this never-gonna-end ordeal. Miriam thankfully is relatively stable. The dramatic oscillations we experienced in years gone by have diminished greatly in magnitude and amplitude. Yes, her pain and spasms still change from day to day and sometimes from moment to moment, but the durations are shorter and more dampened. It is a rare day now that she spends 20 out of 24 hours in the spa or sleeping. That is not to say those days never happen, just not as often. More typically she has several hours a day where she can pay bills, surf the internet, or piddle on her sewing machine.

CHAPTER 19
A Settlement

Why haven't there been more journal entries? I've been busy trying to build the dredging business I started back in '07. The growing business has taken me out of town occasionally. This is a trend I expect to see continue and grow to become a larger part of the business. Another reason the journal writing slowed down was once the house issue was settled, we went to work on the house and generally things quieted down on the litigation front, so we went about living our lives adjusting to our normal.

Soon after returning from our month-long road trip with my parents, the excess insurance carrier flew a lady from California to see us. She came to the house and met with us and Fred to talk about settling the case. Before leaving, she assured us we would hear more in a couple of months. Funny thing is that opposing counsel Ralph, knew nothing about it; because when he caught wind of it, he called Fred to see what was going on. Seven months later, instead of talking settlement, we are girding our loins for another legal battle. It is my opinion that Ralph apparently saw a heap of legal fees slipping from his grasp and convinced the E/I not to settle, because he was going to go to work and could save them lots of money.

The hardball tactics employed by the other side have been tough to endure. So far, the case manager they chose more than 10 years ago has been frustrated into quitting and they are trying to take Miriam's medical care away from people who have Miriam's best interests at heart and replace them with a puppet doctor they can control. Lawyers not only choosing the doctor but dictating patient care, what could possibly go wrong with that plan? While this is going on, with a straight face, they declare, "We are concerned about Mrs. Johnson's health and only want what's best for her."

Fifteen months ago, they replaced the agency providing CNA (certified nursing assistant) level care with one told to provide companion level care. Although at first glance this does not sound so bad, it is a big cost savings to them now, which becomes a big deal when extrapolated over the remainder of her expected life and converted into dollars in a settlement. At this time, under threat of not paying the agency, the legal team began to dictate how the daily reports were to be written. The companions are supposed to watch and "assist" Miriam with ADLs she would love to do but has not been able to perform for years: preparing meals, doing laundry, cleaning house, etc.- if they knew my wife, they would understand being in this condition and needing this level of help was never part of her life's goals! The reports all read "assist" and most things are simply not recorded because they don't want a written record about how much "assistance" is really required to get Miriam through a normal day. They wanted less damning evidence to present to a judge if that became necessary.

Toward the end of 2015, an interest in settling the case shifted into high gear. These negotiations took place in Atlanta around a large conference table with yet another mediator. The other side even flew in a guy from California who owns an agency that specializes in helping settle large cases. By the way, it's not clear to me what the threshold is for a "large" case. This may have qualified because very few work comp cases are this expensive, but in the grand scheme of things we were not arguing over big numbers like take place outside of work comp. Besides "Mr. California," they had at least two lawyers and a financial guy holding down their side of the large table. A mediator was also present to keep us in our respective corners.

On our side of the table was Miriam, Matthew, me, Fred and our own financial guy brought in by Fred. Every so often, after several minutes of collective discussion, one side or the other would retire to a private room for private discussions. Their first offer had me heading to the exit. I thought they were there to talk business, not insult some country bumpkins. Fred talked me back into the room and the discussions continued for most of that day and were continued on at least one other occasion if not two. They begin to run together after this many years. Evidently the first offer was designed to make them appear accommodating with any subsequent proposals. We parted ways without reaching an agreement.

Make no mistake, we wanted desperately to close this chapter of our ordeal. Always having people question and debate each request for something needed for Miriam's benefit was maddening and exhausting. The never-ending legal maneuvering consumed copious amounts of mental energy that needed to be directed at my family and business. We could not afford, however, to allow our desire for resolution to cause us to make a deal that would trade one set of problems for another, like what to do when inadequate funds were exhausted. This was a very stressful time. We have one chance to get it right or we may end up in a homeless shelter somewhere regretting our decision.

Letter to Fred Hill, Ralph McKay, et al

Re: Settlement for Miriam Johnson

December 31, 2015

Hopefully through this document we can clarify our position concerning settlement of Miriam Johnson's Workman's Comp claim.

Yes, we are interested in settling the case.

An agreement must be reached that makes sense for both sides. The proposal on the table has been rejected because it fails to make any sense for our side of the equation. This would transfer enormous risk to us that ultimately inflict even more financial pain than we have already suffered. It simply will not work.

Two years ago, when Ms. Prenda first sat in our living room and talked of settlement, I explained that any settlement would have to "provide for Miriam's care, including 24/7 attendant care."

This has been reiterated in two opening sessions of settlement mediation.

The current proposal does not allow near enough funds to pay for vans, wheelchairs, medications or any other non-MSA expenses out of funds earmarked for attendant care. There are also no provisions for inflation, so this proposal is a non-starter for us. To make this work, I would be forced to quit working and provide her care while forfeiting my income yet again. If one of my maladies makes this impossible or causes my demise prior to Miriam's, our son would be forced to suspend his career to care for YOUR insured. The reward being offered to offset all this risk is that she gets to keep her doctor and you will no longer screw with her life.

The scales in a risk/reward analysis are far from balanced! I submit no one sitting around that negotiating table would accept the proposal we are being asked to take were they in our shoes.

There is no guarantee she will not live longer than the projected 20 years. Right now, she's lived 18 years since the accident and is going pretty strong, even in the face of unfathomable pain. Under Dr. Elliott's care, she has been stable for many years now.

She has the same dreams as everyone else: to hold grandbabies, grow old with her mate and pursue the dreams that are still possible. Far from giving up, she wishes to thrive as best she can. An important component of this is getting the care and medications she needs and not feeling like a burden to those around her. It is not her fault she requires 'round-the-clock care, but she shouldn't have to watch her loved ones interrupt their lives and careers to provide it! Attendant care gives her a measure of independence and her loved ones the opportunity to get adequate rest and provide for the financial well-being of the family.

You know the costs of her care, both historical and future projected; we have calculators too and have a pretty good idea of the money required to provide for her future care.

Although tight and still not without risk, the proposal we have made can work if the funds are managed carefully. It is reasonable and provides benefits for both sides of the equation. You will save at least 50% of projected outlays, in addition to the savings from legal and administration, which have to be substantial.

~ Mark and Miriam Johnson

They rejected our proposal, and a few frustrating weeks went by without any activity. The impasse was broken after I took their last offer and restructured it into something I thought we could live with.

In April of 2016, an agreement was reached and approved by the Georgia State Board of Workman's Compensation to settle this case. The terms cannot be disclosed. Rest assured we failed to get close to what we thought would be fair and reasonable. For this to work, either Miriam would have to die in less than 15 years or Mark would have to work some magic and grow the pie somehow. One of the advisors present while we were negotiating the settlement (our "money guy") suggested we could sign everything over to Social Security and essentially become wards of the state until we died. "Of course, this decision would have to be made soon after settling: he said. We chose not to take this advice.

I have continued to grow and build my dredging business. One day hopefully it can be sold and help shore up our finances enough to get us to the finish line.

Settling the case brought to a close a very stressful chapter in this crisis. Suddenly we were able to make decisions without thinking about how we would defend it before a judge one day. We can employ the doctors, caregivers and courses of treatment of our choosing without needing an outsider's approval for any of it. When new batteries were needed for the wheelchair, we bought them and did not have to wait six months for approval. In other words, control had returned our lives. I no longer spend an inordinate number of my waking hours thinking about Miriam's case, and have not written letters to anyone in years. With a few strokes of a pen and the blessing of a judge, the legal case was over. Only time will tell if we made the right decision.

Do you think Fred and Stacy miss us? I doubt it. I imagine they were very happy to close this career chapter and move on to less problematic clients.

Because we had settled, we were able to pursue an experimental course of treatment that might possibly help Miriam with pain relief. No more dealing with non-approvals from the work comp system.

CHAPTER 20
"Get the Picture"

Long before television brought every game into our living rooms, University of Georgia football fans had Larry Munson. Every fall Saturday, the Bulldog Nation would gather around a radio and listen to Larry Munson bring the action to our ears, where his vivid images would be projected onto our mind's eye. He was so good we were transported to the stadiums and thrust into the action on the field. As I recall, he began each broadcast with the tagline: "Get the Picture." Without pretending to posses his mastery of the art, I will attempt with the written word to bring to life the most important part of our story.

Once the legal case was resolved, we settled into what we thought would be "our normal" for the remainder of our lives. Miriam continued to suffer inconceivable pain, which she fought with the same tools she had employed for many years. Many hours were spent every day in her spa, where she could take naps, read books, listen to music, and exercise. By the time we moved into the accessible house, we had upgraded her spa to one large enough for a variety of exercises and one that had enough seats and jets. She could always find a jet that would apply a blast of warm water to just the right spot for that day.

The spa was a big part of her daily routine. Her caregivers put her in and took her out two or three times most days, and on really bad days, she just stayed in hour after hour. She kept the water temperature around 100, so it was cooler than most hot tubs, and she could tolerate it for longer periods without damaging bodily organs. One thing I never could understand is how well her skin tolerated being immersed. My fingers and toes shrivel up after a few minutes, but hers never did. The prescription drugs were another arrow in her quiver. She hated taking them and didn't like the way they dulled her mind, but she had little choice. For many years I felt like a legal drug pusher. On those occasions when doses got missed for one reason or another, we all usually regretted it. She would try to distract her mind from the pain by reading books, singing songs, praying, watching television, or going places. Sometimes, she'd do two or three things at a time, all in an attempt to keep from screaming out in agony.

This was our life. Once the accessible house was completed and we moved in, I worked to build a dredging business from another of my crazy ideas. Matthew went on and built a life but never forgot about actual and potential obligations and responsibilities back at home.

Miriam is and should be the center of attention, so forgive me when my perspective seems oriented on me instead of her. She is a real life walking. talking miracle in a day and time when people wonder if they still happen in our post-modern world. We live in a "time of enlightenment" that openly questions whether a Creator God exists and if He does exist, does He still function among us? We have first hand experience and evidence that not only does He exist, but He is here and that He's not too busy to touch people.

For more than 22 years, I have watched my once vibrant, intelligent wife career down one slippery slope after another, each steeper than the last, toward what I was certain would be a pain-ravaged, pre-mature death. By default, I became her primary caregiver and decision-maker. In the darkest and hardest of times, I had to make decisions without being able to talk with my best friend and confidant. I harbored a lot of anger about the hand fate had dealt us. If she had died in a car wreck back in '97, I would have grieved, eventually healed, and gone on with life. What was so frustrating was that for more than two decades, we were left dangling from the cliff face of life in a perpetual state of limbo, neither falling to our death nor being hoisted for rescue. My life, our son's life, as well as extended family, were all there with us always supportive and always doing everything they could to help, but at the same time wondering when or if the situation would ever change. Extended family and friends pitied us, sympathized with us, prayed for us, and did what they could, but they were powerless to change our circumstances.

Why would God allow this amazing woman to suffer so much pain and disappointment? I often wondered, sometimes with a clenched fist pointed upward. We twisted in the winds of medical, legal, and financial drama but went nowhere. In this state of perpetual suspended animation, we could only watch Miriam suffer inconceivable pain, day after day, month after month, year after year. You can tell by the preceding pages that I tried to change or improve the situation, but aside from annoying a lot of people, I mostly vented my anger. Maybe this form of venting is what kept me from completely unraveling?

As the years went by, I became increasingly worried about our twilight years. When I was not shaking my fist toward heaven, I did a lot of praying. I begged God to allow me to outlive her and to give me the ability to care for her until her death. I also prayed that He either heal her, or take her home, but one way or another, please take away her pain. Watching her writhe in agony was brutal; why did she have to suffer so? This woman who I have never seen drunk or chemically impaired, was living in a drug-induced haze, taking enough medications to kill large animals. She spent many hours a day (and more than a few nights) in her spa, attempting to keep the pain demons at bay and survive one more day. Even with all of this, she still howled periodically in agony. There was absolutely nothing in the world I, or anybody else could do about it. I sure did not want Matthew to be stuck with this burden, so I begged the Lord above to allow me to outlive her.

I had for years wondered what possible purpose all her suffering could have, but mostly adopted a fatalistic perspective on it. I never considered our fate "unfair" because we somehow "didn't deserve it." In my mind, sickness, disease, death and pain are just part of living in a fallen world. Prosperity theology was developed by humans for humans, by fake preachers who knew if people heard what they wanted to hear, they would send them their money. Being a Christian does not insulate us from the consequences of the Fall; instead, we own great hope for ultimate victory and an eternity free from the consequences of man's sin.

Oh, me of little faith. I had long ago given up any hope of my wife ever walking again. I did relentlessly cling to a shred of hope that she might one day, one way or another, be freed from her pain. The wheelchair was just a tool to facilitate her life, but it did not define her. It was the overwhelming pain that prevented her from coming off the mind-numbing medications and thriving. My prayers were about her pain much more than her ever regaining the ability to walk.

That kind of miracle was just too big of an ask; I would have been very content with one I considered to be much more, uh, "reasonable," if you will. Perhaps I thought we might have a better chance of scoring a smaller miracle than a larger one? Who knows the reason, but I cannot remember the last time I actually prayed that she would be completely healed and walk again. I was, however, so bold as to remind God the Father, that His Son only suffered for three days prior to His resurrection. I know, I know, it is shocking I was not struck by a bolt of lightning! He really is merciful where our stupidity is concerned!

Our path to the twilight years became even more uncertain as I began to experience some health issues of my own. Atrial fibrillation is something both my parents had, and apparently, they were kind enough to contribute to my genes. After having a few short episodes in my 30s and early 40s, it came to stay in my late 40s. It has deprived me of some energy and stamina, but the cardiologist does not think it will be the cause of my demise. In my mid-50s, I was diagnosed with rheumatoid arthritis, which has so far, thankfully, also been managed and is also not debilitating. It has, however, taken away my ability to do much physical work. The more I do, the more I hurt, so I have grasped a really convenient excuse for being lazy. I'm not near as tough as my wife with this pain thing. Thankfully, I have a great crew of younger, healthier employees to do the physical work I once performed myself. At this point in my business, what I know and who I know is more valuable than what I can personally do.

These health problems have also caused great concern about my future ability to care for Miriam. I have really felt for Matthew. This only-child gig that he finds himself in has really put a lot of potential burdens on his life. He had a front-row seat for our train wreck for the last 10 years he lived at home. Then, thankfully, he was able to build a career and family of his own, but his folks have never been far from his thoughts. He has worried about being able to care for Mom should something happen to Dad, and I know he was concerned about whether there would be enough money to provide for her/our care until he can get us in the ground.

Having settled Miriam's case did provide a little financial breathing room. Remember all the dreams we had about traveling during some of our darkest hours? It was cheap therapy while cooped up in a hospital room, and honestly, there was little to no chance of any of those dreams coming to fruition. The necessary pieces to make that puzzle simply didn't exist. But once out of the hospital and with the recovery behind us, we became emboldened and determined to live life to the fullest extent possible. I wondered, could we possibly take a cruise? Would Miriam's wheelchair work on a ship with narrow halls and small rooms? Could we get everything she needed transferred from a car (or airplane) onto a ship? Were we nuts for even considering something as crazy as a cruise? At the very top of our "places to go" list has always been Alaska. *Would an Alaskan cruise be possible?* I wondered. Since we had never been on a cruise, I didn't know if cruising was something we could do or not, or even enjoy.

Rather than jump into the idea headfirst without knowing how "deep the water was," in January of 2017 I booked a five-night cruise that sailed from Tampa, Florida (easy driving distance from central Georgia) into the Caribbean. Upon arriving at the terminal, our luggage was whisked away by porters and taken to our stateroom. It didn't take long to figure out we were having a load of fun and that cruising was something we could do. Before the end of the trip, we were in the Next Cruise office booking an Alaska trip for May of the same year, only a few months away.

Why the rush? For one thing, we wanted more experiences like the one being enjoyed at that moment, and, although I can't recall what it was now, Miriam had a procedure scheduled for the summer that caused me to want to secure the memory of an Alaska cruise beforehand. This would give us/me a memory no one could take away in the event of a bad outcome. The reservation was made during a moment of exuberant excitement. Only later did the logistical challenge that had been created provide a reality check. We had flown on three occasions to New York for surgeries, so I knew flying was possible. When we flew to New York, however, it was before the days of leg bags (for urine), a bi-pap for sleep apnea, and supplemental oxygen, so traveling was somewhat simpler then.

These were two pieces of equipment that would have to make the trip, and the oxygen would be in use during the flight via her portable machine. The leg bag was helpful in one sense, because it eliminated a lot of trips to the bathroom, but created stress in others because there was the constant threat of an infection, or the bag breaking at an inopportune moment. The larger oxygen generator she used at night to plug into the bi-pap filled the largest legal-to-fly-with suitcase and weighed 50 pounds.

Enough luggage was rounded up to transport the portable pharmacy and hospital room we would need to facilitate the trip. The cruise line was alerted to the fact we would need an extension cord for the equipment in the room, as well as distilled water for the bi-pap, and that oxygen would be in use in the room. The airline was notified about the powered wheelchair and supplemental oxygen that would be in use during the flight. This was going to be a nine-night trip onboard the ship. Many people going to Alaska also enjoy an overland adventure, but schlepping luggage, medical equipment, and the wheelchair to and from multiple hotel rooms and buses was going to be more adventure than Mark was willing to take on. With this schlepping thing in mind, flight reservations were made to keep it to a minimum. The chosen schedule had us leave Atlanta early in the morning, change planes in Minneapolis, then fly to Vancouver, before boarding the ship the same afternoon. The return trip would be non-stop Anchorage to Atlanta, but a delay on this leg at least wouldn't mean we would miss the ship. Porters would be employed to assist with the luggage. Fortunately, this ambitious plan worked.

We made our connections and arrived at the ship before it sailed. Did she hurt? Yes. Did she have to take the same number of naps as she did at home? Yes, but even though we couldn't leave the afflictions behind, we still had a wonderful trip! Watching Miriam burst into tears as she tried to take in the spectacular scenery made the effort well worth the stress required to bring the dream to reality. At this point, I want to thank the nice lady at Delta who allowed the slightly oversized and slightly overweight bag containing the oxygen generator onto the conveyor at check-in.

On another occasion, in the fall of 2018, we were traveling with my brother and his wife, trying to get to Quebec City to board a ship for a fall foliage cruise. This time we had flown into Toronto to catch a smaller commuter plane for the short hop to Quebec City. We caused an hour delay for boarding because the ground crew did not know how to affix the shiny new ramp to the door of the airplane so they could facilitate boarding Miriam in her wheelchair. We watched the show from the terminal while they tried one strategy and then another until a supervisor arrived who quickly solved the problem. The rest of that trip also went as planned and was a raging success. Our future was slowly coming into focus and was becoming more interesting. Dreaming resumed!

Ch Ch Ch Changes…

It's the week of Thanksgiving 2019. Our cups truly runneth over. Thanksgiving has always been my favorite holiday of the year, but this one is like no other! My wife, our life, and our future are so different from only a few months ago. I am having a difficult time processing not just the changes but the rate of change.

Things are a changing! Her crisis lasted 22 years and eight months, and before that, we were dealing with a life-and-death crisis with our son's health. After 30 years of playing fireman and being on call and on duty around the clock, I am embracing the changes!

Dr. Sam Downs came into Miriam's life via a referral from Dr. Elliott during 2018. She still saw Dr. Elliott, but he wanted another pair of eyes to examine her case and look for options he may not have considered. Dr. Sam Downs was able to see Miriam because her workman's compensation case had been settled. This put us in charge of who treated her. If the case had not been settled, Dr. Sam Downs or his treatment protocol would never have been approved, at least not without a protracted legal battle, in my opinion.

Dr. Sam Downs spent several months giving her injections at three different sites on her left foot. He was doing this weekly for up to six weeks at a time. The injections provided some temporary relief, but the hoped-for result never materialized. Eventually, as had been the case over and over, hope faded, and we became overwhelmed by frustration, despair, and desperation. In early 2019, he expressed a desire to begin changing and reducing a few of her medications. We understood why; it was a noble goal, but she was taking them because they had been prescribed by well-meaning doctors over the years to help with pain, not because she liked the way they made her feel—she didn't.

"I'd like that too, but what are you going to do about the pain?"

It was a pregnant question posed to every doctor who had treated her for two decades. I guess we hoped an answer would be somehow birthed in the room before our eyes, just because we were bold enough to ask.

Sometime in the early Spring of 2019, Dr. Sam Downs did manage to deliver a treatment idea we had never heard before. "How about hyperbaric oxygen therapy?"

Miriam brought his bundle of questionable suggestions home and laid it before me. We were both skeptical. It sounded like something a snake oil salesman and witch doctor had dreamed up while drinking their homemade Kool-Aid at a séance. Shut her in a tube, pressurize it, pump in medical grade oxygen, and this is supposed to fix her?

"Isn't this what divers use to recover from the bends?" I asked.

Every naval vessel that has sailed the high seas for the last hundred years has had a hyperbaric chamber on board. They have made appearances in a few movies and documentaries over the years. I recall one particularly brutal scene from a James Bond flick. Dr. Sam Downs attended a conference and read some articles about hyperbaric therapy being used successfully to reduce pain for patients with Miriam's condition. He thought it might be worth a try. He would consider it a success if she had a 30% reduction in pain and was able to reduce some of the narcotic medications.

We began our own research and learned that it had been successfully used for burn patients, stroke victims, the treatment of some cancers, wound care, and concussions, to name a few. We learned enough to redirect our thinking and at least become open to trying it.

A hyperbaric chamber is a cylinder into which a person is placed. It is sealed then pressurized with 100% medical-grade oxygen. The oxygen is forced by the pressure into the person's pores and helps the body make stem cells, which helps the body heal itself at the cellular level. Okay, the science maybe was beginning to make sense.

During the next visit, he filled in more details about the treatment. He said it would take 40 sessions to complete the course but not to expect any results for at least 20. He also mentioned that all the success stories for her condition were from patients who had been suffering for only a short period of time. Would Miriam's two-decade battle with RSD produce a less favorable result? He was not sure.

The protocol was stringent for safety reasons. To prevent any kind of static electrical spark that might burst into an instant inferno in the presence of pure oxygen, (we learned of a tragic story about a mother and child who were getting treatment and unbeknownst to the mother, the child had snuck an electronic toy into the chamber. They both perished.) she would have to change into one of their all-cotton scrubs, including socks. Jewelry had to be removed and all electronics had to be left outside. She would then be placed in a cylinder with plexiglass windows, which would allow her to see out, but the door would be shut, and the chamber would be pressurized to two atmospheres, or twice our normal atmospheric pressure, in 100% oxygen. The presence of oxygen is why they take such care to eliminate all possible sources of static electricity. Once the door is closed and the chamber pressurized, immediate help for anything or any reason is not available. Because the chamber pressurizes like a diver being under water, each session is called a dive. For the duration of "the dive," a technician specifically trained in hyperbaric therapy is in the room, and because oxygen is in use, a physician must be in the building. This is obviously something they take seriously. We were concerned about the possibility of a spasm during a session, but she understood that she would either have to solve it somehow or just suffer until the chamber could be depressurized and the door opened. Immediate assistance of any kind would not be available.

Miriam asked Dr. Sam Downs, "Is there any chance I'll be able to walk again?"

His reply minced no words: "No, no way, don't even go there, absolutely not. I'm hoping for a reduction in pain, and that is what you, too, should hope for, but this may not work. There are no guarantees."

I was wondering how a 30 percent reduction in pain followed by a 30 percent reduction in medications (which was his stated goal) would provide much of a net benefit.

What Miriam was thinking (that he did not understand) was that if the pain would go away, she would find a way to walk, no matter what the doctors declared. Miriam was not dissuaded by the fact that her leg was now a shadow of what it once was. That was not going to stop her; she'd deal with strengthening it when and if it was needed.

Some measure of hope was again dangling near the very frayed rope to which we clung. Hyperbaric therapy was not inexpensive, was not convenient, and quite frankly, looked like a long shot. Since there were no other courses of treatment in sight, we went for the Hail Mary. Since the last surgery in New York all the way back in 2001, we had been surviving one day at a time. We had grasped all the possibilities that had been dangled near enough to grab, but each one failed to provide measurable progress. To say we were desperate hardly does justice to our state of mind. Matthew shared our skepticism about shutting Mom in a can of compressed air but agreed with our decision to give it a try. One big advantage hyperbaric therapy offered over many of the other courses of treatment and surgeries, was that, aside from the cost, there appeared to be few downsides. In other words, if it failed, she would not be any worse off than before starting the treatment, just a little poorer.

Dr. Sam Downs had two chambers at his office, but it was even further from home than Dr. Elliott's office. For maximum effectiveness, the 40 sessions needed to be done as close together as possible. We began searching for someplace closer to home that might also be less costly. Miriam thought she had located such an option, but after one session, it was clear their protocol did not provide anything close to the one suggested by Dr. Sam Downs. His chambers would engulf her in 100% medical-grade oxygen; the more convenient and cheaper alternative used compressed room air and did not pressurize to the suggested level, which also was why it was half the cost. We talked about it and agreed that if it failed, we would forever wonder if the failure was due to the corners we cut.

We agreed she needed to go to Kennesaw, Georgia, to Dr. Sam Down's office. Two hours each way through Atlanta traffic, plus two hours in the chamber, add time to dress and undress twice, eat lunch somewhere, and the day is shot, times 40! At this time, thankfully, Miriam had two very capable caregivers who were not afraid of driving in Atlanta traffic, so Mark was off the hook for that detail, anyway.

It went as advertised, down to a lack of measurable progress after 20 sessions.

"Maybe a little less pain" was all I could get her to commit to.

She completed her 40th session on August 23, 2019. Some weeks, she went five times; others, usually because the doctor had to be elsewhere, she went only four days. Her commitment to the treatment made quite an impression on her doctor and technician. Upon completion, she noticed some reduction in pain levels, probably, she thinks, about the 20 to 30 percent that Dr. Sam Downs had hoped for before the treatment began. We resumed our normal routine of medication, daily spa sessions, and trying to distract her from the pain.

The Miracle

In mid-September, she got in the spa for a routine "because she was hurting" session. Caregiver Glenda, as was routine, used the overhead lift and harness to lower Miriam gently into the spa. Let me be clear about something: she got in the spa because she was hurting and went to sleep, which was part of her normal routine. While awakening from a nap, she bumped her foot on the bottom and noticed it didn't hurt, so she pressed harder on the bottom and still felt no pain! The healing miracle took place during that nap. Yes, it was that dramatic; she was in pain when she went sleep, and wasn't in pain when she woke up!Since 2001, her left foot was numb to the touch, but when any pressure was applied, it sent her into fits of agony, usually accompanied by one of her now-patented spasms that we were certain had been engineered by Lucifer himself. In the next few days, she continued applying pressure until the foot was bearing weight. Still no pain! Given her history, she kept any exuberance in check until she was certain something remarkable was going on. At first, she was suspended in the water by a buoyant waist belt so she could exercise her very atrophied left leg. Eventually, she began walking around in the spa AND did not feel pain!

With the pain no longer an issue, her spa sessions went from pain mitigation to rehabbing the leg. She practiced standing, taking steps and began exercising her leg whenever she was in the spa. Twenty years of atrophy was itself, a daunting hurdle to overcome and was among the reasons her doctors kept trying to lower her goals and expectations- a limb this atrophied simply could not be used again, in their mind. Medical professionals do not have protocols for getting people who have been wheelchair-bound for two decades back on their feet, probably because there are no suitable patients to practice on. Before addressing the atrophy, the underlying reason that put them in the chair in the first place had to be fixed, and this normally does not happen. But Miriam had been given a cocktail of hope mixed with a jigger of progress. She was determined to gulp until it was gone. She wasn't about to, at this point, let a little atrophy stand in her way. She worked and struggled and refused to quit. Within a short time, we were all intoxicated with unbridled joy!

A few days or weeks later (we regularly argue about this timeframe) I walked down our hallway and glanced into Miriam's bedroom and saw Miriam standing in front of her wheelchair, on her own two legs, trying on clothes. Her caregiver Glenda was bringing items from the closet to see if they still fit since she had lost weight. This was the first inkling I had that something miraculous was going on in my house, under my nose. She claims she had by this time mentioned having less pain and was walking in the spa, but I am pretty sure I had not grasped what she claims to have told me. Maybe I need to listen better?!

It took a few minutes to regain enough composure for me to go into her room and have a closer look. I was stunned. She was standing there in front of the wheelchair, bearing weight on both legs, like it was normal or something. True, it was only for a few seconds at a time, but she was standing and bearing weight on both legs.

Throughout the fall of '19, Miriam worked on walking. She also exercised her leg in the spa. She walked around the house until she got tired, then returned to the wheelchair. She pushed herself, being driven by pure determination. As she got stronger, she began walking a little bit outside around the house. Some very dramatic moments occurred when she began revealing her "secret" to family and friends. She enjoyed immensely showing off her new "trick" to doctors who had never known her as a walking patient.

Her first "victims" were doctors Downs and Elliott. Her stamina was understandably limited for quite some time, so she rode her wheelchair from the parking lot to the waiting room but stood when called and proceeded to walk to the assigned treatment room. The office staff began reaching for tissues. The doctors were stunned, to say the least.

Perhaps the most dramatic moment was when Dr. Robel saw her rise from her wheelchair and walk toward him as he entered the exam room. This man had followed her case from October of 1997, the date of injury. He was speechless. When he saw her name on his schedule, he wondered what he could possibly do for her that hadn't been done. It gave him great pleasure to prescribe a course of physical therapy to help strengthen her leg.

She was walking, but she had also lost a good bit of weight, evidently another side-effect of her time in the pressurized oxygen and increased activity. Within a few months, the pulmonologist said her oxygen levels had improved to the point she no longer needed to carry an oxygen machine wherever she went; a couple of months after that, the urologist measured enough progress with her bladder function that he removed the suprapubic catheter and accompanying leg bag. Dr. Sam Downs began reducing her narcotic medications as quickly as he could. Progress was happening simultaneously on many fronts at the same time! The frayed rope/lifeline we had been clinging to for so long had been miraculously snatched up, and we were once again standing on something that felt like solid ground. We would not allow anyone to pinch us for fear we'd wake up and find it was all a cruel dream.

The surprise Miriam enjoyed the most was when Matthew came to the house, having no knowledge about what had been happening with Mom. For the first time in 20 years, Matthew saw his mom walk across the room. It was pretty cool to watch! When he arrived at the house, we told him to stand across the room from where his mom was sitting in her chair. She then proceeded to stand up and walk to him while he watched in stunned, speechless amazement. It gave her great joy to give him a hug while standing in front of him. Me? Oh, I was busy blubbering off to the side while wiping my eyes again. I had a front-row seat to observe the miracle my feeble measure of faith dared not even ask for; thankfully, Miriam had not been quite so timid with her prayers.

On one occasion during the early walking phase, Miriam's sister Debra drove her to Dawsonville where they met grandson Boone at a park. It was a victorious time when Miriam got to take Boone's hand and walk with him to the playground herself instead of watching while someone else did it. Since this was not enough, she climbed a few steps with him and slid down a slide! I think her cheeks hurt for days from all the grinning. Her heart nearly burst with joy!

The Sunday she decided to walk into church, Matthew, Olivia, and Boone joined us. A few close friends from our small group were aware she had begun to walk, but her progress had yet to be widely known. That Sunday, watching her carry herself under her own power from the parking lot to her seat was pretty special. Some big-mouthed friends had given the church staff a heads-up that we had planned to do this, so it was not a complete surprise to them, but it did create a celebratory moment before the sermon began.

When Miriam's medications were reduced enough that it was deemed safe, I decided it was time she got reacquainted with driving. We were driving home from somewhere and were on a deserted country road when I pulled over and told her it was time to drive. She hesitated, probably because I caught her off guard, but she walked around the van and slid into the driver's seat. Driving and the independence it provides is one of the things she missed; we all would! The need to be driven everywhere she needed to go further underscored her feeling that she was just a needy burden to her family. Driving again was also not a subject I can recall we discussed much; she was so intensely focused on the other changes taking place that I don't think she gave much thought to driving again. She slid into the driver's seat, fastened the seatbelt, and grabbed the steering wheel so hard it could not possibly escape. Nervous laughter and oversteering punctuated the first couple of miles.

She did well enough during this first session that by the time we got home, she had begun to relax the death grip she had on the wheel which allowed blood flow to change her white knuckles back to pink. It took some time and patience before she got to the point she would go somewhere by herself. People talk about never forgetting how to ride a bike, which may be true, but dulled skills and reactions from a long hiatus are only recovered through practice. The same is true with driving. Muscle memory and reflexes we take for granted, she had to relearn. Teaching her to drive again was a job I enjoyed because it represented one more step toward recovering the life she had been deprived of for so long, AND I could help her with it.

Miriam was scheduled to be completely off of her narcotic pain medications by June of 2020. She had been slowly reducing the doses for a full year, and that process was nearing completion.

Considering the type and doses of medications she had been on, I thought she did great! Were there periods when she suffered symptoms of withdrawal? Yes, but HER determination allowed us to soldier through. She never looked back and never retreated from her progress. She did not like the way the meds made her feel and was glad to get free of them. It took some time for me to get used to looking into her eyes and seeing the clear-headed, intelligent woman I married. We can talk now. She rides in the passenger seat beside me in the van instead of behind me like a chauffeured woman (think "Driving Ms. Miriam"). Now that the night-time-care-givers-so-Mark-can-sleep are no longer coming to the house, "her" bed is once again "ours." We are again savoring with enthusiasm the little "normal" things that "normal" people take for granted. My future may be looking much brighter in the event I require someone to care for me at some point in the future. Hopefully, I have a few "credits" in the caregiving bank. One immediate benefit is that her improving health is reducing my stress level, which can only be good for my health.

I can look at her now and see a face that is relaxed and happy instead of scrunched up in pain. Often now, she wears the smile I fell in love with oh so many years ago. Life is getting simpler. By the spring of 2020, we were going places without wheelchairs. As her core muscles strengthened, the pulmonologist declared oxygen was no longer needed at night either! Also, late in 2020, the suprapubic catheter was removed after she began urinating on her own. The healing miracle touched things we never anticipated or expected. Traveling suddenly became much easier. We will no longer require wheelchair-accessible hotel rooms or accessible staterooms on cruise ships; no, it will be like we're almost normal!

See what I mean by having to adjust not just to the changes but the pace of change? It took more than two decades to get to the dark place where we were at the beginning of 2019. Now she can walk through Walmart, Kohl's, Academy Sports, and Publix after going to physical therapy!

Miriam can fill her own cup with ice and water now, so I am officially no longer needed. I expect to see her spending more and more time in the kitchen we built for her 15 years ago but she was never able to use it. I tease her that she will soon begin looking for a younger, healthier man better able to keep up with her. As her strength improved, we began cutting back on the attendant help that had been a fixture in our lives for so long. We were thankful for the help when it was needed, but we are so glad to get back our privacy!

Yes, big changes are happening for which I am exceedingly thankful. I will just have to do my best to adapt!

CHAPTER 21
Christmas Tidings

It is now the spring of 2022 as these keystrokes are made. Seeing Miriam walk across a room or work in the kitchen still thrills me because she always enjoyed it so much. We were both glad to have me hang up my apron because I'm not much of a cook. She prepares meals and we entertain company, just like we did back before her accident. Her stamina is growing. She has not used a wheelchair for nearly two years now. It was a fine thrill to be able to buy a "normal" vehicle that was not equipped with a wheelchair ramp.

For a dose of pure, unbridled joy, you should see her with our grandson. Three years ago, she could only sit on the porch swing and bawl in frustration as her sister walked across the yard holding his hand. Today, it thrills me to watch her do the same. They have become great friends. Occasionally she drives herself three hours to their house so she can take care of him for a day. She even gets down on the floor to play with him. She is proud to be wrapped around his finger and savors every minute! The joy of being his "Anmaw" provides a lot of motivation for her to look for things to do with him. One project she dove into was to build a butterfly garden, so she could share with him not only the beauty of the creatures but eventually the process by which they get that way.

Physically, she is doing great. I'm amazed at how well her leg muscles have responded to the new activity level after all those years of doing nothing. Her feet get tired and sore after she's been on them for a while. This, too, is improving with time and better footwear. Suddenly, she is putting wear and tear on the soles of her shoes, which is something different for her. She has found that many pairs of shoes she had accumulated over the years were not that well suited to walking, so she's thinned out and made some new purchases.

The temperatures in her legs and feet are now the same, whereas a few years ago, there could be as much as 15-degrees difference! She returned to the hyperbaric chamber for about five sessions in October of 2019, two more weeks in the summer of '20, and two more weeks in the summer of '21. She no longer needs supplemental oxygen day or night but still uses a CPAP at night for sleep apnea. Her spa sessions have dwindled to two or three a month, and a collateral benefit—the power bill has dropped significantly!

I cannot begin to express how proud I am of Miriam. It is so wonderful to look at her face and see a smile instead of anguish and pain. Her zest for life has returned. Now, she's determined to try to make up for all that lost time. I hope the senior citizen she is now married to can keep up.

One disappointment for us is that, as far as we know, Miriam is the only patient suffering from RSD to have experienced this level of success. We were hopeful this could become a pioneering treatment for people suffering from R.S.D. Since this is unfortunately not the case, we are left with the conclusion that Divine intervention was responsible for the complete healing. Yes, I said complete. I think the 60-something Miriam is capable of any activity she did before her accident. Her memory may have suffered from all the years on the intense medications, but this, too, may have diminished on its own with age.

Christmas Tidings and Our Book

I am very grateful to the friends and family members who have patiently guided, coached, corrected, and edited this book to present something encouraging, entertaining, and worth reading. Final editing was finally accomplished with the help of editor Melanie Saxton leading up to Christmas of '23. By the way, Melanie suggested I share excerpts from our latest Christmas Letter to give you a glimpse into our current lives.

It is our desire that our story will help others see that they can navigate and survive difficult times. Despite feeling overwhelmed, you never quit on loved ones or give up on your faith. That is the foundational message in all of this. Our God is still in the miracle business, much like our salvation. We didn't earn it or deserve it, but God, in his infinite wisdom, freely gives it to us. We are truly thankful for Miriam's miracle!

I still begin every day thanking God for our new life and don't take it for granted. As Christmas approaches, our home is filled with the aroma of holiday cooking. Miriam has been cooking for family and friends and making gifts in her craft room. She is wide open and full throttle from the time jumps out of bed in the morning until she falls asleep in front of the television in the evening, with periodic breaks for rest. It is a joy to be able to share her life. We were both in our thirties when she had her accident. Now, we are in our sixties. The locusts have surely had their fill, devouring what should have been the prime of our lives. What's next for us? Miriam is ready for me to sell the business and retire. She wants us to pursue our dreams of traveling, despite giving up on ever being able to do so. No matter what form it takes, we plan to walk over the last hill together, hand in hand, if we are able.

CHAPTER 22
With Love from Miriam

My Thoughts

This is a chapter of my life that frankly, I never even thought would ever come to be. After working 20 years at a job I really enjoyed as a Med Lab Technologist, I had a fall on a freshly waxed floor that sent my life on a tangent I could not have ever foreseen happening. It should have been a quick ACL surgery, a few months of physical therapy and then on back to my job and life.

I thought I would retire at 60-something and hopefully continue my active life. But at the age of 37, I never anticipated that the next 20+ years would be filled with excruciating, constant, intractable pain, more surgeries than I could ever imagine, more time spent in a myriad of doctor's offices, countless hours spent in physical therapy, more hospital rooms than I could even think about, and to end up in a wheelchair with round-the clock-care—not even in my wildest nightmares!

This all did come true, but the overwhelming thought I clung to over the years was this — God, in His everlasting, abundant mercy, grace, and love, sent His Son to earth to live a sinless life, be crucified on a cross, was resurrected from the dead on the third day, so that He paid the debt of my life full of sin, so HE could have a relationship with me! Did this all change the day I fell and my life changed? Absolutely not! Nor did it change as I struggled with failed surgeries, and incredible pain day after day for years! Did I wonder what God was up to? Did I cry out to Him to take this pain away? Of course! However, no matter how much pain I was in, I remembered what Jesus went through on the cross—the incredible amount of torture and pain that He, the Son of God, endured for my sins! My pain that I lived with every day, was NOTHING compared to what He went thru so that I can have life everlasting! But, even if God had not healed me here on earth, I knew that I would be pain-free when He took me home to heaven! And I would praise Him all the days of my life, no matter what.

Over and over during the 20+ years that I suffered, one thing that would so often be going on in my mind was scripture songs, praise songs, and hymns memorized over years of my life. Now, I sound like a frog in a bucket if I sing, but I am thankful for those who sing so beautifully! These songs were a lifeline to me. They brought peace and comfort throughout my days. There were many dark days and long nights, but His Word and songs were there, whether it was the middle of the night or anytime during the day.

There was also spiritual warfare going on. So many times, as my body and mind were worn out from the constant barrage of pain, Satan would send his fiery darts of doubt into my mind. "You are a wimp. God shouldn't make you suffer like this! You are an embarrassment to your family. People pity you. You aren't an asset to anyone! You are such a burden on your family! Why is God making you suffer so? *You don't deserve this* were just a few of the thoughts that Satan sent my way. However relentless those thoughts became; I knew that the same God that saved me had not deserted me. That God is the same yesterday, today and tomorrow (Hebrews 13:8). His promises are true, for all of the past, present and future! Satan wanted to control my mind, to steal my joy, to make me doubt God's faithfulness. So, as Satan fired away his darts, I began to speak to him. Get away from me, Satan, I will not let you control me, I'm a child of God, He is my everything, my Savior, and my Lord. He will be glorified in my life, He is my King and you have no power against Him!" Satan's voice in my head got quiet. When we praise our Lord, Satan has no power! Did he barrage me again and again- of course! But God is greater, He is the victor in all things!

John 4:4 tells us that "The Spirit who lives in you is greater than the spirit who lives in the world." While enduring all the pain, God also showed me that I could pray for others who were in pain or experiencing trying circumstances with a renewed understanding. My mind was not occupied by many of the things that I normally would be thinking about, like what groceries I need, how to plan my day, do

I have gas in my car, etc. So, this time allowed me to intensify my praying like never before. Often, as I was soaking in my spa for some relief from some of the pain, I was having awesome worship sessions with my Lord and Savior! His Word is so comforting and trustworthy!

The Holy Spirit would bring to mind scripture after scripture, bringing comfort, peace, and calmness to my weary body. "We can come boldly to His throne of grace, that we may obtain mercy and find grace to help in time of need!" (Hebrews 4:16) "Let all that I am praise the Lord; may I never forget the good things He does for me." (Psalm 103:2) "My health may fail, and my spirit may grow weak, but God remains the strength of my heart; He is mine forever!" (Psalm 73:26) "For the Lord your God is living among you. He is a mighty Savior. He will delight in you with gladness. With His love, he will calm all your fears. He will rejoice over you with joyful songs." (Zephaniah 3:17) "The faithful love of the Lord never ceases! His mercies never come to an end! Great is His faithfulness; His mercies are new every morning." (Lamentations 3:20-23) Jesus tells us in John 16:33, "In this world, you will have trials and sorrows, but take heart, I have overcome the world."

I can't say enough about my precious husband and son through this time. They went through so much! I can't imagine the anguish as they watched me suffer, and often couldn't do anything about it. They took on activities I could no longer do, sacrificing time, and energy. Their bodies grew weary too, but never did they lag in caring, consoling, being my voice, loving, creating new distractions for me, entertaining me, being tender, compassionate, and always looking for ways to make things better, and so, so much more!

Friends, family members, former co-workers, church family, neighbors, and many more were such an encouragement to our family and me. The support, care, love, and things they did for us was so timely, needed, and graciously poured out upon our weary family. People brought food, took me to appointments, procured needed equipment, loaned us things, loaded and emptied our dishwasher, came to our home to cut our hair, cleaned our floors and kitchen, helped build an addition onto our home for the much-needed spa, visited, encouraged us, prayed for and with us, sat with Mark during my surgeries, got groceries for us, picked up medication, took me out for lunch, helped me wrap Christmas presents for my family, sat with me so Mark could attend events with Matthew, brought books for me to read, brought laughter when we were not sure we could even laugh, transported Matthew to school and other events, and for these things, and much more, we are so eternally grateful!

I hope that this book will give you encouragement and hope. And dear readers, if you don't have a personal relationship with the King of Kings and Lord of Lords, Jesus our Savior, then reach out to Him today. He is faithful, merciful, true, gracious, and loving. God sent His Son, Jesus, to die on the cross for our sins so that we can have fellowship with Him for all eternity. Find a Bible and ask God to reveal Himself to you. Seek for Him. Learn the truth of who He is. Throughout the Scriptures, there are facts, stories, miracles, and prophecies that have all come true. God desires a relationship with you. He created you. He tells us that He has come so that we might have life and have it more abundantly. (John 10:10)

And HE is still working miracles today! I know!

~ Miriam Johnson

PHOTO GALLERY

Spring 1999

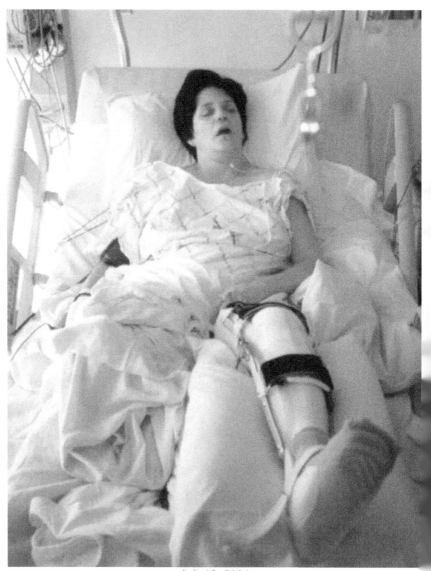

July 12, 2001

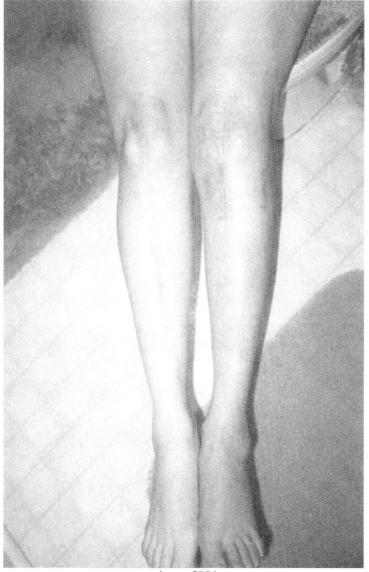

August 2001

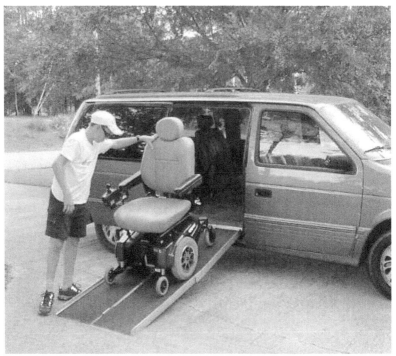

Wheelchair on ramp

Campsite cook

Case Manager

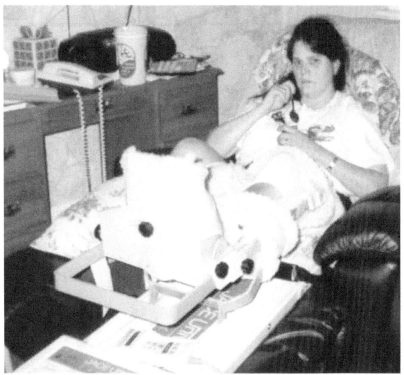

CPM in chair

CPM on couch

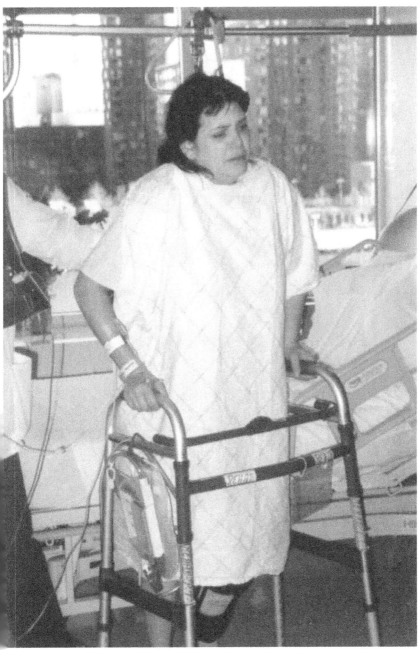

First steps post surgery

Fish slayer

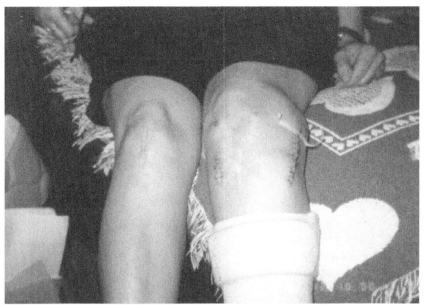

Front view December 2000

Foot drag

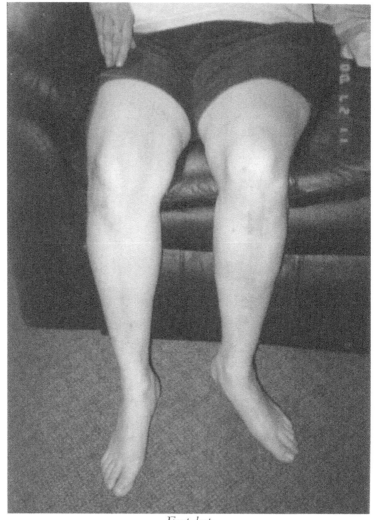

Foot drop

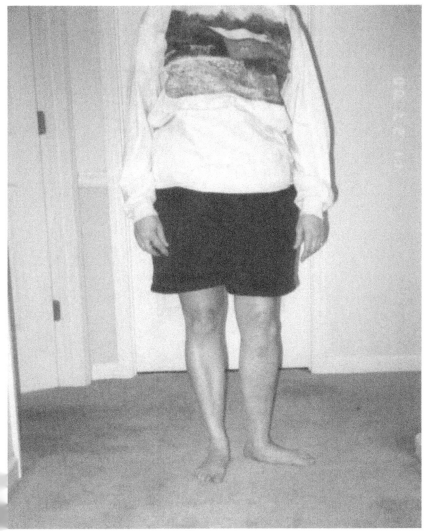

Foot rotation

High school graduation

Her doctor

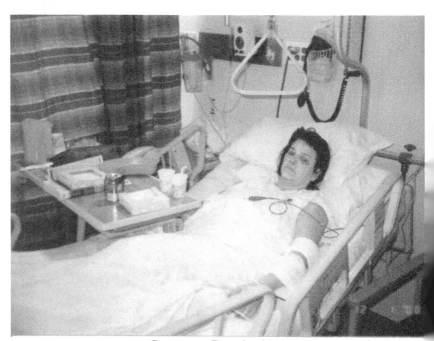

Post surgery December 2000

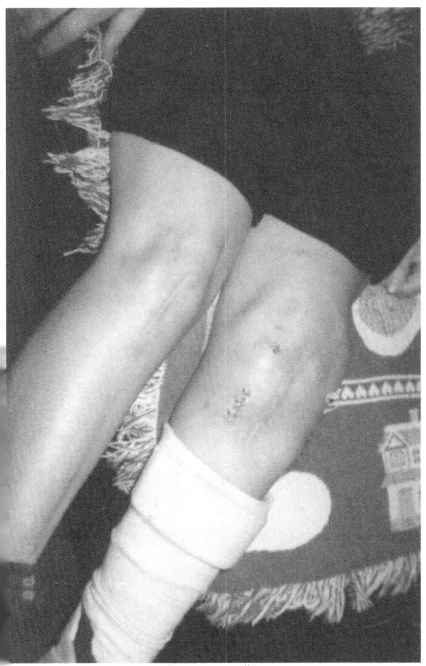

Post surgery swelling

Queen Miriam

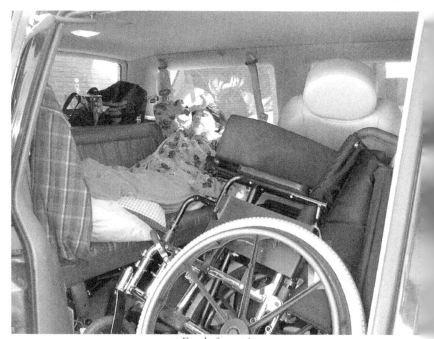

Ready for a trip

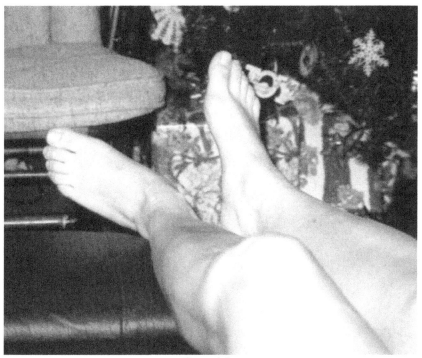

Rotated foot

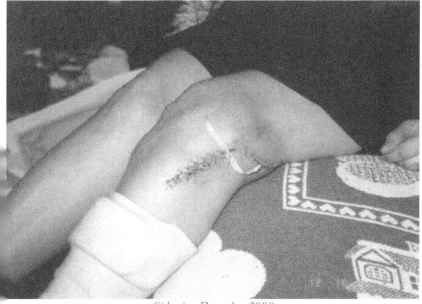

Side view December 2000

Spa time

Spa exercise

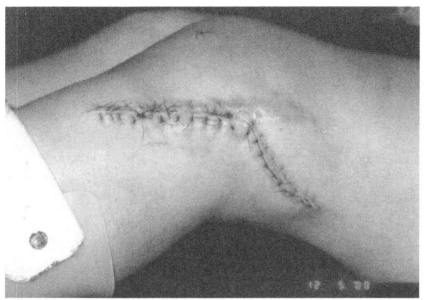

Stitches

Her *aquarium*

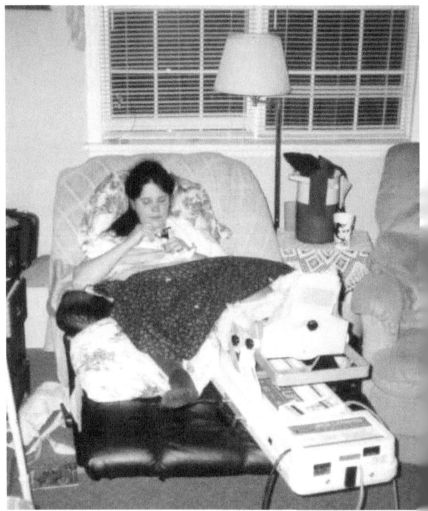

Surgery recovery

Therapy dog

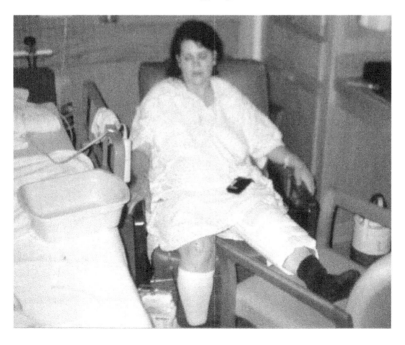

Second ACL

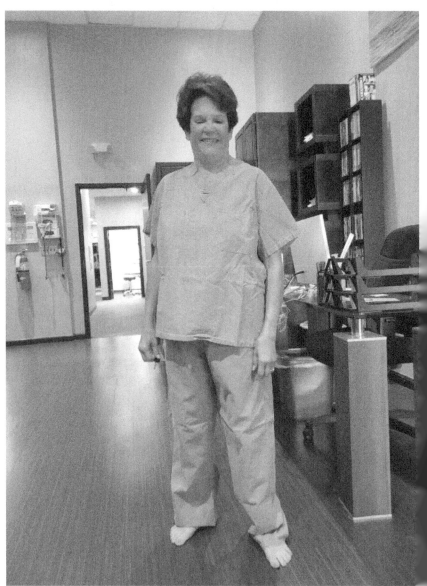

Dressed for chamber

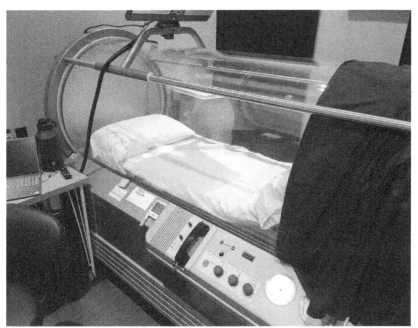

Hyperbaric chamber

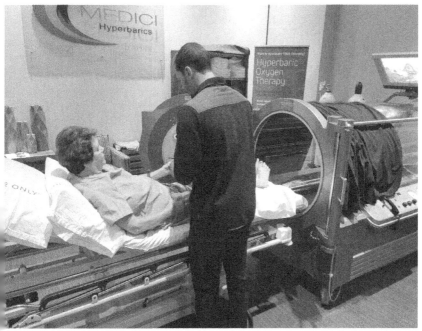

Making ready

Fall 2019 Walked into church

Spring 2020 First day on a playground

CAST OF CHARACTERS

Miriam............................... Injured worker

Mark.................................. Miriam's husband

Matthew............................ son of Mark and Miriam

Debra................................ Miriam's older sister

Wanda............................... Miriam's younger sister

Bruce................................. Mark's brother

Sandy .... Bruce's wife

Fred Hill .... Miriam's Workman's Comp attorney

Joe Hill .... Hospital attorney

Ralph McKay..................... Hospital attorney II

Eddie Hammond................ Lawyer

Tim Boone .... Lawyer

Chris Harris .... Altma, employee health nurse

Julie Adams....................... Neighbor

Kay Shepherd .... Generous friend

FG Servicing Agency .... Managed Worker's Comp case for
Altma Hospital

Dr. Neyland .... Neurologist

Altma Hospital .... Hospital in Athens

Dr. Max Robel .... Orthopedic surgeon and authorized
treating physician

Dr. Ron Hayes .... Orthopedic surgeon

Dr. Cox............................. Orthopedic surgeon, Birmingham

Dr. Wilson .... Orthopedic surgeon, New York

Dr. Watson .... Hand surgeon, NY

Dr. Edwards .... Pain doctor

Dr. Dean .... Pain doctor

Dr. Elliott .... Pain doctor

Dr. Dion .... Pain doctor who monitored drugs while Dr. Elliott was out of town

Dr. Cook .... Neurosurgeon based in Athens

Dr. White .... Atlanta doctor; sent Miriam for IME (independent medical examination)

Dr. Mayes .... Consulting Orthopedist

Dr. Moore .... Consulting Orthopedist

Dr. Sam Downs .... Pain doctor with hyperbaric chambers

Dr. Richard Ware .... Orthopedic

Adams family .... Neighbors

Kathy Siles .... Neighbor

Mrs. Veale .... Mother of my employee Scott

Chris Fannin .... Friend

Rose Bellamy .... Friend

Stacy Casey .... Case manager

Debbie Travis .... account manager at servicing agency

Pastor Ray and wife Sandra ... Pastoral care team

Pastor Charles .... Officiated Mark and Miriam Johnson's wedding

Henry .... Physical Therapist

Lyn Hamby .... Friend

Peggy .... First "professional" attendant

Celia .... a.k.a. St. Tulia, a close friend of the family, later joined the "professional care team"

CONDENSED TIMELINE OF OUR ORDEAL

10/1997 .... Miriam is workplace injured on her left knee due to a fall on a freshly waxed floor. ACL severed, Grade 2 MCL tear.

11/1997 .... ACL #1—reconstruction using patella tendon, L knee. Dr. Max Robel, Athens, GA.

1/1998 .... Miriam returns to light duty.

4/1998 .... Arthroscopy #1—remove scar tissue and perform notchplasty. Dr. Max Robel, Athens, GA.

5/1998 .... ACL #2 using a hamstring graft. Drs. Hayes and Robel, Athens, GA.

1/1999 .... Arthroscopy #2—loose screw removed. Dr. Hayes, Athens, GA.

4/1999 .... Arthroscopy #3—"cyst removal" that turned out to be a fabella, so it was not removed, plus peroneal nerve explored. Dr. Hayes, Athens, GA.

4/1999 .... Heritage Flooring files bankruptcy.

7/1999 .... ACL #3 using patella tendon from right knee plus posterior lateral ligament reconstruction with allograft and removal of the fabella. Dr. William Cox, Birmingham, AL.

9/1999 .... Lake Oconee Flooring purchases assets of

Heritage Flooring; Mark is employed as Sales Manager.

12/1999.......................Filed personal bankruptcy.

5/2000.......................Dr. Cox admitted there was nothing else he could do for Miriam and referred her to Dr. Russell Warren.

7/2000.......................Implantation of spinal cord stimulator for pain control after months of peroneal nerve blocks. Dr. Mark Edwards, Winder, GA.

11/2000.......................Removal of all hardware from prior procedures, bone grafts from hip to tibia, and the dissecting of the peroneal nerve. Dr. Riley Wilson and Dr. Watson, Hospital For Special Surgery, New York, New York.

6/2001 ....Replacement of spinal cord stimulator battery. Dr. Mark Edwards, Habersham County Medical Center, Demorest, GA.

7/2001 ....Reconstruction of ACL, posterior-lateral corner, and replacement of lateral meniscus. Dr. Riley Wilson, Hospital For Special Surgery, NY, NY.

7/2001 ....Hospitalized for treatment of infection in knee following surgery. Dr. Robel, Altma Hospital, Athens, GA

7/2001 ....PICC line installed for 6-week infusion of Vancomycin.

7/2001 ....Lost job at Lake Oconee Flooring.

8/2001 ....Installation of epidural. Dr. Edwards, Demorest, GA

8/2001 ....Admitted to E.R. for overdose. Altma Hospital, Athens, GA

9/2001 ....Meningitis from epidural abscess from tunneled epidural; epidural removed.

9/2001 .... PICC line installed for weeks of Vancomycin treatment.

11/2001...................... Trial for intrathecal pump; single injection.

11/2001 .... Sympathetic block.

12/2001 .... Sympathetic block.

4/2002 .... Intrathecal pump trial; 10 day trial w/morphine, baclofen and dilaudid.

4/2002 .... Removal of intrathecal pump catheter; subsequent leakage of CSF at 1 tsp/11 minutes.

4/2002 .... Blood patch for CSF leakage; post-dural headache.

5/2002 .... Reprogramming of spinal cord stimulator.

Fall of '05 .... Started accessible home.

Spring '06................... Moved into accessible home.

Fall '06...................... Closed furniture business.

2007 .... Started dredging business.

7/2000........................ Implantation of spinal cord stimulator for pain control after months of peroneal nerve blocks.

11/2000 .... Removal of all hardware from prior procedures, bone grafts from hip to tibia, and the dissecting of the peroneal nerve. NYC.

6/2001........................ Replacement of spinal cord stimulator battery.

7/2001........................ Reconstruction of ACL, posterior-lateral corner, and replacement of lateral meniscus NYC.

7/2001........................ Hospitalized for treatment of infection in knee, following surgery.

7/2001........................ PICC line installed for 6-week infusion of Vancomycin.

7/2001........................ Mark lost job.

8/2001 .... Installation of epidural.

8/2001 .... Admitted to E.R. for overdose.

9/2001 .... Meningitis from epidural abscess from tunneled epidural; epidural removed.

9/2001 .... PICC line installed for weeks of Vancomycin treatment.

11/2001...................... Trial for intrathecal pump; single injection.

11/2001 .... Sympathetic block

12/2001 .... Sympathetic block

4/2002 .... Intrathecal pump trial; 10 day trial w/morphine, Baclofen and Dilaudid.

4/2002 .... Removal of intrathecal pump catheter; subsequent leakage of CSF at 1 tsp/11 minutes.

4/2002 .... Blood patch for CSF leakage; post-dural headache.

5/2002 .... Reprogramming of spinal cord stimulator.

2004 .... Removal of non-functioning Spinal Cord Stimulator - Round the clock care provided by family or paid home health care.

7/2017 .... Replacement of Left shoulder joint from torn rotator cuff and overuse from crutches/wheelchair.

1/2018........................ New Pain Management doctor. Changed some meds.

4/2019 .... Pain Dr. talked with me about Hyperbaric Oxygen therapy.

June–August 2019 .... Traveled to Kennesaw, GA Monday-Friday for eight weeks for 40 sessions of hyperbaric oxygen therapy.

September 2019 .... Miriam took her first steps.

May 2020................... Miriam is free of all medications, including narcotics.

Since the injury occurred, there have been:

Note: We quit counting after August of '01

- 50+ visits to Orthopedic Clinic;

- 7 visits to Birmingham to the Orthopedic Clinic.

- 265+ sessions of physical therapy

- 20 visits for nerve blocks

- 3 Trips to NYC

- Etc, etc, etc…

Would you like more information about our journey? Feel free to contact us at miriamsmiracle@gmail.com.

Made in United States
Orlando, FL
09 March 2024

44589154R10222